W9-DCW-772

THE FIDUCIARY

THE FIDUCIARY

An In-depth Guide to Fiduciary Duties—From Studebaker to Enron

Christian D. Rahaim

iUniverse, Inc.
New York Lincoln Shanghai

THE FIDUCIARY
An In-depth Guide to Fiduciary Duties—From Studebaker to Enron

Copyright © 2005 by Christian Deeb Rahaim

All rights reserved. No part of this book may be used or reproduced by any means, graphic, electronic, or mechanical, including photocopying, recording, taping or by any information storage retrieval system without the written permission of the publisher except in the case of brief quotations embodied in critical articles and reviews.

iUniverse books may be ordered through booksellers or by contacting:

iUniverse
2021 Pine Lake Road, Suite 100
Lincoln, NE 68512
www.iuniverse.com
1-800-Authors (1-800-288-4677)

ISBN-13: 978-0-595-34429-1 (pbk)
ISBN-13: 978-0-595-67117-5 (cloth)
ISBN-13: 978-0-595-79189-7 (ebk)
ISBN-10: 0-595-34429-1 (pbk)
ISBN-10: 0-595-67117-9 (cloth)
ISBN-10: 0-595-79189-1 (ebk)

Printed in the United States of America

CONTENTS

LIST OF FIGURES

PREFACE

The Fiduciary contains critical material that results in an informative and compelling body of work. From the evolution of the fiduciary concept to its adaptation in ERISA and its continued evolution in the workplace, the author provides captivating insights that keep the reader engaged, written in a clear, concise, and straightforward manner. The chapters build the necessary framework for the reader to develop an understanding of fiduciary obligations related to pension plans in today's volatile environment.

Upon reading *The Fiduciary*, it is evident that interpretations and applications of ERISA relating to fiduciary responsibility and governance are ever changing. Therefore the concepts offered in this book are evolving. Readers should read with the intention of seeking new insight, awareness, or both and garner knowledge around the aspect of functioning as a fiduciary. The laws are certain to continue to evolve; although the concepts offered are current as of publication, they change quickly and often.

This publication is designed to provide accurate and authoritative information concerning the subject matter covered. It is sold with the understanding that the author is not engaged in rendering legal advice, investment advice, or other professional service herein. If legal, investment, or accounting advice or other expert assistance is required, a competent professional should be sought. The information contained herein represents the author's views and is not intended by the author to represent legal or investment advice. Furthermore, it is not intended to establish an express or implied attorney-client relationship.

ABOUT THE AUTHOR

During author Christian Rahaim's twelve years in human resource management he has provided strategic leadership for benefits, compensation, mergers, acquisitions, and divestitures. He has managed due diligence for government investigations and compliance for some of the nation's Fortune 100 companies. In addition, he was involved in the dismantling and termination of the benefit structure and plans in the nation's most complex bankruptcy.

Chris is the author of *The Employers' Handbook to 401(k) Savings Plans.* Additionally, he has written numerous articles, including "ERISA, OWBPA, & WARN: The Bermuda Triangle of Employment Severance Agreements," "The Doctrine of Respondeat Superior Applied to Electronic Communications," "The Effect of Mandatory Pre-dispute ADR Agreements on Title VII Claims," "Comparison of Cognitive Ability Test and Clinical Assessment on Employment Selection," and "The Success of Skill-Based Pay in Achieving Goals."

The author has negotiated agreements and settlements with the U.S. Department of Labor, the Pension Benefit Guaranty Corporation, and the Internal Revenue Service. Additionally, providing information on pension legislation to the U.S. Senate and House of Representatives gives the author exhaustive insight into workplace pension plans.

The author received his Juris Doctor degree from Loyola University, a Master of Business Administration degree from the University of Mississippi, and a Bachelor of Arts degree in Psychology from the University of Mississippi. While in law school, he received an AmJur award in Criminal Law and Business Planning (for academic achievement).

INTRODUCTION

Slightly more than thirty years ago, Congress responded to abuses in the operation of large private pension plans by enacting important employee benefit legislation—the Employee Retirement Income Security Act of 1974 (ERISA). Although it does not require a company to provide its employees with pension plans, retirement benefits, or any other type of benefits, ERISA does adapt centuries-old concepts of fiduciary obligations and loosely defined trust laws to create fiduciary standards of conduct for persons who have discretionary control over employee benefit plans.

"ERISA is a comprehensive statute designed to promote the interests of employees and their beneficiaries in employee benefit plans."[1] An ERISA fiduciary must act for the exclusive benefit of plan beneficiaries,[2] and must act "with the care, skill, prudence, and diligence under the circumstances then prevailing that a prudent man acting in like capacity and familiar with such matters would use in the conduct of an enterprise of a like character and with like aims."[3] These duties are the "highest known to the law."[4]

The Fiduciary is intended to function as a primer on ERISA fiduciary obligations targeted toward the business professional seeking an overview of the rules governing and the duties of an ERISA pension plan fiduciary. Reference to case law or statutory code section is intentionally minimized. Nonetheless, certain key concepts are best defined by way of the case facts and decisions. Furthermore, if certain fiduciary duties are solidified in the statutory authority the code section is incorporated.

Chapter 1, "Synopsis of the Modern Pension Environment," describes the current pension environment. From increasing fiduciary litigation to shifts in employee investment strategies and objectives, the character of employee benefits and the fiduciary rules that govern their administration, management, and investments is undergoing a radical transformation.

Chapter 2, "Background and History," provides the foundation of fiduciary law—the Roman Civil Code—and traces its interpretation and evolution through European common law, to U.S. Trust Law and finally into the Employee Retirement Income Security Act of 1974 (ERISA). Moreover, ERISA's history, beginning with the development of the U.S. private-based pension plans in the nineteenth century, is traced though its enactment—sparked in part by the collapse of the auto giant, Studebaker.

Chapter 3, "Overview of Pension Plans," narrows the focus of ERISA toward this book's content, which is pension plans. Pension plans generally are divided into two categories—defined benefit and defined contribution. The features, advantages, and disadvantages of each are described as a core foundation before fiduciary concepts are applied. Additionally, the model of a company's retirement benefits program has shifted, which places more ownership on the employee and further confuses the responsibilities of fiduciaries. Finally, current issues and developments of cash balance plans are vetted.

Shifting from background and foundation to application, Chapters 4 and 5, "Determination of a Fiduciary" and "Responsibilities of a Fiduciary," develop the standard for determination of a fiduciary and the obligations set forth in ERISA, government regulations, and applicable case law. Two major elements of an ERISA fiduciary law are the establishment of the person or entity responsible for acting as the fiduciary and the determination of an occurrence of a fiduciary breach. In other words, these chapters examine who fiduciaries are and what their responsibilities comprise. Years of court decisions elaborate the meaning of ERISA and establish the basic framework for these determinations. In addition, an overview of prohibited transactions, fiduciary relationships and structure, and the often-misunderstood ERISA section 404(c) application is provided.

Chapters 6 and 7, "Investment Management for Defined Contribution Plans" and "Investment Management for Defined Benefit Plans," address investment management in a pension plan, which is a critical and often-litigated fiduciary duty. Although duplicative in nature to the responsibilities at a high fiduciary level, the processes and components of investment management by a fiduciary differ greatly between a defined benefit plan and a defined contribution pension plan. From an overview of investment categories, issues with employer securities, development of an investment policy statement to the balancing of elements and constituents in pension plans, these chapters allow the business-side fiduciary to understand the processes employed by pension experts.

Chapters 8 and 9, "Plan Fees and Expenses" and "Administration and Compliance," guide a fiduciary through the basic aspects—often subjects of DOL and IRS audits—of managing the operation of a pension plan. Recent DOL focus on understanding and communicating a plan's fees and expenses, especially in the defined contribution area, enables fiduciaries to fully understand the DOL's position and how best to comply. The issues discussed under compliance, although recently taking a backseat to other issues such as investment management, lie at the very heart of ERISA and the Internal Revenue Code's foundation on pension plans.

Chapter 10, "Communications," conveys that while once merely a compliance icon focused on compliance-type issues, participant communications in today's pension world are highly scrutinized concerning investment management, fiduciary disclosures, and harmonizing Security Exchange Commission regulations. Recent trends in the industry have promulgated that a more sophisticated level of investment advice—that is not clearly distinguished from mere investment education—carries certain fiduciary obligations. Other topics addressed are understanding participant needs and identifying communication problems.

Chapter 11, "Managing Fiduciary Responsibility," provides the fiduciary with a roadmap for developing sound fiduciary structure, policies, and processes to manage pension plans. Not only are the duties and actions conducted while a fiduciary critical, but research and diligence before accepting a fiduciary assignment are of equal significance. Finally, when errors or breaches occur the options for correction are complex and should be considered cautiously and only with appropriate expert advice.

1

SYNOPSIS OF THE MODERN PENSION ENVIRONMENT

The Road to Fiduciary Hell Is Paved with Good Intentions

DYNAMICS IN THE INDUSTRY

A recent survey conducted by the investment advice firm Financial Engines found that 73% of plan sponsors believe their fiduciary responsibilities or liabilities have increased over the past twelve to twenty-four months with only 48% of sponsors believing that their role as a fiduciary is clear.[5] Moreover, current allegations of corporate fraud, late trading, improper market timing, and excessive fees have further complicated the panorama of fiduciary responsibilities.[6]

The percentage of the private sector workforce covered by an employer-sponsored pension plan has remained at about 50% since the early 1970s. Although the number of covered workers has remained relatively unchanged, there has been a substantial shift in the type of retirement coverage from defined benefit pension plans to defined contribution plans, specifically 401(k) plans. Coincidently, while the number of defined benefit plans has declined, the number of 401(k) plans has grown dramatically in just over two decades. Today, there are an estimated 350,000 401(k) plans covering 47 million workers and holding more than $2 trillion in assets.[7]

Although there has been a profound shift in the type of pension coverage, pension law has not changed to keep up with this trend. The collapse of Enron and the loss of more than $1 billion of workers' retirement savings emphasize the need for reform. After the collapse of Enron—at the time, the largest bankruptcy in U.S. history and still the most complicated—some argued that it was an isolated instance of corporate greed. Recent incidents, such as the jury conviction of the Arthur Andersen accounting firm for obstructing justice, the indictment of Tyco Industries' CEO for falsifying merger information, and the misstatement of WorldCom's financial condition by nearly $4 billion before the company filed for bankruptcy (now the largest bankruptcy in U.S. history), indicate a cause for concern.

It is clear that these corporate scandals are not unique to one company or one industry. Like Studebaker, Enron and WorldCom are not isolated instances of corporate greed but examples of the need for broader reform of fiduciary responsibility for employer-sponsored pension plans, which have become the bedrock of America's modern retirement system.

There is a saturnine demand for companies to conduct fiduciary training for the committees, boards of directors, officers, and agents to make them aware of what their responsibilities are and help them fulfill their fiduciary duties. Additionally, the need exists to ensure that the fiduciaries have all the information they need to do their job right—disclosure on fees and fund reviews.

In today's industry, most benefit plans have become commercially outsourced programs with third party vendors administering, for all intensive purposes, a type of account for the employee at the company's request. Nevertheless, the fiduciary duties under ERISA in most cases do not convey to the vendor; more exactly, they remain with the company. As such, the seminal issue facing the employee benefit industry today is fiduciary liability. Unfortunately, many people associated with the employee benefit industry go about their business uneducated about these frightening realities because they lack sufficient knowledge of fiduciary responsibilities. This book, although not a substitute for competent legal advice, does provide the structural foundational understanding necessary for employers.

ECONOMIC REPERCUSSION

A successful retirement has always required a source of steady, dependable income to meet basic spending needs and a source of capital to meet unexpected or unusual expenses. The traditional analogy for retirement security is "a three-legged stool"—social security, employer pension plans, and individual savings. The first two legs of the stool supply the steady income, and individual savings meets the need for capital and supplements the income. As social security gradually erodes and employer pension plans diminish, more pressure is placed on individual savings.

Americans now retire earlier, live longer, and use more medical care than any previous generation—all of which increases the financial resources necessary to assure a secure retirement. Nonetheless, individual savings are falling and many workers contribute minimal amounts to their pension plan. Social security, which was not designed to provide full retirement benefits, is less able to meet retirement income needs. Although many workers are well prepared for retirement, others are unlikely to be able to meet their retirement needs.

Defined benefit plans, most of which were established in the 1950s and 1960s, are a key component of retirement security for 44 million Americans. Providing retirement income to long-term employees on a tax-effective basis, pensions helped organizations retain employees, provide workers a graceful transition to retirement, and lower direct compensation and taxes. In some cases, corporate motives were paternalistic, helping employees save for retirement when they had few resources to do so on their own.

The retirement landscape changed dramatically with the passage of the Revenue Act of 1978, adding Section 401(k) to the Internal Revenue Code. When regulations were issued in 1981, employers quickly added matching 401(k) plans to their portfolio of benefits. During the bull market of the 1990s, many employees believed their 401(k) plan provided for luxurious retirement at an early age. At the same time, pension plan assets grew significantly, and financial executives grew accustomed to holidays from pension funding.

The bear market early in this decade quickly changed these perceptions. Employees now face the prospect of working longer before their 401(k) plan can provide a comfortable retirement, and executives confront sharply higher contributions and expenses for their defined benefit plans.

Some companies have responded by freezing or eliminating pension plans and placing more emphasis on defined contribution plans by making higher contributions and adding more incentives for employee savings. This approach has two shortcomings. First, despite significant incentives and the availability of tax-favored vehicles such as IRAs and 401(k) plans, the savings rate of Americans has declined sharply over the past fifteen years. Data shows that the growth of assets in these plans is due more to a transfer of savings from after-tax accounts to pre-tax accounts rather than to a rise in net savings. Moreover, these retirement accounts tend to benefit those who can most afford to save (or transfer savings) and provide less benefit to lower-paid employees who often fail to participate at significant rates.

A second weakness is that employer contributions to defined contribution plans primarily transfer value from the employer to the employee. This places all the investment risk and longevity risk on the employee and does not generally create additional value.

ORGANIZATION OF THE BOOK

Understanding where the industry currently stands and the evolution of the concepts and laws that support today's fiduciary standards is a prerequisite for everything else. The next step is understanding who is considered a fiduciary and how that classification is applied. Only then can the responsibilities and standard of success or failure be recognized and levied.

Key areas of concern or complication are explored in detail. From understanding fiduciary responsibilities in managing the assets of defined contribution and defined benefit plans to understanding compliance and communication issues, any person involved in managing pension plans will gain a greater understanding of potential pitfalls and measures to prevent such breaches.

While ERISA has been in place since 1974, Enron and other corporate scandals have inspired increased vigilance by the U.S. Department of Labor over employer-sponsored qualified plans. Persons in a position or a potential position of serving as a fiduciary need to understand their roles as fiduciaries. This book provides a template for skilled oversight of their plans, including a program for ongoing review of investments, mechanics to determine fiduciary status, and audit concepts and methods.

Much of this book presents recommended solutions or observations, many of which are alternative methods or that may be disagreed. Nevertheless, the intention of this book is not to provide custom solutions to every situation but instead to emphasize topical areas of concerns and a general structural overview of the world of the pension plan fiduciary. It is strongly recommended that anyone involved with the management of a pension plan consult with experts regarding legal and investment advice.

2

BACKGROUND AND HISTORY

Thrice did Rome conquer the world:
by her arms, by her church and by her law.[8]

In its basic meaning, a fiduciary is a person charged by law and equity with a higher duty to care for another person. A fiduciary is required by law to place the other person's interests equal to or ahead of his or her own in all dealings involving that other person. The relationship is often created when the other person approaches the fiduciary to use the fiduciary's special skills and knowledge, for a fee, to benefit the other person.

Developing from Latin, the word *fiducia* means "trust" and carries connotations of total trust, good faith, and honesty. The most common fiduciary is a trustee of a trust, but fiduciaries can include business advisors, attorneys, guardians, administrators of estates, real estate agents, bankers, stockbrokers, title companies, or those who undertake to assist someone who places complete confidence and trust in that person or company. Characteristically, the fiduciary has greater knowledge and expertise about the matters being handled. A fiduciary is held to a higher standard of conduct and trust than that of a stranger or a casual businessperson. The fiduciary must avoid "self-dealing" or "conflicts of interest" where the potential benefit to the fiduciary is in conflict with what is best for the person who places the trust. For example, a stockbroker must consider the best investment for the client and not buy or sell because of what brings the broker the highest commission. While a fiduciary and the beneficiary may join in a business venture or a purchase of property, the best interests of the beneficiary must be primary, and absolute candor is required of the fiduciary.

From a legal standpoint, the term *fiduciary* is borrowed from civil law. The Roman laws defined a fiduciary heir as a person who was instituted heir and who was charged to deliver the succession to a person designated by the testament. Some say, however, that it properly signifies the person to whom a testator has sold his inheritance under the condition that he should sell it to another. *Fiduciary* may be defined as "to be in trust, in confidence."

ROMAN CIVIL LAW

The roots of the *fideicommissa* and its progeny in civil law can be traced back to early Roman law.[9] While the fideicommissa is often referred to as a civilian trust, this is not quite the case. Originally the fideicommissa was legally unenforceable because the holder of such a position was bound by his conscience, not by law.[10] Additionally, this institution has metamorphosed into a number of subspecies in the modern context and must be examined on a jurisdiction-by-jurisdiction basis. Notwithstanding, there are a number of notable similarities in the development of the civilian fideicommissa and the common law trust.

One of the earliest uses of fideicommissa stemmed from the provision of Roman law that restricted inheritance from the paterfamilias, or head of the Roman family, to non-citizen heirs. Furthermore, there was virtually no substantial means of effecting succession to female heirs irrespective of their citizenship. Establishing a fideicommissa provided the Roman testators or settlors with a means of providing for an ineligible heir or legatee, permitting the heir to benefit from the estate by indirect means. In this arrangement, the Roman citizen appointed a trusted friend to take the estate subject to a moral obligation to restore the true intended recipient.

Testators sometimes charged fiduciaries to give the whole property to the beneficiary and keep nothing for themselves.[11] Not surprisingly, fiduciaries saw no point in accepting such legacies and refused them, so they wholly failed. As a result, in later Roman law the fiduciary had to be given at least one-quarter of the property for himself, and the fundamental notion that fiduciary and beneficiary had entirely separate interests, which each beneficially owned, was passed on to the modern civil law systems.[12]

This purpose closely parallels the early English use, particularly in that the trusted friend, as fiduciary, held dominium over the estate until it was restored to the fideicommissary, that is, the beneficiary. As with the trust, the obligation to the beneficiary was not one for which he could seek legal remedy for there was none. The obligation was one founded on good faith, which Cicero expressed as "The foundation of Justice is good faith—in other words, consistency and truthfulness as regards promises and agreements."[13]

Following this paradigm, an aggrieved fideicommissary appealed to the Roman emperor seeking relief for breaches of moral obligations; The Roman emperor in turn ordered the consuls to fashion an "equitable" remedy. Eventually this practice grew in popularity, and a special proctor, called a *fideicommissarius*, was appointed to deal with fideicommissa. This closely mirrors the English role of the chancellor in the twelfth through the fifteenth centuries. Further, the historian Gibbon said, "[T]he invention of the fideicommissa or trusts, arose from the struggle between natural justice and positive jurisprudence."[14] This is strikingly similar to the symbiotic relationship that developed between the common law and equity, of which Frederic William Maitland said, "[E]quity without the law would be as a castle in the air, an impossibility."[15]

EUROPEAN COMMON LAW

Accordingly, the fideicommissum found its way into modern European legal systems. In France, it became known as the substitution *fidÈicommissaire*. In some countries, it became possible to use the fideicommissum not simply as a testamentary device but also as a contract inter vivos (for example in marriage settlements). Some of the European civil law systems, such as that of Switzerland, not only had the fidÈicommissaire as part of their law of succession, but also recognized the concept of the fiduciary agent who is the legal owner of property vis-à-vis third parties but not against the settlor/beneficiary. This latter relationship is regarded as a kind of mandate and dealt with as part of the law of obligations. Since 1983 Luxembourg has had the concept of the fiducie, or fiduciary contract, under which a Luxembourg bank may hold assets for the benefit of the settlor/beneficiary. This can be used instead of a trust in many commercial situations but is less useful in the personal/social context. Many European systems also recognize the *fondation, fondazione, stichting,* or *Stiftung,* which is a fund of assets dedicated by its founder to a particular purpose and supervised by a public authority, and which acquires a separate legal personality upon registration. The French Parliament is currently considering a *projet de loi* to create a new institution in French law, the *fiducie,* with characteristics similar to those of the trust.

When William the Conqueror introduced common law in England in 1066, the *Corpus Juris Civilis* was already in existence for more than 500 years. To an extent, the civilian experience with equity was a primer for the "King's conscience" and his ecclesiastic chancellor who was trained in Roman law. Even the supposedly unique common law concept of a proprietary right and in rem tracing is found in early Roman law. Quoting Justinian, "But ...if in his lust for wealth he should hastily proceed to sell or mortgage in the hope that the condition will not take effect, let him know that upon the fulfillment of the condition, the transaction will be treated as of no effect from the beginning."[16]

The modern common law trust evolved from English history and is founded in what is considered the uniquely English "legal" concept of equity.

To that extent, the term "common law trust" is largely a misnomer in that English common law and equity are separate legal systems.

Equity

Equity can be looked upon conceptually as a system of fundamental fairness that developed to counteract the harshness and limitations of the common law and its associated legal remedies. Real justice, then, was to be found in the king as the embodiment of the *fons et origo justitiae*, that is, the fountain and source of justice. "Equity grew out of the residuum of justice left in the King"[17] where the common law system of writs resulted in unduly harsh or inadequate remedies. During its early development, the king referred such complaints to the advice of his council. The council in turn referred the matter to the chancellor who in the early period was not a lawyer but an ecclesiastic trained in Roman law and canon law. The chancellor was said to be imbued with the "King's conscience" and possessed the authority to override the abstention or judgment of the common law courts. This function of the chancellor eventually evolved into the Court of Chancery.

In the early sixteenth century, the ecclesiastical reign gave way to lawyers who began to carve out a system of equity that would ultimately be lauded as "[a] noble, rational and uniform system."[18] This point is quite important if scrutinized with an analytical view regarding the theme of this examination. It is also important to note that the term "equity" in a legal context is not exactly what the word denotes in its customary usage. Equity as a system of law is more narrowly tailored than the general proletarian concept of equity and fundamental fairness.

The Trust

Equity's greatest contribution to the world is that it has presented the world with its "largest and most important invention"—the trust. [19] Thus, the trust is believed to be a creature of equity as its genesis is properly found there. The trust developed from the ignoble medieval practice of conveying property to a use. Essentially, a feoffor conveyed his estate in land to a feoffee to hold for the use of a beneficiary or "*cestui que use.*" A curiosity of this system was that the feoffee was given the title to the feoffor's estate with the cestui que use having no enforceable legal rights against the feoffee should he fail to discharge his moral obligation. Notwithstanding the inherent risks, the inability and inequity of the common law in defending the rights of the cestui que use could be tempered by equitable intervention. The scheme thereafter developed rapidly into a viable and frequently used device to avoid conveyance taxes, that is, fines and incidents associated with the feudal system. The trust's use became popular to such a degree that during the reign of Henry V (1413–1422) the majority of the land in England was held in use.

Eventually, Parliament (and King Henry VIII) enacted one of the world's earliest anti-avoidance statutes, the Statute of Uses 1535. The effect of the statute was, however, arguably opposite to its purported purpose. Over the next several centuries, the statute was strictly interpreted by the courts in favor of finding that the statute did not succeed in eliminating the use or the practice of separating a beneficial and legal interest in the estate. The use continued and "what began life as the 'use' came to be known as the trust as a result of the Statute of Uses."[20] This is largely due to the courts' interpretation of the act as not prohibiting a "use upon a use" and the conclusion that the second use was the "trust."

As the trust's popularity expanded, the Court of Chancery had opportunity to broaden and impose its system over common law. Ultimately, equity perfected the concept of duality of estates and the equitable remedies of the cestui que trust. By finding the feoffee to have a legal estate subject to an equitable interest, there are in effect two estates. From this seemingly logical concept comes the proprietary interest of beneficiaries and the arrival of the modern common law trust.

U.S. COMMON LAW OF TRUSTS

Under the common law of trusts, a trustee has several basic fiduciary duties to the beneficiary of the trust. These basic duties are as follows:

- A duty to see that the property of the trust is legally designated as trust property
- A duty not to delegate to others trustee powers over trust property
- A duty of undivided loyalty to the beneficiaries of the trust
- A duty to invest prudently by maximizing returns on and ensuring the safety of trust assets

In sum, the primary themes among these duties are loyalty and prudence. Furthermore, The Restatement of the Law Third of Trusts (1990) and the Uniform Prudent Investor Act identify these principles of prudent investing:

- **Duty to diversify.** If the decision is to forgo the benefits of diversification, good reason is needed.

- **Duty to invest according to a suitable level of risk.** Risk and return must be weighed in the context of the trust's objectives.

- **Duty to avoid unnecessary expenses.** If the decision is to pay higher costs than necessary, good reason is needed.

- **Duty to seek advice when necessary.** If the decision is that help is needed, an advisor must be chosen carefully and actions monitored.

Under the common law of trusts, a trustee's duty of loyalty is the duty to act in the interest of the trust as if the trustee had no other competing interests to protect, especially his or her own. This duty is a component of all fiduciary relationships. In 1928, U.S. Supreme Court Justice Benjamin Cardozo conveyed this high standard of loyalty when he asserted:

> Many forms of conduct permissible in a workaday world for those acting at arm's length are forbidden to those bound by fiduciary ties. A trustee is held to something stricter that the morals of the market place. Not honestly alone, but the punctilio of an honor the most sensitive, is then the standard of behavior. As to this there has developed a tradition that is unbending and inveterate. Uncompromising rigidity has been the attitude of courts of equity when petitioned to undermine the rule of undivided loyalty by the "disintegrating erosion" of particular exceptions. Only thus has the level of conduct of fiduciaries been kept at a level higher than that trodden by the crowd.[21]

This extreme expression of singular loyalty under the common law of trusts sets out strict prohibition against fiduciary conflicts of interest, which has been the hallmark of subsequent legislation and litigation under ERISA.

In addition to the duty of undivided loyalty to the beneficiaries of a trust, a trustee under the common law of trusts has the duty of prudence in managing trust assets. The duty of prudence established a standard of performance in managing trust assets measured as equivalent to the care exercised by a person of ordinary prudence in dealing with the fiduciary's own assets. The standard of skill and care established under the traditional common law of trusts is that of a person of ordinary prudence, or the prudent man rule. This rule owes its genesis to the case of *Harvard College v. Amory* in 1830, which held:

> All that can be required of a trustee is to invest, is that he shall conduct himself faithfully and exercise a sound discretion. He is to observe how men of prudence, discretion and intelligence manage their own affairs, not in funds, considering the

probable income, as well as the probable safety of the capital to be invested.[22]

This flexible standard under the common law proved vague enough that trustees, including fiduciaries of employee benefit plans, found little comfort in making individual investment choices on behalf of the trust. Likewise, beneficiaries who were disappointed in the performance of a trust often found it difficult to maintain a legal action in proving a fiduciary's lack of prudence and breach of trust. The prudent man rule was applied on an investment-by-investment basis rather than looking at the overall performance of the trust's portfolio of assets. Overall, the common law of trusts ultimately proved a poorly stocked toolbox in meeting the special requirements of employee benefit plans.

HISTORY OF ERISA

During the first half of the nineteenth century most men worked in handicrafts or farming and support in old age was provided by their offspring who had taken over the family business or farm. The last third of that century saw manufacturing employment increase at twice the rate of population growth, and these new workers needed to find a different way to provide for their old age. This was also a period when banks, insurance companies, and the stock and bond markets were developing many new financial capital instruments for retirement saving.[23] This was also a period of widespread labor unrest, with violent strikes and the rise of labor unions. As the nineteenth century ended, employers faced an aging workforce with potentially diminished capacity. In response some of the more enlightened employers started providing a variety of benefits for their workers—a response that has been called "welfare capitalism."[24]

The American Express Company, then a railroad shipping company, established the first employer-sponsored retirement plans in 1875.[25] The American Express plan applied only to disabled elderly employees.[26] A worker was eligible only upon completing 20 years of service and reaching age sixty. Additionally, the company's general manager had to recommend retirement, subject to approval by the executive committee of the board of directors. The annual benefit was 50% of the worker's annual average pay during the ten years preceding retirement, up to a maximum of $500 annually. Four decades later in 1915, the company was still operating under the same plan except that the age requirement had been dropped. The following is an excerpt from the company's executive committee resolution approving this program.

Cases [are] constantly arising of application for assistance by employees of the Company, injured or worn out in the service. It [is] therefore
Resolved:
[T]hat all payments on account of the above named application be charged to a separate account to [be] known as the Pension account, and not charged as heretofore to current expenses.
Resolved:
[T]hat the Genl Supt. is hereby directed to report to the Executive Committee [the] names of such employees of the Co. as are now deserving and entitled to such assistance and heretofore from time to time report such additional cases as may arise.
Adopted

Hence, American Express formalized an accessible, informal welfare capitalist program as a ceremonial accounting convenience.

Employer-sponsored pension growth was slow, primarily because of the Depression between 1873 and 1879. In 1880, Baltimore & Ohio Railroad installed the second U.S. private pension plan with similar motives as American Express—an expression of corporate generosity. Moreover, B&O provided old age income protection as part of the first formal and comprehensive employee benefit package in the railroad industry. Unlike American Express, B&O thoroughly specified program details, unambiguously joined pension benefits to its broader welfare scheme, and actively publicized the program. Consequently B&O became the model for railroad welfare-capitalist practice, and other companies over the remainder of the century used similar program structures.

Throughout the late nineteenth century until the Great Depression, pension plans grew primarily in the railroad, banking, and public utility fields. Pension benefits were regarded as a gift from the employer in recognition of long and faithful service. Many of these early arrangements were inadequately funded and ultimately were terminated. During this period, pension plans had minimal government supervision. Employers had no legal obligation to provide retirement benefits. Once a plan was established, an employer maintained the right to deny, reduce, or terminate benefits at its discretion. For the most part, pensions during this period were viewed as a reward rather than a right.

In 1900 the Pennsylvania Railroad, the largest private employer in the country, established the first modern pension. After much study and deliberation, it created a plan that was equal to 1% of an employee's average wage during the last ten years of employment times the number of years worked. The plan, which included a mandatory retirement age of seventy and covered all workers, was justified as a payroll saving because older workers could be replaced with less expensive and more productive younger workers. In order for the company to have complete control, the plan was noncontributory and the pension board did not include labor representation.[27]

During the first two decades of the twentieth century, most large corporations financed their pensions from operating funds and had no reserves. After the well-publicized failure of the Morris Packing Company pension in 1923, suggestions for reform came from government, consultants, and insurance companies, specifically asking that pension costs should be accrued, funds should be held with an independent fiduciary, and workers should be vested. Employers resisted reform on all three counts. From the beginning, most plans were noncontributory so that employers could terminate them at any time. Actuarial costs were difficult to estimate with most plans because benefits were based on final salaries. Building trust funds was expensive and these might be seen as employee assets. Corporations did not want to turn over funds to another institution when they felt they could better use the funds themselves. Finally, vesting was the least desirable idea because employers wanted to give pensions to reward only long-serving employees. In general there was a conflict between the reformers' view of pensions as deferred wages and the corporations' view of pensions as tools for controlling their workforce. In fact, throughout the first half-century of employer pension plan growth (1880–1930), during which more than 400 private pension plans were established, almost all were discretionary. Vesting—the guaranteed right of an employee to a future benefit—was virtually unheard of in the pension plans of the early twentieth century. Undeniably,

> At the turn of the century, when the early pension plans were being established, employers felt little pension obligation to any employee who did not stay alive, stay well, and stay put until retirement. Pensions were hardship payments, charity for nearby and visible former workers. If an employee died before retirement, his family usually did not receive anything. If he became disabled after long service, he might be taken care. If he quit or was discharged, he probably received nothing.[28]

Furthermore, an interesting feature of most early pension plans called for a different retirement age for men and women. According to a 1926 Bureau of Labor Statistics study, a third of the pension plans surveyed established retirement ages that were earlier for women than for men.[29] Therefore, women had to begin working for the company earlier in life to be eligible for pension because most plans made no reduction in the service required for the specific retirement age.

Until the early part of the twentieth century, courts did not know how to handle pension issues. Courts frequently viewed them as gratuitous promises, unenforceable by law because they did not involve any immediate reward for services. By the late 1920s, that had begun to change, as state courts began to apply principles of trust and contract law to pension issues. Despite this increasing sophistication of the state courts, pension regulations were inconsistent from state to state and there were no standards for important matters such as funding, vesting, and monitoring the conduct of the people responsible for governing pension plans.

In 1947, the first major piece of federal legislation governing pension plans was approved. That year, Congress passed the Labor Management Relations Act (LMRA, also known as the Taft-Hartley Act). Intended less as a pension reform than as a means of restraining the power of union-dominated pension funds, the Taft-Hartley Act only applied to plans in which unions representing covered employees were involved in the plans' management and governance.[30] The only significant pension legislation during this period prohibited discrimination in favor of highly paid employees—employee benefits earned were still not protected.[31]

In 1950 during labor negotiations, General Motors proposed a fully funded pension plan managed by financial professionals. Essentially this was the first modern private pension plan[32] and was soon followed by a number of initiatives from other companies. The General Motors pension plan was based on two significant assumptions that have been the basis of the pension investment world ever since. First, the proposal included investing the assets in the stock market rather than providing a fixed income (and no more that 5% in any one stock—diversification).[33] Second, General Motors' proposal, which was stunning at the time, stated that funding would not be invested in General Motors' stock.

In the late 1950s and 1960s, congressional committees conducted repeated investigations into the affairs of pension and benefit plans dominated by corrupt labor unions, especially the Teamsters. These investigations, most notably that of the Senate's McClellan Committee led by chief counsel Robert F. Kennedy, found widespread looting of plan funds through sweetheart deals, kickbacks, and various forms of cronyism.[34]

In the mid-1960s, Studebaker Corporation, the oldest automobile manufacturer in the United States, collapsed, leaving its pension plan with less than 20% of the assets it needed to pay promised benefits.[35] Studebaker started out in the mid-1800s making covered wagons, then horseless carriages, and finally cars, including stylish models like the Avanti and Starliner. A company hand-book promised employees that upon retirement "[Y]ou'll be able to settle down on a farm ...visit around the country or just take it easy ...and know that you'll still be getting a regular monthly pension paid for entirely by the company."[36]

According to the terms of the plan, the first claims went to retirees and employees eligible to retire. This population was approximately 3,600 partici-pants or a third of the total workforce. They were entitled to benefits in full. After Studebaker purchased lifetime annuities from Aetna for $21.5 million of the fund's $24 million, the remaining $2.5 million was paid in lump-sum ben-efits to 4,080 participants who were vested but still too young to retiree. This represented only a 15% replacement value on this total benefit. The final group of 2,900 participants, who had not vested, received nothing.

Fundamentally, the fiasco that resulted from thousands of former Studebaker employees suddenly finding themselves without their promised pension created the public pressure necessary for Congress to pass compre-hensive pension reform. Congress responded with the enactment of ERISA fiduciary and remedy law. The enactment of the Employee Retirement Income Security Act of 1974 (ERISA) was the culmination of more than a decade of investigation into the affairs of pension and employee benefit plans conducted by Congress, presidential commissions, and the Departments of Labor, Justice and Treasury.[37] ERISA was primarily designed to protect pension plan partici-pants and beneficiaries against two hazards: default risk and administration risk that had been revealed spectacularly in pre-ERISA practice.

Furthermore, the drafting of ERISA was driven by Congress' intent to establish a comprehensive federal regulatory scheme for the operation of pen-sion plans and other employee benefit plans based on new and unwavering principles of fiduciary duty that would be enforced with uncompromising rigidity.[38] The new federal law of employee benefit trusts had four major objectives. They were:

1. A uniform legal culture of fiduciary duties would be developed incre-mentally by the federal courts to define further the statutory standards of ERISA on a case-by-case basis that would supersede the traditional common law of trusts, which had been unevenly applied and inter-preted under the individual laws of each state.

2. Those fiduciary standards developed under ERISA would be clarified and modified purposely to accommodate the special needs and pur-poses of pension plans.

3. Employee pension plan beneficiaries would have liberal access to the federal courts in enforcing the fiduciary standards of ERISA, and those plan fiduciaries found to have breached their duties could be held personally liable for resulting plan losses.

4. Fiduciaries of employee benefit plans not utilizing the trust form as a funding vehicle would still be subject to the fiduciary standards of ERISA.

Congress was able to adopt and adapt the familiar trust model as the regulatory system. Moreover, ERISA subjected ERISA-covered plans to a "belt and suspender" application of trust law.[39] ERISA requires a mandatory trusteeship, obligating that "all assets of an employee benefit plan shall be held in trust by one or more trustees,"[40] who are subject to the strict fiduciary duties discussed below. Furthermore, ERISA extends the realm of fiduciary duty far beyond the plan's trustees. ERISA requires every plan to "provide for one or more named fiduciaries" who are "to control and manage the operation and administration of the plan,"[41] and the statute treats anyone as a fiduciary to the extent that person exercises material discretion over the plan or its assets.[42] Therefore, ERISA subjected all significant aspects of plan administration to fiduciary duties and remedies derived from trust law and hence exclusively from equity.

There are two great principles of trust fiduciary law: the rules of loyalty and the rules of prudence. ERISA codifies both. The loyalty rule forbids self-serving behavior. ERISA's version, patterned on the Restatement of Trusts,[43] requires that "a fiduciary shall discharge his duties with respect to a plan solely in the interest of the participants and beneficiaries and ...for the exclusive purpose of...providing benefits to participants and their beneficiaries."[44] The prudence rule imposes an objective standard of care, comparable to the reasonable person rule of tort law, holding trustees to the standard of conduct expected of similarly situated decision makers.[45] ERISA's prudence rule tracks this standard, obliging the ERISA fiduciary to exercise "the care, skill, prudence, and diligence" of a "prudent man acting in like capacity."[46]

In transposing the trust model as the regulatory system for this new field of federal law, Congress chose not to replicate much of the detail of traditional trust law.[47] Instead, the drafters of ERISA propounded the two grand principles of loyalty and prudence, leaving most of the details to be worked out in fiduciary practice under regulatory and judicial oversight. As the Supreme Court held "Congress intended that the courts would look to the settled experience of the common law in giving shape to a federal common law of rights and obligations under ERISA-regulated plans."[48] Congress also gave extensive regulatory authority over ERISA fiduciary law to the U.S. Department of Labor, which has produced an important body of regulations interpreting ERISA. The drafters surely decided to be discreet with the understanding that the courts would apply the subordinate rules of trust fiduciary law that were not spelled out in ERISA as manifestations of the core norms of loyalty and prudence that ERISA preserved. Thus many familiar rules of trust administration did not find their way into the text of ERISA. Examples of exclusion were:

- The duty to inform beneficiaries about significant aspects of trust administration
- The duty to collect
- The duty to segregate, earmark, and protect trust property
- The duty to enforce and defend claims[49]

Nevertheless, courts, including the U.S. Supreme Court, have understood to import these principles as appropriate in the course of applying ERISA's duties of loyalty and prudence. ERISA also omits large swaths of traditional trust law that is structurally inapplicable to pension and employee benefit trusts. For example, having originated as a branch of the law of donative transfers, the law of trusts has been particularly attuned to the problems associated with successive (usually life and remainder) estates.[50] By contrast, pension and employee benefit plan trusts are commercial arrangements arising from the employment relationship.[51] In ERISA Congress had no need to carry over doctrines of trust law that are oriented to intrafamilial wealth transfer.

Conversely, in a number of important respects ERISA went beyond the common law of trusts in establishing or extending new legal standards of conduct to plan fiduciaries. Some of the more significant distinctions are:

1. By combining the exclusive benefit rule under the Internal Revenue Code with the "sole benefit standard" as stated under the Labor Management Relations Act, ERISA now required plan fiduciaries to act solely in the interest of the plan's participants and beneficiaries for the exclusive purpose of providing plan benefits or defraying reasonable administrative expenses of the plan. This established the sole benefit standard of fiduciary conduct under ERISA.

2. A plan fiduciary now could take little comfort in managing a plan with only the ordinary prudence required under the traditional prudent man rule. Instead, under ERISA a fiduciary needed to act with the care, skill, prudence, and diligence under the circumstances then prevailing that a prudent man acting in a like capacity and familiar with such matters

used in the conduct of an enterprise of a like character and with like aims. This established the prudent expert rule of ERISA.

3. A fiduciary was still required to diversify the investment of a plan portfolio to minimize the risk of large losses unless under the circumstances it was clearly not prudent to do so. This closely resembled the fiduciary principle known under the common law of trusts as the diversification rule.

4. A fiduciary needed to follow strictly the terms of the written plan document (unless otherwise in violation of ERISA) and to administer the plan in a fair, uniform, and nondiscriminatory manner. This principle has come to be called the plan document rule.

5. Unless otherwise exempted, a fiduciary could not allow a plan to engage directly or indirectly in transactions prohibited under ERISA, a caveat known as the prohibited transaction rule.

ERISA DEFINED

ERISA section 3 broadly defines the term "employee benefit plan" to include any pension benefit plan or any welfare benefit plan. A pension benefit plan is "any plan, fund, or program" that provides retirement or deferred income to employees. A welfare benefit plan is "any plan, fund, or program" that provides, through the purchase of insurance or otherwise: (1) severance pay; (2) medical benefits; (3) benefits in the event of sickness, accident, disability, death or unemployment; (4) vacation benefits; (5) apprenticeship or training programs; (6) day care centers; (7) scholarship funds; (8) prepaid legal services; or (9) any benefit described in the Taft Hartley Act § 302(c) (other than pension benefits).[52]

ERISA is applicable to any "employee benefit plan" established or maintained by an employer engaged in interstate commerce or an employee organization representing employees of such employers or both.[53] Employee organizations include both labor unions and beneficiary associations. The principal exceptions to ERISA's coverage are: (1) governmental plans,[54] (2) church plans,[55] and (3) plans maintained solely for the purpose of complying with workers' compensation, unemployment compensation, or disability laws.[56] Department of Labor (DOL) regulations[57] also carve out exceptions for benefit programs that an employer offers without endorsement or administrative support, such as payroll deduction, and for certain payroll practices.

ERISA's Four Titles

ERISA has four titles. Title I, "Protection of Employee Benefit Rights," is the focus of this book. Title I establishes reporting, disclosure, and fiduciary responsibility standards for all ERISA-governed plans. It creates standards for plan participation, benefit vesting, benefit accrual, and benefit funding for pension plans; it also sets forth administration and enforcement provisions concerning those standards. In addition, Title I establishes plan design rules for group health plans.

Title II, which applies only to tax-qualified retirement plans, contains amendments to the Internal Revenue Code, many of which parallel the provisions of Title I. Title III includes various jurisdictional and administrative provisions, and Title IV creates an insurance program administered by the Pension Benefit Guaranty Corporation for defined benefit retirement plans that terminate without sufficient assets to cover vested benefits.

The Player Line-Up

ERISA defines five key functions: plan sponsor, plan participant, plan administrator, plan trustee, and plan fiduciary.

- The plan sponsor is the employer or employee organization that establishes the plan. In the case of a plan maintained by two or more employers or by an employer and an employee organization, the sponsor is the joint board of trustees or other similar group of representatives that establishes or maintains the plan.[58]

- A plan participant is an employee or employee organization member who is or may become eligible for employee benefit plan coverage. (A covered dependent is considered a "beneficiary.")[59]

- The plan administrator is responsible for compliance with ERISA's reporting and disclosure obligations. The plan sponsor is the plan administrator unless a different party is named in the plan document. It is better practice to avoid naming an individual person as plan administrator because the administrator is liable for ERISA reporting and disclosure noncompliance penalties.[60]

- A plan fiduciary is a person with discretionary authority over either plan administration or plan assets.[61] In a funded plan, the party with discretionary authority over plan investments is a fiduciary. In both types of plan, the party with discretionary authority over claims payment decisions is a fiduciary. The courts have recognized, however, that plan design decisions, even if made by a named plan fiduciary, are plan sponsor actions that are not subject to ERISA's fiduciary responsibility rules discussed below.[62] ERISA prohibits persons who have been convicted of certain crimes from serving as an administrator; fiduciary; officer; trustee; custodian; counsel; agent; or employee of, or consultant to, an employee benefit plan during a court-established period of three to thirteen years after such conviction or release from imprisonment, whichever is later.[63]

3

OVERVIEW OF PENSION PLANS

The pace of change will not slow and it will continue to be influenced largely by participants.[64]

A "qualified retirement plan" with its accompanying trust is a plan authorized to provide benefits to employees. Qualified retirement plans provide special tax benefits for both employers and employees, but they must satisfy rigorous tax requirements.

There are two basic categories of pension plans: defined benefit and defined contribution. Defined benefit plans promise to make payments at retirement that are determined by a specific formula, often based on average earnings, years of service, or other factors. In contrast, defined contribution plans use individual accounts that may be funded by employers, employees, or both; the benefit level at retirement depends on contribution levels and investment performance.

During the post–World War II era, the number of employer-sponsored U.S. pension plans grew dramatically. Although significant in terms of percentage of a companies' basis, it has paled in comparison to the volume of the last twenty years. Figure 3-1 illustrates the growth in the number of U.S. private pension plans from 1875 through 2000.

Figure 3-1: The Number of U.S. Private Pension Plans from 1875–2000

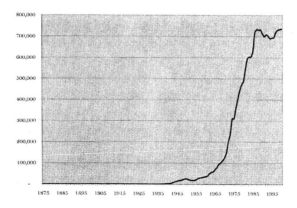

Over the past quarter century, employment-based private pensions have shifted dramatically from defined benefit plans to defined contribution plans, as illustrated in figure 3-2. Data from the U.S. Department of Labor (DOL) indicates that between 1975 and 1997 growth in defined contribution plans outpaced defined benefit plans in every major measure of comparison—assets, benefits paid out, active participants, and contributions.[65] The number of participants in these plans has grown from nearly twelve million in 1975 to over fifty-eight million in 1998. Over three-fourths of all pension-covered workers enroll in either a primary or supplemental defined contribution plan. Assets held by these plans increased from $74 billion in 1975 to over $2 trillion today.

Figure 3-2: Defined Contribution Pension Plans as a Percent of Total Pension Plans

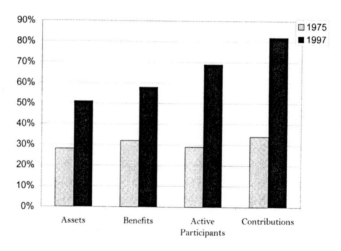

Most of the new pension coverage has been in defined contribution plans. Nearly all new businesses establishing pension plans choose to adopt defined contribution plans, specifically 401(k) plans. In addition, many large employers with existing defined benefit plans adopt 401(k)s and other kinds of defined contribution plans to provide supplemental benefits to their workers.

Most workers whose 401(k) plans are invested heavily in company stock have at least one other pension plan sponsored by their employer. Just 10% of all company stock held by large 401(k) plans (plans with 100 or more participants) was held by stand-alone plans in 1996; the other 90% was held by 401(k) plans that operate alongside other pension plans, such as defined benefit plans covering the same workers.

Although there has been a shift to defined contribution plans, defined benefit plans remain a vital component of our retirement system. Under defined benefit plans, workers are assured of a predictable benefit upon retirement that does not vary with investment results.

The trends in the pension system are a reflection of fundamental changes in the economy as well as the current preferences of workers and employers. Three influences explain the increased use of defined contribution plans. First, governmental regulations have an overwhelming influence on plan choice.[66] Second, a changing workplace has contributed to the rise of defined contribution plans.[67] Third, the economy in general has led to more flexibility in the plan's design.[68]

First, the impact of the government has been the most significant force driving the shift to defined contribution plans. Intentional or not, government legislation, regulations, and court rulings have greatly increased the attractiveness of defined contribution plans versus defined benefit plans. The most influential governmental actions contributing to this shift are detailed as follows:

- Administrative complexity and frequent regulatory change have an asymmetrical influence for defined benefit plans.

- Increasing Pension Benefit Guaranty Corporation (PBGC) premiums add to the cost of private defined benefit plans.

- Full-funding limitation and liquidity requirements mitigate a defined benefit advantage.

- Tax changes related to reversions increase the desire to switch to a defined contribution structure.

- Impact on defined benefit plans by suspension of 30-Year Bonds may have a negative affect.

Second, the movement from a manufacturing-based economy to a service-based economy, the growth in the number of families with two wage earners, the increase in the number of part-time and temporary workers in the economy, and the increased mobility of workers has led to the growing popularity of defined contribution plans. Employers' views have similarly changed. Increased competition and economic volatility have made it much more difficult to undertake the long-term financial commitment necessary for a defined benefit pension plan. Many employers perceive defined contribution plans to be advantageous. Moreover, employees have also embraced the idea of having more direct control over the amount of contributions and the kind of investments made to their pension account.

Finally, as global competition increased with the onset of widespread globalization in the 1980s, many companies sought benefit plans that aligned benefits with employee performance. In a time of uncertain profits, defined contribution plans, because of fewer regulations, are preferred over defined benefit plans.

DEFINED BENEFIT PENSION PLANS

Once the cornerstone of private retirement security, defined benefit pension plans today face a number of severe challenges. They include complex funding rules, significant investment and interest rate risks, and looming accounting changes that will increase balance sheet volatility. Many employers question the need for pension plans with unfunded liabilities. Employees appear to prefer the portability, control, and transparency offered by 401(k) or comparable defined contribution plans. Since 1985, the number of defined benefit plans insured by the U.S. Pension Benefit Guaranty Corporation has declined from 114,500 to less than 32,000.

Despite the challenges and declining numbers, defined benefit pension plans can create value for employers and employees by providing the same benefit for a lower cost than could otherwise be obtained or a greater benefit for the same cost. Employer-sponsored health and life insurance plans, for example, create value by pooling risk and purchasing power. Benefits are provided to all employees (many of whom may be uninsurable on an individual basis) at a lower cost than if individuals purchased the insurance. Pension plans have similar characteristics, but these features are often overlooked because of the deferred nature of the benefits.

Defined benefit pension plans can also create value directly for the employer by lowering overall employment costs and increasing workforce productivity. Pension contributions, which are allocated primarily to those employees who stay with the organization, encourage continued employment, thus lowering turnover costs and helping to retain intellectual capital. Moreover, well-designed defined benefit plans can overcome the perceived shortcomings of pensions.

Differences between a Traditional Formula Defined Benefit Plan and a Cash Balance Formula Defined Benefit Plan

Cash balance plans are the most common form of hybrid pension plan. Hybrids are defined benefit plans with defined contribution characteristics. Like all defined benefit plans, a cash balance formula plan "defines" or specifies the retirement benefit that will ultimately be paid out. Nevertheless, the way in which retirement benefits are calculated is not the same as with traditional defined benefit pension plans. Cash balance plans have been created largely by means of conversions of traditional defined benefit plans.[69] Bank of America created the first cash balance plan in 1985 yet most conversion occurred in the late 1990s.[70]

Under a traditional formula defined benefit pension plan, retirement benefits are based on a formula such as a set dollar amount for each year worked, or a specified percentage of earnings. Often, these traditional formula pension plans calculate an employee's retirement benefit by averaging the employee's earnings during the last few years of employment, taking a specified percentage of the average, and then multiplying it by the employee's total years of service. This typical end-of-the-career approach of a traditional formula defined benefit plan can increase an employee's retirement benefit by emphasizing the usually higher salary of the last years of employment.

By contrast, with cash balance formula plans the retirement benefit paid is the total accumulation of all contributions over the employee's working career and earnings "credited" to the employee's hypothetical account as of retirement age. A cash balance plan does not give as much weight to the last years of salary—it looks at an employee's entire salary history.

A cash balance formula plan may allow participants to elect distribution of their vested benefits before attaining retirement age (e.g., upon separation from service). In this case, the amount the participant is entitled to receive may or may not exactly equate to the participant's hypothetical account balance. The amount the participant is entitled to receive is actually the present value of the future benefit (calculated by actuaries) at retirement age.

Although a cash balance formula plan is a defined benefit plan, on a hypothetical basis it resembles a defined contribution plan. With a cash balance formula plan, each participant has his or her own individual account into which employer contributions are credited. The contributions are generally based on a percentage of pay. Each participant's individual account also is credited with interest. Upon withdrawal, by law cash balance plans must provide an annuity option. A lump-sum option also may be provided, but this is at the discretion of the employer.

A cash balance formula plan is different from a defined contribution plan and most other kinds of defined benefit plans. The cash balance plan does not define employer contributions but instead defines the future pension benefits that will accrue in each individual account. Because the cash balance plan stresses the current lump sum of an individual participant's benefit, the plan's assets have no direct relationship to the individual account accruals.

Employer contributions are based on actuarial valuations. Because the actuarial valuations are not present value valuations, the employer contributions may be less than the sum of the additions to the participant's account.

The interest-rate by which a cash balance plan account is promised to grow generally is some specified rate related to a bond index rate or Treasury bill fund rate.

The sponsor of the plan determines how the assets from the plan will be invested. The sponsor therefore legally assumes all the risks. Nonetheless, they can definitely acquire all short-term rewards and the potential for getting all future rewards. A cash balance plan can be worthwhile to the sponsor if there is a large positive difference between the rate of return promised to the employee and the rate at which the assets earn when invested. The investment gains and losses also will affect the employer's future contributions to fully fund the pension plan. If the employer can earn a high enough differential between the promised rate of return and the actual rate of return, the plan can become self-funded. Those managing a cash balance plan's portfolio seek the highest long-term rate consistent with the appropriate risk levels. Although management may not achieve the required interest rate in one year, over time they are likely to earn a return on the investment portfolio that is greater than or equal to the set rate.

Cash balance plans are subject to the same ERISA regulations as other defined benefit plans. The vesting is required to meet the minimum vesting requirements under both cliff (five years) and graded vesting (three to seven years). The funding rules for the plan are the same as for other defined benefit plans. Unlike defined contribution plans, however, the PBGC must insure cash balance plans. By definition, a defined contribution plan is always fully funded, and therefore plan termination insurance is not needed. Insurance is required under the cash balance plan, however, because it is possible for participants to lose part of their accrued benefits.

Under a typical defined benefit plan, two employees with equal pay but differing years of service will earn the same amount of retirement income for each new year of service. Nevertheless, note, because the money invested for an older employee (who is closer to retirement), the employer's cost of funding the pension obligation for a younger employee is less than that for the older employee. Also note that the combination of a defined benefit, a low promised interest rate, and a bull market may create a fully funded plan running years into the future solely on self-funding, thus eliminating the employer's obligation for any current contributions. For employees who terminate employment at younger ages, both the accrued employee benefits and the employer's costs are low. No doubt this is one of the reasons why younger employees place low value on non-portable defined benefit plans.

Traditional pension plan benefit formulas are oriented toward the total retirement benefit, taking into account the retirement age and the length of service of the employee. In stark contrast, cash balance plans emphasize annual accumulations and therefore may not be as flexible as traditional plans in providing specific levels of retirement income.

Issues with Cash Balance Plans

The process of converting and administering cash balance plans has received considerable attention in recent years. Until Congress and the Treasury Department resolve these open issues, the continued role of this type of pension plan is aleatory at best. In 1999 the IRS imposed a moratorium on determination letters for cash balance conversion pending clarification of applicable legal requirements.[71] Under the moratorium, all determination letter requests regarding cash balance plans are sent to the national office for review; however, the national office is not currently acting on these plans. [72] The Treasury Department recently issued proposed regulations addressing certain issues relating to cash balance plans.

There are three issues facing cash balance plans: (1) whether limits and non-discrimination testing should be based on benefits or contributions, (2) whether cash balance formulas are age discriminatory by their precise nature, and (3) whether the manner by which a company transitions from a traditional defined benefit formula to a cash balance formula reduces the benefits.

The first issue is whether limits in cash balance plans should continue to be based on benefits. The Internal Revenue Code establishes two key requirements for private pension plans: the limits set on pension plans and the non-discriminatory effect of pension plans with respect to higher-versus lower-paid employees. Defined contribution plans have limits based on contributions and defined benefit plans have limits based on overall benefits. The nature of hybrid plans calls for clarification of the rules regarding limits and non-discrimination provisions.

The second issue stems from the fact that benefits accrued at retirement under a cash balance plan are frequently related to the age of a participant. For example, assuming all else is equal, under a cash balance plan a younger participant's accrued benefit at retirement than an older participant's accrued benefit because the effect of interest credits will have applied for more years. Cash balance formulas and current guidelines for defined benefit plans are incompatible, which causes an age discrimination issue.

Recently cash balance plans won a significant victory. A court concluded that cash balance plans were not inherently age discriminatory under ERISA.[73] This case provides positive precedent for cash balance plans that is needed to ensure the continued viability of all hybrid pension plans.

In 2003 two court decisions increased the legal uncertainties surrounding hybrid plans. In the IBM case, the court found that IBM's pension equity plan and cash balance plan violated the age discrimination rules of ERISA.[74] Additionally, in the Xerox case the court ruled that Xerox's calculation of the lump-sum benefit for participants below normal retirement age was not actuarially equivalent to the normal retirement benefit as required by ERISA.[75]

The publicity generated by these cases led to detrimental legislative activity. In January 2004 the Consolidated Appropriations Act of 2004 was signed into law. This bill includes a provision that prohibits the Treasury Department from issuing regulations on age discrimination issues and requires the Treasury Department to present a legislative proposal to Congress on transition relief for older workers in a cash balance conversion. Because of this provision, on June 15, 2004, the Treasury Department and the IRS decided to withdraw the proposed regulations on age discrimination that had been issued in December of 2002.

The third issue relates to the potential for a reduction of benefits based on methods used when transitioning from a traditional formula to a cash balance. A key transition component is wearaway, which is a period when a participant earns no additional pension benefit following a plan conversion. The two primary causes of wearaway are the elimination of early retirement subsidies and the use of alternative interest rates when calculating initial account balances in cash balance plans.

The first cause occurs when the value of an employee's benefit at conversion under the traditional formula is higher than the value of the employee's converted benefit. Although ERISA mandates[76] that the employee's benefit remain intact as under the traditional formula, some companies freeze the benefits under the cash balance formula until they exceed those of the traditional formula at the time of conversion. There are alternative methods to remedy this cause of wearaway. There are three common remedies:

- **Wearaway (or "greater of" approach):** Under a wearaway approach, a participant does not accrue any additional benefits after the conversion until the participant's benefit under the cash balance formula exceeds the preconversion accrued benefit. Because of this effect, plans with a wearaway are also referred to as using the "greater of" method of calculating benefits. Plan design can greatly affect the length of any wearaway period. Upon a conversion to a cash balance plan, participants are given an opening account balance. The pay and interest credits provided under the plan are then added to this opening balance. The opening account balance may be determined in a variety of ways and is generally a question of plan design. For example, an employer may create an opening account balance that is designed to approximate the benefit a participant would have had based on the participant's compensation and years of service if the cash balance formula had been in effect for the prior years. Depending on the interest and mortality assumptions used, this lump-sum amount may or may not equal the actuarial present value of the participant's accrued balance as of the date of conversion, determined using the statutory interest and mortality assumptions required for lump-sum calculations. Under the wearaway approach, the participant's protected benefit is compared to the normal retirement benefit that is provided by the account balance (plus compensation and interest credits), and the participant does not earn any new benefits until the new benefit exceeds the protected accrued benefit. For example, suppose the value of the protected benefit is $40,000, and the opening account balance under the cash balance formula provides a normal retirement benefit of $35,000. The participant will not earn any new benefits until the hypothetical balance under the cash balance formula increases to the extent that it provides a normal retirement benefit exceeding $40,000.

- **No wearaway (or "sum of" approach):** Under a plan without a wearaway, a participant's protected benefit under the cash balance plan consists of the sum of the benefit accrued before conversion plus benefits under the cash balance formula for years of service after the conversion.[77] This approach is more favorable to plan participants than the wearaway approach because they earn benefits under the new plan immediately. This approach is also referred to as the "A + B" method, where A is the protected benefit and B represents the benefits under the cash balance formula.

- **Grandfathering:** For older and longer-service participants, benefits under a cash balance formula tend to be lower than the benefits a participant may have expected to receive under that traditional benefit formula (the "old" formula).[78] The employer might therefore provide some type of "grandfather" to participants already in the plan or to older or longer-service employees. For example, the participant might be given the choice between the old formula and the cash balance formula for future benefit accruals or, in the case of a final average pay plan, the plan may stop crediting service under the old formula but continue to apply post-conversion pay-increases. This approach goes beyond preserving the benefit protected by the anticutback rules.

The second cause of wearaway occurs when a company uses a higher interest rate when establishing the opening account value under the cash balance formula than that used in the traditional formula. This cause of wearaway can be avoided by using the same interest rate assumptions.

Another transitional component is whipsaw, which results from an awkward accounting procedure that may lead to a mismatch between hypothetical and actual accounting values. For example, to determine the actual account value of a lump-sum benefit at any given point, the hypothetical account value must be projected forward to the normal retirement age, converted to an annuity, and then discounted back to the present. In this process, if the interest-crediting rate matches the discount rate, the hypothetical account and actual value will be equal. On the other hand, if the interest-crediting rate is greater that the discount rate, the hypothetical account balance will exceed the actual lump sum received, and vice versa.

DEFINED CONTRIBUTION PLANS

A defined contribution plan, on the other hand, does not promise a specific amount at retirement (see figures 3-3 and 3-4). In these plans, employees, employers, or both contribute to an individual account under the plan, sometimes at a set rate, such as 5% of earnings annually. These contributions generally are invested either on the participants' behalf or at their direction. Participants ultimately receive the balance in their account, which is based on contributions plus or minus investment gains or losses. The value of their account will fluctuate due to changes in the value of investments. Examples of defined contribution plans include 401(k) plans, 403(b) plans, employee stock ownership plans, and profit-sharing plans. The general rules of ERISA apply to each of these sorts of plans, but some special rules also apply.

Figure 3-3: Differences between Defined Benefit and Defined Contribution Plans

Key Differences Between Plan Types	
Defined Benefit	**Defined Contribution**
Benefit is known	Benefit is unknown
Cost is unknown	Cost is known
Employer bears financial risk	Employee bears financial risk
Generally provides higher benefits for long-service employees	Can provide substantial benefits to short-service employees
Separate account for each employee is not required	Separate account for each employee is required
Requires an enrolled actuary	Actuary is not required; however, a recordkeeper is required
Subject to PBGC premiums	Not subject to PBGC premiums

Figure 3-4: Advantages and Disadvantages of Defined Benefit and Defined Contribution Plans

	Defined Benefit	Defined Contribution
Advantages	Guaranteed retirement income security for workers No investment risk to participants Cost of living adjustments Not dependant on the participant's ability to save	Tax deferred retirement savings medium Participants have a certain degree of how much they choose to save Can be funded through payroll deductions Lump sum distributions may be eligible for special 10 year averaging Participants can benefit from good investment results Easily understood by participants
Disadvantages	Difficult to understand by participant Not beneficial to employees who leave before retirement	Difficult to build a fund for those who enter late in life Participants bear investment risk Annual employee salary reductions is limited annual limits

Money Purchase Pension Plans

A money purchase pension plan is a defined contribution plan in which the employer is obligated to make contributions based on a fixed formula. The plan is subject to certain funding and other rules because a money purchase pension plan requires regular, fixed contributions.

Simplified Employee Pension Plans (SEPs)

SEPs are relatively uncomplicated retirement savings vehicles. A SEP allows employers to contribute on a tax-favored basis to individual retirement accounts (IRAs) owned by employees. SEPs are subject to minimal reporting and disclosure requirements. Under a SEP, the employee must set up an IRA to accept employer's contributions. Generally, the employer can contribute up to 15% of pay into a SEP each year, up to a maximum of $30,000.

If a company employs twenty-five or fewer people, the employer may establish a salary reduction SEP. If the employer has such a plan, in addition to any employer contributions to the SEP the employees may also elect to have SEP contributions made on their behalf from salary on a before-tax basis, up to the lesser of 15% of pay or within annual limitations. The deferral contributions are added to any employer contributions to determine the annual limit ($30,000 or 15% of pay). Other limits may apply to the amount that may be contributed. State and local governments and tax-exempt organizations are not eligible to establish salary reduction SEPs.

Profit Sharing Plan or Stock Bonus Plans

A profit sharing or stock bonus plan is a defined contribution plan under which the plan may provide—or the employer may determine, using a pre-determined formula—how much will be contributed to the plan. The plan contains a formula for allocating to each participant a portion of each annual contribution. A profit sharing plan or stock bonus plan may include a 401(k) plan. Despite the name, contributions are not required to come from profits and contributions can be made even though the employer has no profits.

401(k) Plans

A 401(k) plan is a defined contribution plan that permits contributions under the Internal Revenue Code (the "Code") section 401(k), which allows eligible employees to elect to make pre-tax contributions from their compensation, if certain requirements related to contributions, vesting, nondiscrimination, and distributions are satisfied. A 401(k) plan may provide for matching contributions, which are subject to specific requirements under the Code, and may include other contributions such as profit-sharing contributions. The features of a 401(k) plan may be associated with an employee stock ownership plan. Design-based "safe harbor" and SIMPLE plans are special class of 401(k) plans that avoid some of the nondiscrimination testing requirements in exchange for meeting certain plan design requirements. The adoption of 401(k) plans by a state or local government or a tax-exempt organization is limited by law.

Employee Stock Ownership Plans (ESOPs)

An ESOP is a form of stock bonus plan designed to invest primarily in qualifying employer securities, generally the stock of the employer. Often an ESOP involves a plan loan to purchase the employer securities. This type of ESOP is commonly referred to as a leveraged ESOP. Congress authorized the creation of ESOPs as one method of encouraging employee participation in corporate ownership.

Target Benefit Plans

A target benefit plan is a money purchase plan in which the employer's fixed contributions to an employee's account are determined by reference to the amounts necessary to fund the benefit level stated in the plan. Unlike a defined benefit plan, the participant is not guaranteed the target benefit.

Comparatively, the contribution is guaranteed, with the participant bearing the risk of investment performance not reaching the future target.

4

DETERMINATION OF A FIDUCIARY

It is not the title, but the function that makes a fiduciary

Under ERISA, there are two categories of people whose conduct or activities are subject to legal constraints and standards: plan fiduciaries and parties-in-interest.[79] Fiduciaries, as discussed later, are those people with some true influential power or discretion over a plan. This definition includes those people who have the authority and responsibility with respect to the management of the plan and its assets, regardless of their formal title. Such a person is considered to have such power over the plan to require the application of special fiduciary responsibility provisions. Figure 4-1 depicts the various classes of fiduciary.

Parties-in-interest, on the other hand, include people who have a close relationship to the plan or the sponsor but do not have discretion over the plan or its assets. Because of their close relationship to the plan and the opportunity for abuse, any transaction with a party-in-interest must be reviewed to see whether it violates ERISA's prohibited transaction provisions. These prohibitions along with the definition of party-in-interest are discussed later in this chapter.

FIDUCIARY STATUS

As a practical matter, the issue about whether a person is a fiduciary of a plan only arises when someone is alleging a violation of some fiduciary responsibility. In the case of pension plans, this issue might arise when there has been a loss of assets due to poor investment practices, failure to monitor investments, or failure to perform due diligence regarding the plans' investment advisors. In any event, when such instances occur, participants may look to the fiduciary as a way to regain losses.

Figure 4-1: Fiduciary Classifications

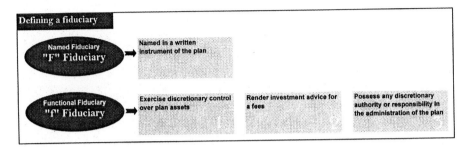

Any person who exercises discretion or authority with respect to the control or maintenance of employee benefit plans will be deemed a fiduciary under ERISA section 3(21). Therefore, the definition of fiduciary under ERISA includes any person who meets any of the following criteria:

- Is named in the plan document as a fiduciary or is appointed as a fiduciary in accordance with a procedure in the plan document
- Exercises any discretionary authority or control over the management of the plan generally or with respect to the management or disposition of plan assets
- Renders investment advice with respect to plan assets for a fee or other compensation
- Exercises any discretionary authority or responsibility in the plan's administration[80]

Named Fiduciary

The first category is a named fiduciary or—in analogous terms to the SEC's insider trading classification of a capital "I" insider—a capital "F" fiduciary. A named fiduciary is the fiduciary pursuant to ERISA's requirement that a plan's written instrument, or document, actually name a fiduciary. The named fiduciary can be an individual, a group of individuals, the employer or company, or a third-party company. The sponsoring employer and trustee are always named fiduciaries.

Every important decision concerning the plan's administration, compliance, communication, and investments originate from the named fiduciary. Even when a named fiduciary delegates duties, he or she retains the onus of selection, monitoring, and retention.

The normal procedure for appointment of a named fiduciary is through the plan document or a written instrument of the plan—the trust document. Nevertheless, the DOL has stated that the named fiduciary requirement of ERISA may be satisfied through a clear identification of persons in a plan document and a statement that they have the authority to control and manage the plan, without referring to them as named fiduciaries.[81]

The legislative history and court decisions indicate that the intention of Congress in requiring a named fiduciary was to concentrate responsibility and liability for the appropriate management of employee benefit plans and their assets.[82] Furthermore, the importance of the named fiduciary is confirmed by its occurrence as the first requirement of section 402 of ERISA. That section provides:

(i) Every employee benefit plan shall be established and maintained pursuant to a written instrument. Such instrument shall provide for one or more named fiduciaries who jointly or severally shall have authority to control and manage the operation of the plan.

(ii) For purposes of this title, the "named fiduciary" means a fiduciary who is named in the plan instrument, or who, pursuant to a procedure specified in the plan, is identified as a fiduciary (A) by a person who is an employer or employee organization with respect to the plan or (B) by such an employer and an employee organization acting jointly.[83]

Moreover, the DOL has stated that the act of appointing such fiduciaries is itself a fiduciary act.[84] Generally, a company's board of directors will designate the named fiduciary either by approving a procedure established in a plan document or by approving a plan document designating a named fiduciary. In such circumstances, the board of directors is a fiduciary with respect to the appointment process. Previous case law treats a board's appointment of a named fiduciary as a functional role—limited to only the appointment. However, recent cases—albeit mostly in dicta—attempt to extend a duty to appoint to a duty to monitor, in essence treating a board member as a named fiduciary.

Functional Fiduciary

The next three categories are considered functional fiduciaries or—in analogous terms to the SEC's insider trading classification of a lowercase "i" insider—a lowercase "f" fiduciary. A functional fiduciary is a person who exercises control over the plan or its investments, or gives investment advice, but who was not formally appointed to perform those roles. While certain positions by their description are without a doubt fiduciaries, such as named fiduciaries discussed above, more frequently courts characterize ERISA's test for fiduciary status as a functional one focusing on whether the person has or has exercised any of the functions defined by ERISA.

In attempting to determine whether a given person is a functional fiduciary, forget about applying any fixed rule. There simply is no bright line test to apply in determining whether one is a fiduciary or is rendering fiduciary-type functions with regard to the plan. For these reasons it becomes even more important for anyone associated with a plan to understand the fiduciary responsibility provisions, as well as the type of activities that might cause a person to be deemed a fiduciary with respect to the plan.

Moreover, it is extremely important to keep sight of the fact that courts have generally interpreted fiduciary status broadly and continue to broaden the definition to include people once thought to be safely beyond the definition. Accordingly, many prudent plan advisors, service providers, and company insiders should assume that they are in fact fiduciaries under ERISA and take appropriate measures to ensure that they do not violate ERISA's fiduciary responsibility provisions.

Deciding whether a person has any of the authority just described is a factual question, demanding an examination of the facts and circumstances of each case. Under this functional approach, a person holding no position with the plan nevertheless becomes a fiduciary if he or she exercises control over a fiduciary function. In other words, formal titles are not controlling. Thus, a person's status as a fiduciary depends on his or her function, authority, and responsibility, regardless of that person's own belief about whether he or she is a fiduciary. The test for determining fiduciary status therefore focuses on whether the person exercises any of the functions described earlier and in section 3(21) of ERISA.[85] Examining each function that establishes fiduciary status is instructive.

Exercise Any Discretionary Authority or Control over the Management of the Plan or Its Assets or Both

To date, the regulations issued by the DOL defining fiduciary status do not set forth the conditions that must exist in order for a person to be deemed a fiduciary based on the level of discretionary authority or control he or she has over the plan's management. On the other hand, other interpretative releases, advisory opinions, and court statements indicate who might be deemed a fiduciary based on such discretionary control:

- **Investment committee members and trustees**
  Generally, the individuals serving on the investment committee of a plan who bear the responsibility for managing plan assets and appoint-

ing investment managers for the plan are plan fiduciaries under this section. Similarly, plan trustees are fiduciaries because of the nature of their functions with respect to the plan. Trustees who act only on direction generally are held to be fiduciaries but with lessened fiduciary obligation, provided the instructions or lack thereof were in accordance with the plan documents and consistent with ERISA. Such persons routinely perform discretionary responsibilities with regard to the plan.

- **Board of director members**

  Members of the board of directors of any employer that maintains a benefit plan will be fiduciaries only to the extent that they personally have responsibility for the discretionary management functions described earlier. For instance, the board of directors might be responsible for the selection and retention of investment managers. In such a case, the board of directors is exercising "discretionary authority or discretionary control respecting the management of the plan," and the directors are therefore fiduciaries.

- **Other officers and employees**

  Note that an officer or employee of an organization that sponsors a benefit plan is not a fiduciary to that plan solely based on holding a particular office in the employer's organization if he or she performs none of the discretionary functions noted earlier. An officer or employee is not a fiduciary unless he or she has or exercises authority, responsibility, or control over the management of the plan. Still, an officer or employee of a plan sponsor is a fiduciary if he or she exercises control through the selection of investments by means of participation on the investment committee of the plan. Such control might exist even when the officer or employee does not formally sit on the committee but has such influence that he or she effectively controls the committee's actions.

- **Benefit managers**

  Other officers and positions in an organization should always be examined to determine whether they perform any of the discretionary functions described earlier. For instance, most companies that sponsor benefit plans have plan benefit managers who have no power to make any decisions about plan policy, interpretations, practices, or procedures, but who do perform administrative functions within a preexisting framework of practices and policies made by other plan fiduciaries. Such persons are generally not deemed fiduciaries because they lack any discretionary authority respecting the management of the plan or the disposition of plan assets. Rather, from the standpoint of ERISA, their functions tend to be ministerial in nature. In addition to ministerial functions, many benefit managers regularly report to plan fiduciaries about certain matters within the discretion of the benefit manager. Such matters might include the preparation of an investment management summary report. As long as the benefit manager does not exercise or participate in the fiduciary decisions, that person is not a plan fiduciary. It is common, however, for benefit managers to sit on plan committees that determine, for instance, which investment advisory firm will manage the assets under the plan. Such a decision is a fiduciary decision and to the extent the benefit manager participates in that decision, he or she is a fiduciary of the plan.

- **Attorneys, accountants, and consultants**
  Although the ordinary functions of attorneys, accountants, and other consultants to plans (other than as investment advisors) may not at first glance be considered fiduciary functions, there will be situations in which such persons, because of their special expertise or their position, may be exercising discretionary control or authority in the management of the plan or its assets. In such situations, it is not at all far-fetched that these persons may be regarded to have assumed fiduciary obligations.

Apart from the apparent situations (that is, those for the trustee, investment committee members, and plan sponsors), the general trend of fiduciary case law has been to test the outer edges of the fiduciary definition. These cases have involved plan service providers who have argued that they are not plan fiduciaries. The trend in these cases appears to be finding fiduciary status where it was not found in earlier cases.

Accordingly, although attorneys, accountants, and other plan consultants performing their usual professional functions will ordinarily not be considered fiduciaries, if the factual situation in a particular case falls within one of the kinds of conduct noted under section 3(21)(A), such a person may be deemed a fiduciary under the plan.[86]

Additionally, DOL regulations provide that a person who performs purely ministerial functions (for example, clerical functions not requiring the exercise of discretion) within the framework of policies, interpretations, rules, practice, and procedures made by other persons is not a fiduciary. The DOL lists the following ministerial, administrative functions that do not fall within ERISA's definition of fiduciary:

- Applying rules to determine eligibility
- Calculating service or compensation credit for benefits
- Preparing employee communication materials

- Maintaining participant service records
- Preparing government agency reports
- Calculating benefits
- Orienting new participants and advising participants of their rights and options under the plan
- Collecting and transmitting contributions as provided in the plan
- Processing claims
- Making recommendations to others for decisions about the plan administration[87]

Rendering Investment Advice for a Fee or Other Compensation

Section 3(21)(A)(ii) of ERISA provides that any person who renders investment advice to a plan for a fee or other compensation, direct or indirect, or has any authority or responsibility to do so is a fiduciary to the plan. This provision has been interpreted and applied broadly to impose fiduciary status on those persons associated with the investment management of the plan.

The DOL's regulations attempt to specify conditions in which a person would be deemed a fiduciary because of the rendering of investment advice.[88] Generally, a person is rendering investment advice to a plan in a manner that will make that person a fiduciary only if that person does the following:

- Makes recommendations about the valuing, buying, holding, or selling of securities or other property
- Has, directly or indirectly, (a) discretionary authority or control over buying or selling securities or other property for the plan, whether or not pursuant to an agreement, arrangement, or understanding; or (b) regularly renders advice to a plan pursuant to a mutual agreement, arrangement, or understanding that such advice will serve as one of the primary bases for the investment of plan assets and that this advice will be based on the particular needs of the plan from the standpoint of investment policy, strategy, diversification, or portfolio composition

In other words, merely rendering investment advice is not enough to make a person a fiduciary of a plan. In order for a person to be considered a plan fiduciary, the investment advice must be given to the plan for a fee or other compensation. In addition, that person must have some level of actual control over buying or selling securities for the plan or must be operating within an agreement or understanding that this advice will be used to make investment decisions.

Consultants, Agents, Brokers, and Salespersons

A more difficult question arises concerning whether the people who suggest or recommend investment vehicles to the benefit plan are fiduciaries. Such people might include pension consultants, mutual fund representatives, insurance agents, investment management consultants, or brokers. As a practical matter, any advice and recommendations made by these people to plans and plan fiduciaries about the advisability of investing in, purchasing, or selling securities; hiring or firing an investment manager; or otherwise selecting an investment vehicle for the plan could constitute investment advice so that the persons who furnish such advice could be classified as fiduciaries under certain circumstances.

These circumstances must include, as noted earlier, the payment of a fee or other compensation to such a person, either directly or indirectly. This includes brokerage commissions, mutual fund sales commissions, insurance sales commissions, and consulting fees.

In addition, because they ordinarily would not have discretion or control over plan assets, these people can be deemed fiduciaries only by virtue of their rendering of investment advice to the plan. As mentioned previously, in order for someone to be considered a plan fiduciary, he or she must offer such advice within a context wherein it is expected that the fiduciary will rely on the advice in making various plan investment decisions.

In this way, some investment brokers have been deemed fiduciaries because of their purported influence over plan clients, even though the brokers technically had no discretionary power over plan assets. In a particular instance, a stockbroker's recommendations were routinely rubber-stamped by the plan trustees.[89] Thus, even though the broker lacked actual discretionary authority, his advice was routinely followed with the tacit understanding that it would form an important basis for the fiduciary's investment decisions. Thus, the court found that he had effectively exercised authority because of his influence over the client and therefore had achieved fiduciary status.

In such instances, the person is said to render investment advice because he or she makes recommendations about buying or selling securities and regularly renders advice with the understanding that it will serves as a primary basis for plan investment decisions. Thus, a broker's practice of merely recommending investments should not make that broker a fiduciary in the absence of any agreement, arrangement, or understanding referred to above. Still, to the extent a plan fiduciary can be shown to rely heavily on a broker's recommendations, such an "understanding" can be inferred, and the broker could theoretically be deemed a fiduciary.

Plan Administrators

One confusing title used in ERISA is the plan administrator. ERISA requires every plan to designate a plan administrator within the plan instrument. When such a designation is absent, ERISA designates the employer-sponsor as the plan administrator.

It should be noted that the plan administrator as designated under ERISA is not the same thing as the identical term used to describe participant record keeping or actuarial functions. Such people, although performing administrative functions, are technically not plan administrators as defined under ERISA.

In general, the plan administrator designated under the plan will have certain responsibilities for making decisions with respect to eligibility and other similar functions. Regardless of duties performed, the plan administrator of any plan is a fiduciary by definition under ERISA section 3(21).

In conclusion, any people with influence or power over the management of the plan need to be cognizant of their potential status as fiduciaries. As the impact of the regulations becomes clearer through practice and litigation, it is apparent that bodies charged with enforcement of ERISA are anxious to paint as many people as possible with the fiduciary brush, and the courts are beginning to fashion a body of law along these lines. Accordingly, it is always best to be well aware of lines of conduct governing a fiduciary's activities, even if one does not consider oneself a fiduciary.

QUALIFICATIONS OF A FIDUCIARY

Although ERISA does not prescribe parameters detailing the qualifications necessary to be a fiduciary, it does require fiduciaries to conduct responsibilities to the plan with the same degree of care as a reasonably prudent person who is experienced in the matter at hand. In general, a fiduciary position requires a person who can understand and fulfill a complex legal role. Fiduciaries must understand that the role of a fiduciary is to represent and act in the exclusive best interest of plan participants as a whole——and not to represent the narrow interests of various constituents.

Factors to consider in determining a proposed fiduciary's qualifications include:

- Experience in the administration of ERISA plans or the investment of plan assets or an understanding of how to appoint and monitor a person who does

- Educational credentials and employment experience that would demonstrate ability to exercise independent judgment

- References or reputation in the field
- Any record of past performance with respect to managing plans as a fiduciary

Particular individuals are prohibited from holding fiduciary positions. Any individual convicted of, or imprisoned for, any of a number of serious crimes specifically expressed in ERISA may not be a fiduciary. For example, any individual involved in such crimes as robbery, bribery, extortion, embezzlement, larceny, grand larceny, murder, kidnapping, perjury, rape, or other violations of various federal statutes is prohibited by ERISA from holding a fiduciary position.

5

RESPONSIBILITIES OF A FIDUCIARY

A pure heart and an empty head are not good enough[90]

The central purpose of ERISA is to protect the benefits and rights of participants and their beneficiaries. All IRS-qualified plans are regulated by ERISA, which imposes significant fiduciary responsibilities on plan managers and sponsors. Under ERISA plan sponsors are required to act with care, skill, prudence, and diligence in the best interests of participants and beneficiaries. In the current complex regulatory and investment environment, satisfying the fiduciary responsibility provisions of ERISA is more difficult than ever.

WHAT EVERY PERSON INVOLVED WITH ERISA BENEFIT PLANS NEEDS TO KNOW

Many people involved with overseeing pension plans fail to understand that they are subject to the same fiduciary responsibility provisions as any other type of benefit plan.[91] As a result, a multitude of people associated with a plan may be making decisions or otherwise acting in a way that could raise an issue of personal or corporate liability. This liability might arise because of inadvertent or careless conduct with respect to the pension plan. The fiduciary responsibility provisions under ERISA establish such liability.

Anyone having any relationship with respect to a pension plan needs to have a basic familiarity with the fiduciary responsibility provisions of ERISA. Even if just to establish sensitivity for the kinds of conduct that might give rise to claims of liability, these people need to be aware. In recent years, the frequency of litigation over the issue of fiduciary violations has increased dramatically. People whose functions once were thought ministerial in nature suddenly find themselves on the defense regarding claims by disgruntled plan participants as well as the U.S. Department of Labor (DOL).

One purpose of this chapter is to set forth the minimum rules governing the conduct of fiduciaries who operate a pension plan. A second purpose is to illustrate the unresolved issues in the area of fiduciary responsibility as it pertains to participant-directed 401(k) plans. The final purpose is to develop a full understanding of pending issues in the role of all plan fiduciaries.

Participant-Directed Plans

At the outset of this discussion dealing with fiduciary responsibility under ERISA and how these provisions apply to self-directed pension plans, it is useful to draw several distinctions. First, as discussed throughout this chapter, the majority of defined contribution plans today are structured to give employees some measure of control over how their money is invested in the plan. These plans are arranged in an effort to be treated as participant-directed or self-directed plans (these terms are used interchangeably throughout this chapter).

Participant-directed plans are useful for a number of reasons. First, they enable employees to make their own investment decisions and thereby offer employees a greater feeling of control over their retirement savings. In addition participant-directed plans, if properly structured and administered, offer some measure of insulation to plan fiduciaries with regard to the ultimate investment allocations made by participants in their individual accounts. This theory holds that if an employee is given the power to allocate his or her own account between several investment options according to his or her own wishes, there is no reason to hold some other person responsible for how the employee chooses to allocate the account. Unfortunately, as will be discussed later, this theory is subject to some wrinkles.

Despite the protections offered by participant-directed plans, they raise as many unresolved issues as they solve. As we will discuss later, for an ordinary employer-directed plan, in which the plan fiduciaries make the investment decisions with regard to the entire portfolio, it is straightforward to determine what to do to stay within the bounds of ERISA's fiduciary structure. This is not to say that doing so is easy; rather, it means that there is considerable guidance available to trustees through DOL interpretations, court decisions, and public commentary, which allow trustees to make these decisions within an established framework. Hence, employer-directed plan fiduciary responsibilities are somewhat less ambiguous than self-directed plans.

On the contrary, the same cannot be said with regard to participant-directed plans. Although it appears that there is some measure of reduced responsibility for the investment allocation decisions in these plans, the argument can be made that this was not a big problem in the first instance. A prudently managed employer-directed pension plan would not place participants in a position to claim fiduciary breaches.

Furthermore, by placing investment authority in the hands of employees, plan fiduciaries create responsibilities that they never had before, particularly in the area of participant communications. Once a plan gives employees this substantial investment power, the obligation to educate and inform participants increases dramatically. Recent lawsuits have been brought by participants in participant-directed plans who were not given enough information to exercise this substantial responsibility.[92]

One of the biggest problems facing fiduciaries of participant-directed plans is that this obligation to inform cannot be estimated. There is little guidance in the nature of regulations or case law for plan fiduciaries to look. This chapter will attempt to define standards; nevertheless, in reality these are nothing more than commonsense solutions. Eventually, standards will be created as they always are—in the courts, at the expense of plan fiduciaries. Thus, many of today's well-meaning plan fiduciaries may find themselves liable because they could not determine how far to go in informing participants about the investment selections of the plan.

Finally, the fact that a plan is participant-directed does not relieve the plan's fiduciaries from any and all other fiduciary responsibility for the plan. Rather, such a setup simply relieves the fiduciary of the responsibility for asset allocation in participants' accounts. Thus, the extent of benefits achieved by offering a self-directed plan is questionable when weighed against the unknown fiduciary risks.

Above all, there is no mandate that pension plans be participant-directed; this is optional. Thus, the reason that the majority of pension plans are moving in the direction of participant direction is twofold:

- Having already given this power to employees, it would be nearly impossible to revert to employer-directed plans. Employees overall would never accept this result; they have become used to it and view it as a right, rather than a privilege

- Possibly more important, plan fiduciaries are overall mistaken about the true nature of the protections offered to them in a participant-directed plan under section 404(c)

Unless plan sponsors as a group gain a more refined understanding of the entire landscape of ERISA's fiduciary responsibility provisions and the limited, though useful, protections offered under section 404(c), it is possible that today's decisions could actually increase (rather than decrease) potential fiduciary liability among plan fiduciaries. These thoughts will be explored in depth throughout this chapter.

Employer-Directed Plans

As noted earlier, so-called employer-directed plans (also known as trustee-directed plans) differ from participant-directed plans insofar as the investment decisions are made uniformly for all participants by either a plan fiduciary or an investment committee. Today, although most defined contribution plans attempt to be participant-directed, the majority of defined benefit plans are employer-directed.[93] Noticeably, there is a greater measure of predictability in employer-directed plans about what the fiduciary responsibilities are with respect to the management of plan assets and their obligation to communicate with employees.

Besides the normal fiduciary obligations discussed later, the practical risk to plan fiduciaries in maintaining an employer-directed plan is that participants will second guess the fiduciaries' investment judgment, believing that it was either too conservative or too aggressive to be prudent under ERISA. Plan fiduciaries who are well informed about their responsibilities should be able to live with this risk. Prudent management and common sense, combined with an understanding of the landscape in which trustees operate, offer the best protections.

THE BASIC FIDUCIARY RESPONSIBILITIES

Overview and History

As noted earlier, pension plans are subject to the extensive fiduciary responsibility provisions that apply to qualified plans generally. Nevertheless, defined contribution plans are generally burdened with more potential for fiduciary pitfalls because of the presence of employee contributions and the likelihood that participants will have some say in the investment decisions that affect their individual accounts. As a result, people associated with the management of the defined contribution plan need to be aware of their overall responsibilities as they relate to the plan, as well as some sensible ways to manage these substantial responsibilities.

In its most basic terms, ERISA section 404(a) directs fiduciaries of all plans to act solely in the interest of the plan's participants and beneficiaries and for the exclusive purpose of providing benefits for these people. Furthermore, a fiduciary must act prudently, diversify the investment of plan assets, and generally act in a manner consistent with plan documents.

In addition to this general requirement, plan fiduciaries are subject to the prudent man standard of care. This standard requires a fiduciary to act "with the care, skill, prudence, and diligence under the circumstances then prevailing that a prudent man acting in a like capacity and familiar with such matters would use."[94]

With these standards, there is little mystery why plan fiduciaries can become confused about the scope of their responsibilities under ERISA. This nebulous standard forms the foundation of ERISA's fiduciary responsibility provisions that control the conduct of all plan fiduciaries. It is from this language, as well as the legislative history of ERISA, that the DOL and the courts have fashioned a body of law governing the conduct of plan fiduciaries. In view of the fact that this language is open-ended, it is easy to see how plan fiduciaries might be nervous about how their investment decisions might be interpreted after the fact.

Nowhere in the fiduciary body of law are there more developments than in the area of participant-directed plans. At the time of publication of this book, several cases raise questions regarding aspects of participant-directed plans. As a result, plan fiduciaries are left with little guidance about how they should manage their fiduciary responsibility in these plans, where the likelihood for employee dissatisfaction runs higher than in any other type of plan. Accordingly, plan fiduciaries must be especially careful in determining how they will proceed with these plans.

Finally, the significance of the fiduciary responsibility provisions—particularly about how they relate to pension plans—cannot be emphasized enough. This fiduciary duty is perhaps more stringent and less understood than any standard ordinarily applied in normal financial matters. The industry is on the threshold of developing content to define this standard. Today's decisions and actions will dictate tomorrow's potential liability. Plan fiduciaries have in their own hands the power to manage this liability.

In summary, plan fiduciaries are required under ERISA to discharge their duties "with respect to a plan solely in the interest of the participants and beneficiaries."[95] These duties are outlined in figure 5-1. Courts have interpreted this language as requiring fiduciaries to act "with an eye single to the interests of the participants and beneficiaries."[96] The statute also establishes four general standards of conduct: the duty of loyalty or exclusive benefit rule, the duty of prudence, the duty to diversify plan assets, and the duty to follow the terms of plan documents unless doing so would otherwise breach the foregoing duties.[97]

Figure 5-1: Fiduciary Duties of ERISA

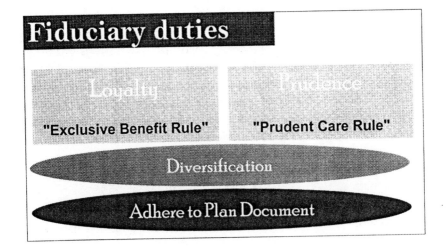

The Exclusive Benefit Rule

Under section 404(a)(1)(A) of ERISA, a fiduciary of a plan must discharge his or her duties for the exclusive purpose of providing benefits to participants and beneficiaries. Courts have taken a narrow view of this provision, requiring that any action with respect to the investment or expenditure of plan assets be made for the sole purpose of benefiting participants and beneficiaries. Although the exclusive benefit rule is phrased in terms of "never," "solely," and "exclusively," the courts have recognized that a verbatim reading of the statute is nonsensical and have readily acknowledged that incidental benefits may flow to the fiduciary or the plan sponsor as long as the fiduciary's primary motivation is to benefit the plan. This rule in essence conveys a duty of loyalty.

In the case of pension plans, one of the more apparent risks of violating this provision would be in decisions that are made because of business objectives or priorities. For instance, the decision to hire a commercial bank as the plan's investment advisor in exchange for a favorable interest rate on business loans or a more favorable line of credit terms would violate ERISA's exclusive purpose rule.

Building on the historical perspective in Chapter 2, loyalty is a word rich in both meaning and connotation ensuing in two uses. First, through its early usage in the English language, it has remained close to its old French meaning of remaining loyal or loyal to the end. This use is of a substantive element and evokes an image of brave knights defending their sovereigns to their last drop of blood. Carried forward to the ERISA fiduciary standards, this use of loyalty is essentially a duty of management that includes a requirement to act in a certain way and to take certain steps to protect the plan participant.

Second, loyalty also connotes fidelity of faithfulness from its Latin origin under Roman law. This use is of a psychological kind—something the law imposes on a fiduciary in order to assure peace of mind and trust—and focuses on the state of mind of one who is loyal. Applied to fiduciary standards, this use generates a duty of preference. Under this use of loyalty, duty is breached not by any particular action but rather by affiliation and association, and by taking positions that raise the threat of harm to the participant.

ERISA requires that fiduciaries act for the exclusive benefit of plan participants and beneficiaries.[98] Furthermore, ERISA requires fiduciaries to act with "an eye single" solely in the interest of participants and beneficiaries.[99] While some courts have interpreted these as two separate and distinct duties, others have viewed them as one. Nevertheless, ERISA's rules impose the duty of undivided loyalty on fiduciaries.

Although the duty of loyalty under ERISA has been broadly applied to all areas of a pension plan's operations, such as excess contributions, expenses paid from plan assets, and operational errors, recently courts have focused on aspects of communication. Three prominent themes raised by the courts are the duties to provide no misleading statements, to support no harmful silence, and to disclose relevant and material facts.

First, a fiduciary cannot materially mislead those owed a fiduciary duty.[100] In other words, when a plan fiduciary speaks, he or she must speak truthfully.[101] Plan fiduciaries have a duty to not mislead participants. Moreover, the fiduciary making the representation need not know it is false.[102] In *Fischer v. Philadelphia Electric Co.*, the third circuit court stated, "when a plan administrator speaks, it must speak truthfully."[103] The Fischer court further stated "the fiduciary obligations owed to participants ...could not be circumvented by building a 'Chinese wall' around those employees on whom plan participants reasonably rely for information and guidance about retirement."

This duty includes a prohibition against lying: "[L]ying is inconsistent with the duty of loyalty owed by all fiduciaries and codified in section 404(a)(1) of ERISA."[104] Fiduciaries can also violate their duty of loyalty by misleading participants and beneficiaries, whether through action, inaction, or silence.[105] In fact, ERISA fiduciaries are charged with more than the duty to refrain from misleading plan participants or to correct their own misstatements. They also have a duty to protect plan participants from misleading information. Thus, if a fiduciary is aware that participants have been misinformed about facts that implicate the stability of their retirement assets, he or she must take action to protect the participants.

Second, the duty recognized by the courts not only precludes misleading participants and beneficiaries, but also imposes an obligation to inform them when silence or withholding information might be harmful.[106] As held by one court "[The] duty to inform is a constant thread in the relationship between beneficiary and trustee, it entails not only a negative duty not to misinform, but also an affirmative duty to inform when the trust knows that silence might be harmful."[107] Therefore, this duty of loyalty may require the fiduciary to correct the inaccurate or misleading information so the participants and beneficiaries will not be injured because of it.[108] An "ERISA fiduciary that knows or should know that a beneficiary labors under a material misunderstanding of plan benefits that will inure to his detriment cannot remain silent—especially when that misunderstanding was fostered by the fiduciary's own material representations or omissions."[109]

Third, the duty of a fiduciary to disclose material information to participants is evolving. Unlike the two previously discussed duties where the law is clear that plan fiduciaries have the duty not to lie to participants or affirmatively mislead them about plan terms or important aspects of the plan, it is not clear whether a plan fiduciary has a duty to disclose truthful information on his or her own accord. For example, it is unclear whether a fiduciary must inform participants about a company's business problems that may negatively affect company stock held under the plan.

Recently, an *amicus curiae*[110] brief filed by the DOL suggests that a plan fiduciary does have an affirmative duty to disclose material information about the plan and its investments. If the DOL's view is correct, then it would be in the best interests of a fiduciary to disclose the information as soon as possible. If the information that the fiduciary possesses is insider information and disclosure would violate federal securities law, plan fiduciaries could be in an untenable position.

In summary, when a fiduciary is aware of material facts that would harm plan participants, the fiduciary may have a duty to disclose facts necessary to protect the participants. An affirmative duty of a fiduciary to act clearly goes beyond the more obvious obligations of a fiduciary to avoid lying to participants, to speak truthfully in response to participant inquiries, and to correct the fiduciary's own prior misstatements. Not surprisingly, the DOL takes an expansive view of the affirmative duties of a fiduciary.

The Prudent Man Rule

Under section 404(a)(1)(B) of ERISA, a fiduciary of a plan must discharge his or her duties with the care, skill, prudence, and diligence under the circumstances then prevailing that a prudent man acting in a like capacity and familiar with such matters would use in the conduct of an enterprise of a like character and with like aims.

Although this rule is referred to under the common law as the prudent man rule, ERISA regulations added "prudent expert" to the fiduciary lexicon, elevating the prudent man standard to include a requirement that a plan fiduciary also act as "one familiar with such manner."[111] The reason for this is that courts and the DOL have interpreted fiduciaries' actions by using a standard of what an expert would do in similar circumstances.

Most fiduciary breaches are the result of lack of prudence. Under ERISA, prudence is a design standard, not a performance standard.[112] In other words, it is process oriented rather than results oriented. As such, a fiduciary must gain a full understanding of each element making up the definition of ERISA's prudence rule. In examining the prudent expert rule, a fiduciary must satisfy the following elements: care, skill, prudence, and diligence. Additionally, a fiduciary must act: based on the circumstances then prevailing, as a prudent expert acting in a like capacity and familiar with such matters, and consistent with an enterprise of a like character and like aims.

A fiduciary must discharge duty with care

The care element of the prudence standard under ERISA section 404(a)(1)(B) requires that a fiduciary be careful and thorough in investigating and understanding the alternatives available to the plan. Evidence of this care includes documentation of vendor searches, investment review and selection, materials regarding alternatives, and expenses. As discussed in Chapter 11, this documentation should be maintained as part of a due diligence file to show that proper care was exercised.

Fiduciaries breach their duty of care under section 404(a)(1)(A) whenever they act to benefit their own interests.[113] For example, ERISA expressly prohibits fiduciaries from "dealing with the assets of the plan in his own interest or for his own account," or "receiving any consideration for his own personal account from any party dealing with such plan in connection with a transaction involving the assets of the plan."[114] The requirement that an ERISA fiduciary act "with an eye single to the interests of the participants and beneficiaries"[115] is the most fundamental of his or her duties and "must be enforced with uncompromising rigidity."[116] This duty—the violation of which subjects a fiduciary to liability under 29 U.S.C. §1109, n7—is directed particularly at schemes "tainted by a conflict of interest and thus highly susceptible to self dealing."[117]

A fiduciary must discharge duty with skill

It is simply not enough to gather information about the plan's operation and administration. That information needs to be reviewed by a person who has the skills necessary to properly understand the importance of the data and its significance in the context of the plan. Fiduciaries can acquire the necessary skill to fulfill their fiduciary responsibilities in two modes. First, they can become an expert through study and investigation. Alternatively, they can hire the expert. Blind reliance on an expert's opinion is inadequate.

Since the seminal ERISA case of *Donovan v. Bierwirth*,[118] courts have held that "a pure heart and empty head" are insufficient to discharge the fiduciary duties under ERISA. Applying *Donovan* in the J. Geils Band case,[119] the court pointedly observed that before serving as this plan's fiduciary, the named fiduciary had no significant financial background or experience. In other words, if a fiduciary does not understand the investments and fiduciary issues of plan, he or she had better hire someone who does.

The court in *Harley v. Minnesota Mining and Manufacturing Company* explained that the law "does not impose a rule that fiduciaries be 'experts' on all types of investments they make."[120] If fiduciaries, however, lack the ability to manage the plan's investments prudently, they must get assistance. The DOL, as well as a number of courts, has taken the position that fiduciaries who are not qualified to fulfill their duties are legally required to seek assistance from competent sources. The DOL states "Unless they possess the necessary expertise to evaluate such factors, fiduciaries would need to obtain the advice of a qualified, independent expert."[121] In *Liss v. Smith*, the court held "where the trustees lack the requisite knowledge, experience and expertise to make the necessary decisions with respect to investments, their fiduciary obligations require them to hire independent professional advisors."[122]

Simply hiring an advisor is not enough. The advisor must be prudently selected and monitored, and the advice must be carefully evaluated before being relied upon. The court in Bisceglia v. Bisceglia stated "Although reliance on an adviser will not immunize a [fiduciary's] actions, it is a factor to be weighed in determining whether a trustee breached his or her duty."[123] As noted in Unisys I, the Third Circuit held "While we would encourage fiduciaries to retain the services of consultants when they need outside assistance to make prudent [decisions], we believe ERISA's duty to investigate requires fiduciaries to review the data a consultant gathers."[124]

A fiduciary must discharge duty with prudence

The decisions of a fiduciary must be prudent. Alternatively, the decisions must be both reasoned and based on an understanding of the information that has been reviewed and evaluated. At a minimum, the element of prudence requires that fiduciaries have procedures in place so that they may review and evaluate whether their decisions are adequate.[125] For example, prudence is satisfied by requiring periodic reports on their decisions and the plan's performance, and by ensuring that they have a prudent process for obtaining the information and resources they need.

While the DOL does not suggest that a fiduciary must follow one prescribed set of procedures, fiduciaries need to apply some procedure to assure themselves that they have properly discharged their responsibilities. Elements of a prudent process could include inquiring, investigating, understanding, and determining.

Moreover, in many instances prudence trumps settlor functions. For example, many fiduciaries incorrectly assume that if a plan provides for or requires investment in employer stock, any such investment cannot be challenged as an ERISA violation because the choice of investment is a plan-designed settlor function. Courts, however, have held that in some circumstances—such as extreme financial distress that threatens the ongoing vitality of the company—ERISA's prudence rule may require diversification out of employer stock even when plan terms call for such investment.[126]

As another example based in part on the cases and advice discussed in the previous topic regarding hiring an expert, the criteria considered in those cases are informative about the requirements for prudently selecting experts to advise plan fiduciaries. The following list is developed from those cases and other sources:

1. **Is the expert qualified?** Fiduciaries are required to select and monitor advisors prudently. As stated in *Liss v. Smith* "Failure to utilize due care in selecting and monitoring a fund's service providers constitutes a breach of the trustee's (i.e., the appointing fiduciary's) fiduciary duty."[127] In selecting the advisors, fiduciaries should consider whether the advisor has the investment credentials, experience, and expertise to warrant being considered an expert:

   • Experience with other ERISA plans

- Education credentials
- Registration with appropriate regulatory authorities
- Reputation
- References
- Past performance with investments of the type contemplated

2. **Does the expert provide quality services adapted to the plan?** Fiduciaries are required to determine whether the investments are suitable and appropriate for the needs of the plan and its participants. As stated by the court in *Liss*: "[Fiduciaries] have an obligation to …select the provider whose service level, quality and fees best matches the fund's needs and financial situation".[128] For example, fiduciaries should ensure that their expert will take into account the investment abilities of the participants and will consider the plan's needs.

3. **Is the expert independent?** Courts have emphasized the importance of the independence of the expert. One court has held that "[o]ne extremely important factor is whether the expert advisor truly offers independent and impartial advice."[129] While fiduciaries are entitled to rely on the expertise of their advisor if the advisor is qualified, the courts appear to permit greater reliance on the advice of independent investment experts whose compensation is not affected by the advice given. Stated slightly differently, if the compensation of the expert can be affected by the advice given, then prudence would require that the fiduciaries understand the nature and amount of that compensation and consider it in evaluating the advice rendered.

4. **Does the expert provide full disclosure of fees and expenses for all investments?** Fiduciaries are required to know all expenses that are being paid by the plan, directly or indirectly, and to determine if they are reasonable (that is, whether the expense is competitive in the marketplace and whether the plan and its participants receive value commensurate to the cost).[130] They are not required to choose the least expensive services but should ensure that they are getting adequate value for the plan's money. In explaining this requirement, the DOL has said, "employers must …ensure that fees paid to service providers and other expenses of the plan are reasonable in light of the level and quality of services provided."[131] To ensure compliance, fiduciaries should obtain, and the advisor should offer, written disclosure of all compensation and other payments, direct or indirect, related to the investments being recommended.

Fiduciaries must also evaluate the costs and fees associated with the investment services of the person advising about investments, who may be an investment advisor, broker, or consultant. The first step is for the fiduciary to obtain complete information about all payments, direct or indirect, being made to that person, whether by the plan or by a third party (e.g., the mutual fund complex, an insurance company, or a broker-dealer). The second step is to evaluate that information and determine whether the plan is receiving adequate value for the cost. A key factor in that analysis is the cost of a similar service in the marketplace. For example, it would usually be imprudent to pay significantly more than the price of comparable investments or services from another source.

5. **How is the expert being paid for his or her services?** Fiduciaries should make sure that a prohibited transaction does not occur because of the manner in which the expert is paid. Under ERISA Section 406, fiduciaries have a duty to avoid prohibited transactions. Under ERISA, the most likely prohibited transaction would be an advisor (for example, a broker or an investment advisor) giving conflicted advice (advice that results in the payment of variable or undisclosed compensation).[132] To avoid these prohibited transaction issues, the advisor should be independent (that is, not affiliated with or compensated by a provider) or should receive level compensation (that is, compensation that does not vary based on the funds recommended by the advisor).

A fiduciary must discharge duty with diligence

A diligent fiduciary ensures that all the steps necessary to research or reasoned have been taken. If information is missing or if questions are raised, the diligent fiduciary gathers the additional information or gets answers to those questions. In its most basic terms, diligence is demonstrated by a quality of care. Furthermore, a fiduciary must be able demonstrate diligence. Therefore, all decisions by a fiduciary should be well documented. At a minimum, a plan fiduciary should build a record that will demonstrate diligence and withstand scrutiny, especially with respect to questionable actions such as investments that are risky or prone to perceptions of self-interest.

A fiduciary must discharge duty under the circumstances then prevailing

A fiduciary has a responsibility to understand what is currently available in the marketplace and through a prudent process decide what is appropriate for the plan. While many factors exist that are impacted by altering circumstances, two prevalent and significant ones related to pension plans are participants and marketplace. Although the correlations and interdependencies are high, each offers unique opportunities. At the inception of ERISA, alternatives in the market were limited. Most plan sponsors administered their plans internally with a limited number of resources available for services. Moreover, the process was simplified and hindered by the reliance on paper-driven processes. In short, there were few options. Today industry is driven by dynamic Internet systems, open architecture with access to endless name-brand investments, on-line investment advice, and plan-sponsor fiduciary advisors. Ultimately, today's world will soon be tomorrow's. Therefore, the fiduciary must continually reassess the circumstance because prevailing circumstances will continue to change. As noted by Ted Benna, creator of the 401(k) plan, "The pace of change will not slow and it will continue to be influenced largely by participants."

As the industry has advanced, participants have become more investor savvy, therefore demanding more investment tools. Nevertheless, some participants have not developed their investment rapport as well as others. To fully understand the prevailing circumstances, the plan sponsor and fiduciaries must assess the level of investment knowledge. As Fred Reish reveals, given the "circumstances then prevailing" language of the fundamental ERISA rule, "[i]f a plan sponsor knows the workforce is unsophisticated about investing, ...[then] under the general prudence rule an argument could be made that the plan fiduciaries cannot fulfill their duty to act prudently if they do not make investment advice available."[133] Even though Mr. Reish was specifically addressing the issue of investment advisory services, his argument can just as easily apply to investment education or professional management services.

A fiduciary must act as a prudent man acting in a like capacity and familiar with such matters

This element essentially modifies the prudent man standard to that of a prudent expert and requires that the fiduciary understand the responsibilities of a person familiar with such matters and acting in a like capacity.

A fiduciary's conduct must be consistent with an enterprise of a like character and aims

Essentially the aim of a pension plan is to provide meaningful and secure retirement benefits to the participants and their beneficiaries. Therefore plan fiduciaries have an obligation to select investments and services consistent with that goal.

In attempting to fulfill these responsibilities, fiduciaries should bear in mind certain principles that have been established by courts applying these fiduciary rules in real-world situations:

1. **A fiduciary's lack of familiarity with investments is no excuse**
   Under an objective standard, a fiduciary is to be judged according to others acting in like capacity and familiar with such matters. This means that a plan fiduciaries is held to the standard of a prudent fiduciary with experience. A plan fiduciaries may not blindly make investment decisions or blindly rely on others; he or she must make decisions within a meticulous framework.

2. **The standard is not of a prudent layperson but that of a prudent fiduciary who has experience dealing with similar situations**
   It is not sufficient that a plan fiduciary act prudently in his or her mind. Instead, that person must act prudently by comparison with a standard based on an experienced professional fiduciary. Thus, when the fiduciary lacks this experience, there is an affirmative obligation to seek independent advice.

3. **The test of prudence focuses on the fiduciary's conduct in investigating, evaluating, and making the investment**
   In other words, the fiduciary's independent investigation of the merits of a particular investment is at the heart of the prudent man standard. A fiduciary's decision to hire a particular investment advisor becomes central to his or her fulfillment of ERISA's fiduciary responsibility provisions.

4. **A fiduciary has an affirmative obligation to seek independent advice when he or she lacks the requisite education, experience, and skill, and must go to great lengths to establish a record for his or her actions**
   When selecting a professional investment manager to manage all or a piece of a plan's portfolio, a fiduciary has an obligation to seek the advice of independent consultants. The failure to make any independent investigation and evaluation of a potential plan investment is in and of itself a breach of fiduciary obligations.

5. **The plan fiduciary maintains the fiduciary obligation to monitor the performance of that manager and to take corrective action if necessary**
   Even after the selection of the investment advisor, the plan fiduciary must monitor the performance of that advisor. The plan fiduciary is not permitted to ignore the plan after the delegation has been made; rather,

the plan fiduciary should monitor the investments on an ongoing basis by referring to an objective and relevant series of indexes.

ERISA section 402(c)(2) permits either a named fiduciary or a fiduciary designated by a named fiduciary to employ others for the purpose of rendering advice regarding any responsibility the fiduciary has under the plan. Section 401(c)(3) further permits the named fiduciary to appoint an investment manager or managers to manage the assets of the plan. When this appointment is properly made, the plan fiduciaries are not liable for the acts and omissions of the investment manager. It has been well established that the decision to hire an investment manager to manage assets of a plan is a fiduciary decision in and of itself that requires the application of ERISA's prudence requirements.

In this regard, the DOL has supported guidelines that may be followed in the prudent selection of a person or entity to invest ERISA plan assets.[134] These guidelines, which are also examples of common sense, would require a plan fiduciary to do the following:

- Evaluate the person's or organizations' qualifications
  - Expertise in the particular area of investments under consideration and with other ERISA plans
  - Educational credentials
  - Registration with the Securities and Exchange Commission under the Investment Advisors Act of 1940
  - Overall qualifications determined by an independent assessment of the person or entity by means of: (i) widely enjoyed reputation in the business of investments; (ii) client references; (iii) the advice of a professional third-party consultant
  - Record of past performance with investments of the type contemplated;
- Ascertain the reasonableness of fees
- Review documents reflecting the relationship to be established
- Ensure adequate, periodic accountings and monitoring in the future

Thus, fiduciaries of any plan who seek to delegate investment responsibilities to independent investment advisors should follow the framework just given, or a comparable one, to ensure that their decisions are prudent from the standpoint of ERISA. It is not enough to blindly hire an asset manager to manage all or a portion of the assets in the plan; rather, the plan fiduciary must undergo a fairly rigorous process in order to justify that the decision to hire any given manager was prudent in light of the circumstances surrounding that decision.

To ensure that the fiduciary does not engage in a prohibited transaction when he or she arranges for an independent investment advisor, the DOL outlined in an advisory opinion known as the "SunAmerica Opinion" certain facts that make an advisor independent.[135] The following facts were provided as evidence that an investment advisor is independent:

- The fees received did not exceed 5% of the sponsor's annual gross income

- The fees paid were not affected by the investments made by participants based on the investment advice given

- Neither the choice of the investment advisor nor any decision to continue or terminate the relationship would be based on fee income to the advisor

- There was no other relationship between the sponsor and advisor

- The advisor was obligated to use investment methodology and output developed independently

The Diversification Rule

Generally, the investment diversification requirement of ERISA section 404(a)(1)(C) places an affirmative duty on a plan fiduciary to diversify plan investments unless under the circumstances it is clearly prudent not to diversify. While the DOL has established certain standards for diversification, no specific yardstick to measure diversification has been provided. Informal limits, however, do exist and have been used by DOL enforcement officials. When determining whether assets have been properly diversified, they use the objectives outlined in the plan's investment policy statement, plan document, summary plan description, and other participant communications.

The Conference Report of ERISA makes it clear that once failure to diversify is established, the burden shifts to the fiduciary to demonstrate that non-diversification was prudent under the circumstances.[136] While some court decisions may lead to the belief that diversification and asset allocation are synonymous, they are not. Asset allocation determines the distribution of assets among various investment categories. Diversification is the risk-reduction process of choosing a broad range of different investments within a particular asset category. Recent cases bring to light three situations where violations of the diversification rule have occurred:

1. A substantial portion of the plan's assets are loaned to the sponsoring employer, generally triggering other types of ERISA violations

2. A large percentage of the plan's assets are placed in a single investment that for one reason or another was imprudent or the fiduciary should have known was imprudent under ERISA's prudence rule

3. Investments, although not necessarily imprudent, are misrepresented or not properly disclosed by the fiduciary

Significant to plans that offer employer securities, under ERISA section 404(a)(2) an eligible individual account plan may acquire and hold qualifying employer securities or qualifying employer real property without regard to the diversification requirements or the diversification element of the prudent man rule. Profit sharing, stock bonuses, thrift, or savings plans may qualify as eligible individual account plans, as may certain money purchase pension plans.

Adherence to the Plan Document

The fourth responsibility imposed by ERISA on a fiduciary is adherence to the plan document. ERISA requires that a plan fiduciary discharge his or her duties in accordance with the terms of the documents and instruments governing the plan to the extent that they are consistent with applicable law. Failure to follow the terms of the plan can be an ERISA violation.

To satisfy this duty, the fiduciary must obtain the governing documents and familiarize himself or herself with the powers conferred and the limitations or restrictions imposed. Failure to obtain, read, or understand the plan documents apparently will not excuse a fiduciary who behaves in a manner prohibited by the documents. While the cases are clear regarding the duty imposed, they are less clear regarding the definition of what makes up the documents and instruments governing the plan beyond the trust agreement and a separate plan document.

The ERISA "Trump Card"

The ERISA "Trump Card" or "Override" originates from the trailing phrase of ERISA section 404(a)(1)(iv) that reads, "insofar as such documents are consistent with ERISA." The section of ERISA that requires plan fiduciaries to discharge their duties in accordance with the "documents and instruments" governing a plan is qualified by the notion that the management of the plan must be consistent with the requirements of ERISA. For example, a fiduciary is theoretically legally obligated to adhere to plan provisions relating to investments as long as the investments can be made in keeping with the ERISA prudence requirement, but the fiduciary is obligated to disregard plan provisions the moment the investment becomes imprudent. In other words, a fiduciary cannot hide behind plan language or blindly follow it.[137]

For most of the thirty years since ERISA was promulgated, courts have upheld the plan fiduciary's ability to rely on the fact that the express terms of the plan required particular provisions, generally related to certain contributions being invested in company stock. The fiduciaries had neither the duty nor the right to override those terms. Nevertheless, some courts, supported by the DOL, are no longer allowing fiduciaries to avoid liability by following the express terms of the plan and trust.[138]

This means that a plan fiduciary would be required to ignore the terms of a plan document requiring the plan to be primarily invested in employer stock if such investment would violate the fiduciary duty of prudence or loyalty to plan participants. For example, if the employer stock decreases significantly in value, a plan fiduciary's duties of prudence and loyalty might require the fiduciary to suspend or discontinue employer stock as an investment alternative under the plan. In short, a claim that a fiduciary imprudently purchased or retained employer stock on behalf of a plan cannot be defeated by language in the plan document requiring the plan's assets to be primarily invested in employer stock. Therefore plan fiduciaries must recognize that the long-standing defense of following the terms of the plan may no longer be available in many cases.

In light of this recent authority, fiduciaries should question whether a particular plan provision seems reasonable under the circumstances and should seek a legal opinion from qualified counsel regarding their fiduciary duty if there is concern about the provision. Assuming the fiduciary discloses all relevant facts to qualified counsel and the legal advice appears to be reasonable, the fiduciary should be able to avoid personal liability by acting in reliance on the legal advice.

FIDUCIARY DUTY OWED TO WHOM

In general terms, fiduciary responsibility under ERISA is simply stated. The statute provides that fiduciaries shall discharge their duties with respect to a plan "solely in the interest of the participants and beneficiaries," that is, "for the exclusive purpose of (i) providing benefits to participants and their beneficiaries; and (ii) defraying reasonable expenses of administering the plan."[139] The fiduciary's duty is to the plan's participants and beneficiaries.

A participant is defined as "any employee ...who is or may become eligible to receive a benefit of any type from an employee benefit plan.[140] The U.S. Supreme Court interpreted this to mean either (1) employees in, or reasonably expected to be in, currently covered employment; or (2) former employees who "have …a reasonable expectation of returning to covered employment" or who have "a colorable claim to vested benefits."[141] To prove that a claimant "may become eligible" for benefits, he or she must present a credible request that (1) he or she will prevail in a lawsuit for benefits, or (2) eligibility requirements will be prospectively satisfied. The definition of employee, although circular in ERISA, was clarified to mean the common law definition of employee.[142] A beneficiary is defined as a person designated by a participant or by the terms of the plan who is or may become entitled to a benefit from the plan.[143]

The fiduciary duty is owed to the plan members taken together. Elevating the fiduciary duty owed to the individual participants of an employee benefit plan far above the duty owed to the plan as a whole prevents fiduciaries from fulfilling their statutory duty. In other words, there is no fiduciary duty owed to a subgroup of constituents, notwithstanding the duty to them as aggregate members of the plan.

Furthermore, the duty is owed to the member of a plan and limited to only that plan. While ERISA contemplates that fiduciaries wear two hats—one in the fiduciary role and another in the corporate role, they also wear separate hats between benefit plans. For example, the responsibility owed to Participant A of Plan B is not necessarily comparable to the responsibility owed to Participant A of Plan C.

Under ERISA, however, a fiduciary may have financial interests adverse to beneficiaries. Employers, for example, can be ERISA fiduciaries and still take actions to the disadvantage of employee beneficiaries when they act as employers (e.g., firing a beneficiary for reasons unrelated to the ERISA plan) or even as plan sponsors (e.g., modifying the terms of a plan as allowed by ERISA to provide less generous benefits). Furthermore, the U.S. Supreme Court ruled that changes in plan design are settlor functions, not fiduciary functions, and therefore do no fall within the scope of fiduciary duty.[144]

ERISA does require, however, that the fiduciary with two hats wear only one at a time, and wear the fiduciary hat when making fiduciary decisions. Thus, the statute defines an administrator, for example, as a fiduciary only "to the extent" that he or she acts in such a capacity in relation to a plan.[145] In every case charging breach of ERISA fiduciary duty, the threshold question is not whether the actions of some person employed to provide services under a plan adversely affected a plan beneficiary's interest, but whether that person was acting as a fiduciary (that is, was performing a fiduciary function) when taking the action subject to complaint.

Finally, there is no fiduciary duty owed to the appointing authority. For example, a named fiduciary appointed by the plan sponsor's board of directors owes no fiduciary duty to that board. Stated differently, while there is a duty by the appointer to monitor the appointees made by a fiduciary, there is no such duty from the appointee to the appointer.

FIDUCIARY RESPONSIBILITY IN PARTICIPANT-DIRECTED PLANS

The fiduciary responsibility rules take on special application in plans that allow for participant-directed investments. In those instances, plan fiduciaries transfer the investment allocation responsibility to employees and as a result may receive a reduction in their own level of personal liability.

For several years, the DOL struggled to finalize the section 404(c) regulations that govern the transfer of investment control to participants. The final regulations were issued on October 13, 1992. In essence, section 404(c) of ERISA relieves plan fiduciaries of liability for investment losses if the plan permits its participants to exercise control over the investments and the losses resulted from the participants' exercise of control. This section of ERISA offers a compelling feature to plan sponsors, and this feature has largely fueled the movement toward participant-directed plans.

Compliance with the requirements of section 404(c) is optional. Plans that elect not to comply with the requirements do not violate ERISA solely due to that election. Yet, an election that is not treated as a section 404(c) plan means that the plan fiduciaries may continue to be held responsible under ERISA for the results of participants' investments. For this reason, compliance with the regulation is advised.

Finally, it should be recognized that plan fiduciaries who seek the protection of section 404(c) always have the burden of proof in litigation—they must prove that they complied with the regulation.

Residual Fiduciary Responsibilities

Sponsors should be cognizant that section 404(c) is an exception to a larger rule and alleviates the plan fiduciaries only from potential liability for investment losses resulting from participants' exercise of control over their own accounts; it does not provide categorical relief from all of ERISA's fiduciary responsibility provisions.

Rather, section 404(c) insulates plan fiduciaries from the results of individual participants' own investment allocation decisions. Thus, before a plan fiduciary can ever hope to be protected under section 404(c), ERISA's general prudence requirements must be satisfied with respect to all of the following:

- The actual prudent and diverse selection of investment vehicles
- The periodic performance review of these investment vehicles
- The ongoing due diligence determination that the alternatives remain suitable investment vehicles for plan participants

Only after having completed this process are plan fiduciaries in a position to take the final step under section 404(c) and move control of investments into the hands of participants under the procedures specified in the regulations. Most important, a plan fiduciary who merely transfers to participants the control over investments, ignoring his or her nondelegable fiduciary responsibilities as just outlined, fails to gain any protection under section 404(c) and may actually increase his or her potential liability under ERISA.[146] The requirements are detailed in the following section and figure 5-2.

THE FOUR HURDLES TO MANAGING FIDUCIARY RESPONSIBILITY IN PARTICIPANT-DIRECTED PLANS

Figure 5-2: Hurdles to Managing Fiduciary Responsibility

Hurdle #1	Hurdle #2	Hurdle #3	Hurdle #4
Prudent Selection of Investment Fund or Advisor	Participants Must Be In "Control" Over Their Investments	Monitoring the Investment Managers	Ongoing Due Diligence

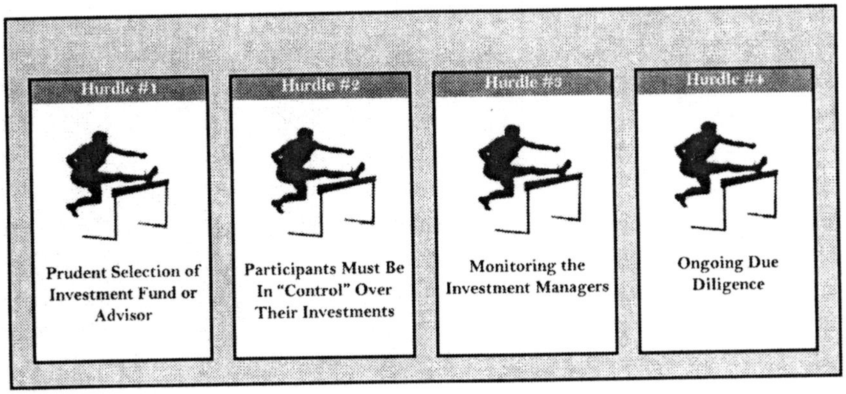

Hurdle 1: Prudent Selection of Investment Fund or Advisor

Fiduciaries of participant-directed plans have a special relationship with participants. Because they are essentially pre-selecting the investment options that will in turn be provided to plan participants, they are engaging in a substantial fiduciary function. The exercise of this function requires plan fiduciaries to act prudently in their selection of these different investment options.

In making this prudent selection, plan fiduciaries need to follow the same fiduciary prudence guidelines outlined earlier. As a practical matter, plan fiduciaries need to take an active role in selecting investment managers for each category in the plan, applying the standards of prudence as well as the exclusive benefit requirement. The selection of each investment manager should be made after exhaustive due diligence and a determination that the manager is the most appropriate of all those surveyed.

Again, because of the relative immaturity of participant-directed plans in the scheme of fiduciary responsibility law, it is too soon to look to the courts for the direct establishment of standards to be used in selecting the particular investment options in a self-directed plan. The DOL has indicated, however, that the standard to be applied is nothing more than an extension of the standard applied in ordinary employer-directed plans.

The DOL emphasizes that the act of designating investment alternatives in an ERISA section 404(c) plan is a fiduciary function to which the limitation on liability provided by section 404(c) is not applicable. All of the fiduciary provisions of ERISA remain applicable to both the initial designation of investment alternatives and investment managers and the ongoing determination that such alternatives and managers remain suitable and prudent investment alternatives for the plan.[147] Therefore, the particular plan fiduciaries responsible for performing these functions must do so in accordance with ERISA.

In selecting the investment fund or manager, plan fiduciaries should consider carefully their conduct in investigating, evaluating, and hiring. The process in which a fiduciary engages in making this decision is the central question in determining whether a fiduciary fulfilled his or her responsibilities in selecting the investments for plan participants. In litigation, plan fiduciaries will be required to prove that they engaged in a thoughtful and prudent selection process. Therefore, it is essential that the plan's decision-making process be thoroughly documented. Additionally, an investment policy statement should describe the process and criteria for the decisions.

Considering the substantial risk of litigation, plan fiduciaries should further bear in mind that they have an affirmative obligation under ERISA to seek independent advice from a qualified professional when they lack the requisite education, experience, and skill. Once again, in litigation, the plan fiduciary would be required to prove that he or she either possessed the requisite expertise or received independent advice from a qualified professional.

The following might serve as a general guideline for plan fiduciaries in their selection of investments to be offered to participants as selections in the plan:

- Use the advice of a professional third-party advisor or consultant to review competitors and to define asset categories
- Establish a competitive bidding procedure; no organization should be pre-selected or precluded (except for parties-in-interest)
- Request written proposals from all bidding organizations
- Review the competitors for any party-in-interest relationship
- Evaluate the organizations' qualifications, from an asset management standpoint, including all the considerations noted earlier
- Ascertain the reasonableness of fees relative to proposed services by establishing a grid comparison
- Ensure adequate, periodic monitoring in the future

The Use of a Financial Advisor or Consulting Organization

The use of third-party financial advisors or consultants to assist the plan fiduciary in the selection of investment management organizations is simply an extension of what has long been the practice of prudent plan fiduciaries. This practice is gaining prominence in the benefits area in view of the substantial responsibility in selecting investment options for participants.

As a practical matter, the plan fiduciary is entitled to rely on the information, data statistics, or analyses provided by the financial advisor or consulting organization in exercising his or her fiduciary duties, provided that the fiduciary exercises prudence in selecting, monitoring, and retaining the advisor or consultant. Generally, the plan fiduciary will be deemed to have acted prudently in the selection and retention of the advisors or consultant if he or she has no reason to doubt the competence, integrity, or responsibility of such persons or organizations.

Choosing a Provider for the Wrong Reasons

Although there is always the powerful consideration of administrative convenience and simplicity, plan fiduciaries must be careful not to select a provider to handle all aspects of the plan investments solely for the reason of administrative convenience. Although this is an important consideration, convenience is not a valid reason in and of itself from the standpoint of ERISA.

Plan fiduciaries must keep in mind the exclusive purpose rule of ERISA, which directs a fiduciary to act solely in the interest of participants and beneficiaries and for the exclusive purpose of providing benefits to participants. It is questionable, to say the least, whether the selection of an organization because of administrative convenience or the attainment of a corporate line of credit, rather than on the merits of that organization's investment expertise in all relevant asset categories, is a prudent decision for the exclusive benefit of participants. Rather, the decision to hire a particular investment manager should be based on an objective evaluation of the standards mentioned earlier.

Select Experts in Each Asset Category

As discussed later in this chapter, participant-directed plans need to offer participants a minimum selection of investment options among various investment categories. In the discussion of those categories, it is important to note that from the standpoint of fiduciary responsibility the company selected to manage the participants' assets should have breadth of experience in all relevant asset classes. A few providers today have such breadth; others have teamed up to create unbundled multi-fund products. Still, certain multi-fund products still have administrative shortcomings as described in Chapters 6 and 7.

Hurdle 2: Participants Must Be In "Control" of Their Investments

In essence, ERISA section 404(c) attempts to immunize plan fiduciaries from any liability resulting from participants' control over investment allocation decisions. Any protections provided under section 404(c) exist under the theory that a plan fiduciary should not be responsible for that which a participant is in control of. Thus, the primary inquiry under section 404(c) focuses on whether the participants are in control of their investments.

This is reflected in the DOL's core requirements for section 404(c) compliance:

- The plan must provide the participant with the opportunity to exercise control over the assets in his or her account
- The participant must in fact exercise independent control with respect to the investment of these assets[148]

Requirement 1: Opportunity to Exercise Control

There are a number of practical requirements set forth under the regulations to ensure that participants are given the opportunity to exercise control over the investments.

Broad Range Requirement

The DOL has consistently adhered to the view that a participant only has an opportunity to exercise control if he or she is offered a broad range of investment alternatives. The definition of "broad range" requires that the plan offer its participants the opportunity to direct their investments into three different investment categories. Each of these three categories must have "materially different risk and return characteristics."[149] Taken together, these three investment categories must permit participants to construct an appropriate investment mix with appropriate corresponding risk and return characteristics. Each investment alternative must also be of a type that, when combined with the other investment alternatives, tends to minimize through diversification the overall risk of a participant's portfolio.

Some commentators have argued that these broad range requirements are vague and therefore difficult to apply.[150] Yet, the final regulation of the DOL is intended to give plan sponsors broad latitude in developing combinations of investment alternatives that meet the broad range requirement. Because the determination of what constitutes a broad range requires considerable expertise, plan sponsors are strongly urged to rely on the advice of a qualified investment management consultant.

Diversification Requirement

In order for the categories to be deemed a broad range of alternatives, each investment alternative must be diversified in and of itself so that participants are given the opportunity to minimize the risk of large losses. For this reason, employer securities cannot be used as one of the core investment alternatives intended to satisfy the broad range requirements of the regulation. Employer securities would not themselves represent a diversified investment alternative.

In order to accomplish the diversification requirement, the regulations permit the plan to offer so-called look-through investment vehicles. These consist of mutual funds, bank collective funds, insurance company–pooled separate accounts, GICs, or a separately managed account for the plan. In essence, these look-through investment vehicles permit employees to achieve instant diversification in any given asset category.

ERISA's legislative history offers guidance on the diversification requirement. A prudent fiduciary must consider the facts and circumstances of each case. The factors to consider include: (1) the purpose of the plan; (2) the amount of plan assets; (3) financial and industrial conditions; (4) the type of investment; (5) distribution based on geographic location; (6) distribution based on industries; and (7) the dates of maturity.[151] Against a claim of failure to diversify, the fiduciary must demonstrate that it was clearly prudent not to diversify.

Frequency of Opportunity to Give Investment Instructions

To exercise control, participants must be able to change their investment allocations with some frequency. The regulations have created a relatively complex set of standards governing the required frequency for opportunities to change investments in different instances.

The general rule provides that the opportunity to exercise control will not exist unless participants are given the opportunity to give investment instructions with a frequency that is appropriate in light of the volatility to which the investment may reasonably be expected to be subject. This principle is known as the "general volatility rule."[152] Nonetheless, regardless of the frequency required under the general volatility rule, with regard to the three core investment vehicles constituting the broad range, investment changes must be permitted once every three months. This is known in the regulation as the "three-month minimum."[153]

Although there is no restriction on a plan's ability to offer other investment alternatives in addition to the three core alternatives, it should be noted that there would be no section 404(c) relief for plan fiduciaries with respect to amounts invested in investment alternatives that do not permit investment instructions with a frequency commensurate with the reasonably expected volatility of the investment alternative.

This rule provides a difficult standard for plan sponsors because no examples are provided in the regulation demonstrating the classes of investments that would require investment changes more frequently than once every three months. Moreover, the DOL has imposed an ongoing obligation on the part of plan fiduciaries to review the volatility of all investment selections.

Fiduciaries of an ERISA section 404(c) plan should periodically review the volatility of its investment alternatives to ensure that the transfer frequency permitted with respect to each alternative continues to be appropriate.

As a result, plan sponsors are well advised to (1) determine the appropriate transfer frequency given the expected volatility of the investments and (2) monitor the volatility of the investment alternatives to ensure that the transfer frequency continues to be appropriate.

The Volatile Investment Transferability Rule

In those instances where a plan permits participants to invest in additional noncore investment alternatives in which investment transfers are allowed more frequently than once every three months, the regulation imposes additional complex rules governing the transfer frequency. These rules, called the volatile investment transferability rules, are necessary because the ability to transfer assets to or from a volatile investment has meaning only when there is in fact another investment vehicle available that can just as readily transfer out or accept assets. In essence, this rule requires that participants be given the opportunity to direct their investment alternatives with a frequency commensurate with the volatility of the more volatile investment vehicle.

Under the regulation, there are two methods for accommodating transfers between core and noncore investments. Under the first method, at least one of the core investment alternatives must permit participants to give investment instructions as frequently as they are permitted to give investment instructions with respect to any additional non-core investment alternative made available by the plan. In addition, the core investment alternative selected to satisfy this requirement need only permit such instructions with regard to transfers into the core alternative.

Rather than permitting transfers directly into core alternatives, the regulation also permits the plan to allow participants to direct the transfer from the more volatile investment into a temporary holding account until such time as they may, under the terms of the plan, further direct the assets into at least one of the three core investment alternatives.

Special Transfer Rules for Employer Stock

In general, the methods for accommodating transfers from employer securities are essentially the same as for all other alternatives except that participants must be given the ability to direct their investments from employer securities into any of the available core investment alternatives.[154] In short, all of the core investment alternatives must permit participants to give investment instructions with regard to transfers into each of the alternatives as frequently as they are permitted to give investment instructions with respect to employer securities.

Disclosure to Participants

In addition to the above requirements, the regulation requires that participants receive sufficient information so that they are able to make informed investment decisions. The regulation requires that certain information be furnished to all participants and that certain other information be furnished when requested.

The requirements listed here should form the skeleton of any participant communications program. As such, these requirements are the minimum of what must be provided to participants so that they are able to make informed investment decisions. Sponsors should work with their plan providers to flush out these minimum standards in an effort to provide sufficient information given the particular characteristics of their plan, company, and employee base.

The following information must be provided for all participants:[155]

- An explanation that the plan is intended to constitute a section 404(c) plan and that plan fiduciaries may be relieved of liability for losses that are the result of participants' investment instructions

- A description of investment alternatives in the plan, including a general description of the investment objectives and risk and return characteristics of each

- Identification of any designated investment managers

- An explanation of how to give investment instructions, any limits or restrictions on giving instructions, and any limits on the exercise of voting, tender, or similar rights

- A description of any transaction fees or expenses that are charged to the participant's account

- A description of the information available by request and the identity of the person or persons responsible for providing the information

- A copy of the most recent prospectus immediately following an investment in an investment alternative subject to the Securities Act of 1933, unless the prospectus was furnished immediately before the participant's investment

- Materials provided to the plan relative to the exercise of voting, tender, or similar rights, to the extent such rights are passed through to participants subsequent to an investment

The following information must be provided on request to participants:[156]

- A description of the annual operating expenses borne by investment alternatives, such as investment management fees

- Copies of any prospectuses, financial statements, and reports furnished to the plan relating to investment alternatives

- A listing of the assets that make up the portfolio of an investment alternative that holds plan assets; the value of such assets; and, in the case of fixed rate contracts of banks or insurance companies, the name of the issuers of the contract, the terms of the contract, and the rate of return of the contract
- Information concerning the value of shares or units of investment alternatives available to participants, as well as information concerning the past and current investment performance of the alternatives
- Information concerning the value of shares or units in investment alternatives held in the account of the participant

These standards are rigorous and probably require more disclosure than any other regulation designed to protect the interest of an investor (participant). Interestingly, these standards provide only a starting point for fiduciaries of participant-directed plans. Plan fiduciaries still must work with their plan providers to be certain that these required disclosures (and other information) are communicated in a way so all participants are able to fully understand the plan. Plan fiduciaries that approach these as boilerplate, fine-print disclosures will continue to be susceptible to liability.

Requirement 2: Actual Exercise of Independent Control

The entire regulatory structure of section 404(c) hinges on whether a participant is in fact in control over his or her investments. When it can be shown that the participant in fact exercised control over the assets in his or her account, the plan fiduciary will be insulated from the results of a participant's investment control. The corollary to this rule is also true: When it can be shown that a participant was not in fact in control over his or her investments, the plan fiduciary can be held liable for the results of the participant's investment decisions.

The regulations state that whether a participant has indeed exercised such independent control is to be determined on a case-by-case basis.[157] This is problematic because there is no real guidance in the regulations for making this determination, and it is the fiduciary's obligation to prove that any given investment decision was in fact controlled by the participant.

Under the regulation, a participant will not be considered to have exercised control over the assets in his or her account unless the participant has provided affirmative investment instructions with respect to such assets.[158] In other words, plan fiduciaries will not be relieved of responsibility for investment decisions under section 404(c) unless participants who have exercised independent control have affirmatively made those decisions. Thus, when participants fail to give investment instructions, the common practice of placing the participant's assets in a so-called safe investment will not provide any protection to plan fiduciaries. As in other non-404(c) type plans, fiduciaries of ERISA section 404(c) plans have a duty to provide for the investment of idle plan assets, and lack of participant direction will not absolve a fiduciary of such duties. In short, until an affirmative instruction is received, there can be no relief of responsibility under section 404(c) of ERISA.

Yet, where a participant is afforded the opportunity to exercise voting, tender, or similar rights and is provided the information necessary to exercise such rights, the regulation provides that a participant will be considered to have exercised control with respect to such rights even if the participant takes no action. In addition, a participant does not in fact exercise control if the plan fiduciary fails to reveal facts that would bear on the suitability of the transaction from the participant's standpoint, unless disclosing these facts would violate securities or banking laws.

Moreover, a participant is not in control when he or she has been subjected to improper influence. Thus, plan fiduciaries should not render any advice to participants. Instead, fiduciaries should rely on the consultants to the plan to provide advice to participants.

Finally, if the fiduciary knows that a participant is legally incompetent, he or she must disregard that participant's investment instructions.

Hurdle 3: Monitoring the Investment Managers

As noted earlier, the actual selection by the plan fiduciary of an investment manager is itself a fiduciary decision subject to the prudent man standard and other ERISA safeguards. Thus, if the plan fiduciary considers hiring the manager or managers, the fiduciary cannot be held liable for this decision unless it can be shown that the hiring decision was somehow imprudent or unreasonable.

The duty of the plan fiduciary in a plan does not end with the appointment of investment managers. The DOL has set forth the following general ongoing responsibilities:[159]

- At reasonable intervals the performance of trustees and other fiduciaries should be reviewed by the appointing fiduciary in such manner as may be reasonably expected to ensure that their performance has been in compliance with the terms of the plan and statutory standards, and satisfies the needs of the plan. No single procedure will be appropriate in all cases; the procedure adopted may vary in accordance with the nature of the plan and other facts and circumstances relative to the choice of the procedure.

- Although this requirement applies universally to all plans regardless of type, the DOL has specifically extended the requirement to participant-directed plans.

- The plan fiduciary has an obligation to periodically evaluate the performance of such vehicles to determine, based on that evaluation, whether the vehicles should continue to be available as participant investment options.

In addition, as noted earlier, the DOL has created a new obligation for plan fiduciaries of participant-directed plans to review the volatility of the plan's investment alternatives to ensure that the transfer frequency permitted with respect to each alternative continues to be appropriate.

From these statements and from court rulings, it is clear that the plan fiduciary must take certain actions in order to discharge his or her obligation to monitor the performance and volatility of the asset manager or managers. The following standard is recommended as an appropriate methodology for performance monitoring:

- Require the trustee or investment manager to prepare periodic reports about the specific investments of the plan assets under the manager's control, including investment performance and volatility

- Compare actual investments and investment performance to the goals of the plan as communicated to the asset manager and to the investment guidelines set forth in the investment management agreement

- Review investment performance and volatility of common indexes or other similar investment portfolios for comparison to the investment results of the investment manager

- Obtain an evaluation by an independent entity experienced in evaluating investment performance of the investment performance and volatility versus relevant benchmark indexes

Hurdle 4: Ongoing Due Diligence

As a final matter, to manage fiduciary responsibility in a participant-directed plan, the plan fiduciary must exercise ongoing due diligence over the investments and the investment managers. In this regard, the DOL has stated that the ongoing duty to consider the suitability of a designated investment vehicle encompasses a continuing determination that the vehicle remains a prudent investment option.[160]

SECTION 404(C) PROTECTION

One of the common themes throughout this chapter is the notion that ERISA section 404(c) does not relieve plan fiduciaries of all their fiduciary obligations under the plan. As noted earlier, plan fiduciaries are still required to perform all their nondelegable fiduciary obligations such as prudent selection, ongoing monitoring, and due diligence. These obligations are in fact identical to the general obligations imposed on a fiduciary in an employer-directed plan. This raises the question of whether maintaining a participant-directed plan offers any real advantage to plan fiduciaries by reducing their potential exposure.

Compliance with 404(c) is unlikely to significantly decrease the incidence of lawsuits alleging fiduciary misconduct when a participant-directed investment goes sour. The proposed regulation's requirement that section 404(c) relief will be unavailable if the fiduciary has not disseminated sufficient information to participants to allow them to render prudent investment decisions affords participants and the DOL an effective enforcement tool by which to continue to impose liability on plan fiduciaries for imprudent investments. Rather than assert that a fiduciary has authorized a substantively imprudent investment, participants will simply argue that they did not receive enough information to render a prudent investment decision.

Given the scope of disclosures required under the regulation, and that plan fiduciaries retain all of their prior responsibilities under ERISA, it appears unlikely that merely maintaining a participant-directed plan actually reduces a plan fiduciary's potential liability. Nevertheless, to the extent that a plan allows participants to direct their own investments, prudent plan fiduciaries should do the following:

- Continue to perform all of their basic responsibilities
- Comply with the regulations
- Make every attempt to communicate information in a straightforward and sufficient manner

Diversification Requirements in an ESOP

Employee stock ownership plans (ESOPs) are unique in that they are intended to be invested primarily in company stock and are an accepted method of transferring ownership of a company to its employees. Therefore, requiring diversification in an ESOP would make it virtually impossible to accomplish its philosophical purpose. Still, ESOPs are subject to diversification rules.

Current ESOP law allows employees who are fifty-five years old and have ten years of participation in the plan to diversify up to 25% of their company stock in an ESOP, which increases to 50% at age sixty.[161]

In *Hall Holding*, the DOL successfully challenged the ESOP fiduciaries for failing to conduct a prudent and independent investigation to establish the fair market value of employer stock purchased by an ESOP.[162] The appeals court affirmed the district court finding, including finding the fiduciaries personally liable for an award of money damages to ESOP participants to compensate for the fiduciaries' failure to determine the "adequate consideration" that should have been paid for the stock.

FIDUCIARY LIABILITY UNDER ERISA

In addition to ERISA's strict parameters on fiduciary conduct, the act further permits legal action to be brought by a participant, beneficiary, or other fiduciary against a plan fiduciary for a breach of duty. In those cases where the fiduciary is found to in fact have violated these duties, the fiduciary may be found to be personally liable for any losses to the plan that result from the breach of duty, and any profits earned by the fiduciary through the illegal use of plan assets must be turned over to the plan. ERISA also gives the court the power to order other appropriate relief such as the removal of the fiduciary.

A fiduciary may not, however, be held responsible for any breaches of fiduciary duty that occurred before the time he or she became a fiduciary or after the time he or she ceased to be a fiduciary. All fiduciaries should be mindful of the principle of ongoing fiduciary breach, which holds that even though a fiduciary may not be personally liable or responsible for the original breach, if he or she knows of the breach, that fiduciary is required to take measures to remedy the situation. The failure to take remedial steps might constitute an independent breach of fiduciary duty in and of itself.

Determination of Losses to the Plan

A disturbing trend in fiduciary responsibility cases is the tendency of some courts to define broadly the word "loss," which means that plan fiduciaries may find themselves liable for violations that at first glance do not appear to have resulted in an economic loss to plan assets.

Consider the following examples as illustrations about how some courts have defined loss and held that the fiduciary violated his fiduciary duties.

1. A plan actually experienced a healthy and positive return on an investment that violated ERISA, but the court compared that return to the return that would have been realized if the funds had been invested in an alternative, proper investment over the same period of time. When several alternatives were equally plausible, the court assumed that the funds would have been invested in the most profitable investment and required the fiduciary to make up the difference.

2. The investment manager failed to follow investment policy that limited equity investment to 50% of the portfolio. The plan nevertheless earned a healthy return on those equity investments, but the court held the investment manager liable for the amount the plan could have earned had the assets not been improperly invested.

3. The court found a violation of fiduciary duty when the investment manager invested 70% of the assets of a profit-sharing plan in thirty-year Treasury bonds. Because of required distributions, the investment manager was forced to sell some bonds at a loss. The court faulted the manager for failing to know the cash-flow requirements of the plan. As a result, the court ordered the manager to pay the plan the difference between what it would have earned had it been funded with bonds containing staggered maturity dates and what it actually earned.

4. The court ordered an investment manager found in fiduciary violation to pay the difference between the plan's actual earnings and what the plan would have earned during the relevant period, as measured by the Standard and Poor's 500 Index.

Return of Profits or Equitable Relief or Both

In addition to having to recoup "losses" to the plan under fiduciary liability theory, a violating fiduciary is always required to return to the plan any profits realized through the abuse of his or her position or trust. Moreover, equitable relief for a breach of fiduciary duty is authorized under section 409 of ERISA even if there are no losses to the plan and no disgorged profits.

The following are examples of the sorts of equitable relief fashioned by some courts:

- Removal of trustee of fiduciary
- Rescission of employment agreement and order to pay back all salary paid
- Prejudgment interest
- Postjudgment interest

Civil Penalties

In addition to possible liability to the plan or to participants for breaches of fiduciary obligation, the DOL may impose a 20% civil penalty under section 502 of ERISA. This penalty is at the discretion of the DOL, which may seek to impose the penalty by court order or by direct settlement with the violating fiduciaries. In some instances, the DOL may choose to reduce or waive the penalty if the fiduciary acted in good faith or will not be able to restore the plan losses without severe financial hardship. The penalty may be avoided by participating in the DOL's Voluntary Fiduciary Compliance (VFC) Program. The VFC Program is discussed in detail in Chapter 11.

Co-fiduciary Liability

In addition to liability for a fiduciary's own breaches, a fiduciary may also be held liable for the breaches committed by other co-fiduciaries if the first fiduciary does any of the following:

- Knowingly participates in or undertakes to conceal a co-fiduciary's breach, aware that such act or omission is a breach
- Fails to meet his or her own responsibilities and, as a result, enables another to breach a fiduciary obligation through neglect of duties, enabling the other fiduciary to commit a breach
- Becomes aware of another fiduciary's breach and makes no reasonable efforts under the circumstances to remedy the breach

Examples of each type of breach are as follows

Participating knowingly in or concealing a breach. E and F are co-trustees and the terms of the plan allow no investments in commodity futures. If F invests in such futures at the suggestion of E, both E and F will be liable for the breach. Similarly, if F independently invests in commodity futures and tells E of this investment, E would be liable as well as F for the breach if E concealed the improper investment.

Enabling the breach. Co-trustees E and F jointly manage the plan assets. E improperly allows F to have sole custody of the plan assets and makes no inquiry as to his conduct. F is thereby enabled to sell the property and embezzle the proceeds. E is liable for a breach of fiduciary responsibility.

Failure to remedy. Based on the first example above, if E has authority to do so and it is prudent under the circumstances, he may be required to dispose of the commodity futures acquired by F. Alternatively, the most appropriate steps may include notifying the plan sponsor of the breach, proceeding to an appropriate federal court for instructions, or bringing the matter to the attention of the secretary of labor.

Plan fiduciaries always should attempt to remedy any breach by other plan fiduciaries. When a plan fiduciary believes that a co-fiduciary has committed a breach, resignation by the fiduciary as a protest against such a breach is not generally considered sufficient to discharge the fiduciary's affirmative duty under section 405(a)(3), which requires the fiduciary to make reasonable efforts under the circumstances to remedy the breach.

Possible ways to remedy the breach might include disposal of an asset, notification to the sponsoring organization, instigation of a lawsuit against the co-fiduciary, or notification of the breach to the DOL.

The DOL has provided guidance regarding remedial measures necessary to prevent co-fiduciary breaches. Co-fiduciaries must take all reasonable and legal steps to prevent the breach. Such steps might include obtaining an injunction in federal court, notifying the DOL, notifying the plan sponsor, or publicizing the breach. Furthermore, all meetings concerning management and control of plan assets should be documented, and any objections alleging potential violations of fiduciary responsibilities should be made part of the record. If a fiduciary believes a co-fiduciary has already committed a breach, the DOL has warned that resignation as a protest against a breach will not generally discharge the duty to make reasonable efforts to remedy the breach. As far back as DOL Interpretive Bulletin 75-8, the DOL has stated, "[T]he board of directors may be responsible for the selection and retention of plan fiduciaries. In such a case, members of the board of directors exercise 'discretion authority or discretionary control respecting management of such plan' and are therefore, fiduciaries with respect to the plan."[163] Nevertheless, the DOL stated the liability was limited to the selection and retention of fiduciaries.

In re CMS Energy ERISA litigation, the court ruled that the discretion given to the employer under the plan provisions was broad enough to support a finding that they were fiduciaries under ERISA:

> [W]here the Board of [Directors] may choose a Plan administrator, and the Employers may choose an Investment Manager, but the Plan does not delegate investment policy or decision making power to such manager, administrator, or any other individual or committee, but in fact reserves the broadest administrative and management responsibility to the Employers, the court is convinced that it is premature to dismiss inside directors of the Employers as non-fiduciaries

absent specific findings on what responsibilities were actually assumed by them.[164]

Regarding the duty to monitor, the court stated:

> ...[T]he allegations are that the Employer Named Fiduciaries and the Insider Director Defendants breached their fiduciary duties by failing to adequately monitor the Plan Committees, the Plan Administrators, and other persons, if any, to whom management of Plan assets was delegated. These Defendants knew or should have known that the other fiduciaries were imprudently allowing the Plan to continue offering CMS stock as an investment option and investing Plan assets in CMS stock when it no longer was prudent to do so, yet failed to take action to protect the participants from the consequences of the other fiduciaries' failures.[165]

Furthermore, in its Enron brief the DOL went beyond the positions it has stated in the past. For example, with respect to the DOL's discussion of the duty to monitor a fiduciary, it is at best unclear what actions a company's board of directors should take with respect to supervising a plan fiduciary appointed by the board. Apparently, the DOL believes that the appointing fiduciary has a duty to disclose information to the appointed fiduciary that could affect the plan. This creates a slippery slope concerning the dissemination of sensitive corporate information.

Co-trustees

Section 403 of ERISA provides that the trustees of a plan must have the "exclusive authority and discretion to manage and control the assets of the plan." As mentioned above, co-trustees may allocate so-called "trustee responsibilities" (which are responsibilities that relate to the management or control of plan assets) between themselves, but trustee responsibilities generally may not be allocated to others. This general rule is subject to three exceptions.

Possibly the most important exception is that a plan may provide that the trustee is subject to the direction of a named fiduciary that is not a trustee. A plan also may permit the appointment of an investment manager with authority to manage, acquire, or dispose of plan assets. If an investment manager is properly appointed, the plan trustee no longer has the responsibility for managing the assets controlled by the investment manager and is not liable for the investment manager's acts or omissions. In addition, a plan trustee may follow the directions of plan participants if the plan and the directions comply with the requirements of ERISA section 404(c). The requirements of section 404(c) are discussed below.

If a plan provides for co-trustees, plan assets are to be jointly managed unless the trustees agree (in accordance with the trust instrument) to allocate specific responsibilities, obligations, and duties among themselves. If trustee duties are allocated in this fashion, a trustee to whom a duty has not been allocated is not liable for losses due to acts and omissions of the trustee to whom the duty has been allocated. If plan assets are held in more than one trust, the trustee of only one of the trusts is not liable under ERISA's co-trustee rules for the acts and omissions of the trustee of any other trust.

Directed Trustee

A directed trustee is a trustee who acts only on direction provided by a named fiduciary or investment manager. A directed trustee is usually held to be a fiduciary but with a lessened fiduciary delegation. At minimum, he or she must determine whether the instructions received are proper in accordance with the terms of the plan and are consistent with ERISA.

Figure 5-3: Trustee Responsibilities

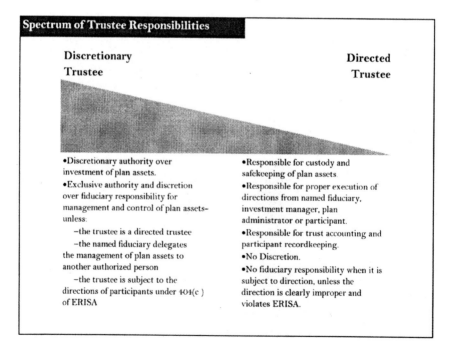

Spectrum of Trustee Responsibilities

Discretionary
Trustee

Directed
Trustee

•Discretionary authority over investment of plan assets.

•Exclusive authority and discretion over fiduciary responsibility for management and control of plan assets–unless:

  –the trustee is a directed trustee

  –the named fiduciary delegates the management of plan assets to another authorized person

  –the trustee is subject to the directions of participants under 404(c) of ERISA

•Responsible for custody and safekeeping of plan assets.

•Responsible for proper execution of directions from named fiduciary, investment manager, plan administrator or participant.

•Responsible for trust accounting and participant recordkeeping.

•No Discretion.

•No fiduciary responsibility when it is subject to direction, unless the direction is clearly improper and violates ERISA.

The DOL's guidance has stated that trustees, by the character of the duties provided, exercise the level of discretion necessary to bestow fiduciary status.[166] Sample duties of directed trustees and discretionary trustees are highlighted in figure 5-3. Moreover, the DOL has stated that a directed trustee has some level of fiduciary responsibility under ERISA section 403(a)(1).[167] In contrast, a number of courts have held that directed trustees are not fiduciaries, concentrating on the definition under ERISA section 3(21) and the lack of investment discretion and responsibility typically accorded to directed trustees.[168] Nonetheless, other courts have concluded that directed trustees have some amount of fiduciary status and liability. These courts have generally ignored whether the directed trustee agreement granted discretion to the trustee and concluded that the directed trustee had some residual discretion based on the language of ERISA section 403(a)(1).[169]

The law is vague about what constitutes "proper" directions or what liability is attached to the directed trustee if things go wrong, even if the trustee was just following orders. There are three possibilities:

1. The directed trustee is liable whenever the fiduciary who gave the instructions was breaching his or her duty, regardless of whether the directed trustee knew or should have known about the breach.

2. The directed trustee is only liable if he or she had actual knowledge of the breach. The directed trustee has no duty to inquire or investigate.

3. The directed trustee can safely follow directions unless he or she knows or should have known that the directing fiduciary was breaching fiduciary duty, in which case the directed trustee has a duty to conduct a "reasonable" investigation.

In the Enron case, the court chose the third option, rejecting the "actual knowledge" argument and establishing a broad basis for liability. This is in keeping with the rest of its approach to fiduciary responsibilities. But in its dicta, the court went even further, stating that in any ERISA retirement plan holding company stock, when there are significant red flags regarding a company's financial statements, it is an issue of fact whether the directed trustee had a fiduciary duty to investigate the advisability of purchasing the company's stock for the plan. This assessment of responsibility by the directed trustee goes beyond even the allegations raised by the plaintiffs in their complaint. It also runs counter to ERISA's legislative history, as well as to the decisions of several other courts.

The DOL filed an *amicus curiae* brief in the Enron case, which argues in part that directed trustees cannot follow directions that they know or should know are imprudent or violate ERISA. In *Enron*, the plaintiffs allege that there were sufficient red flags suggesting the imprudence of the lockdown, such that the directed trustee may have had a duty to override the fiduciary's direction to freeze participants' accounts.

Liability Related to Employer Stock Investments

The emergence of recent lawsuits where participants claim fiduciary breach for the investment of plan assets in employer stock raises awareness of fiduciary duties. The claims, which remain in the trail stage as of publication, fall in the following two categories:

- The fiduciaries breached their duty of loyalty by failing to disclose pertinent information to the participants
- The fiduciaries breached their duty of prudence by not diversifying assets invested in company stock

A fundamental tenet of ERISA is that a person can wear "two hats," or serve in a dual roll, acting both as a fiduciary to an ERISA plan and as an officer or board member with an obligation to the company. Yet one of the most problematic allegations in ERISA tagalong claims is that the plan fiduciaries had an inherent conflict of interest by serving as both a plan fiduciary and as an officer or director of the sponsor company. In recent cases, plaintiffs argue that because of this dual capacity the plan fiduciaries took actions primarily for the benefit of the company rather than plan participants, and that plan fiduciaries knew but failed to disclose material, non-public information that injured plan participants. To avoid or at least minimize the effect of those allegations, companies should consider appointing independent fiduciaries to manage and monitor the plan's investment in company stock. These independent fiduciaries should have no actual or perceived relationship with the company or its directors and officers, and they should have exclusive control over all investment-related decisions for the plan. Because liability exposure for plan administration is much less than liability exposure for plan investments, independent fiduciaries could be appointed solely with respect to plan investments, thereby allowing the plan sponsor and its officers to control various noninvestment administrative tasks. Alternatively, company officials who typically do not have access to the company's non-public information could be designated investment fiduciaries, although such a practice invites arguments that the fiduciary in fact knew or should have discovered the non-public information because of his position with the company.

Federal securities laws require a company to disclose material information to investors only at certain designated times, such as when an SEC filing is due or when the company is purchasing or selling its own securities. In contrast, ERISA may require plan fiduciaries (including company officers) to disclose material information regarding the company on a more current basis if the information could reasonably be viewed as important to plan participants in making plan investment decisions. These conflicting disclosure obligations under the securities laws and ERISA place company officers who are plan fiduciaries in a classic catch-22. If they disclose the non-public information to plan participants, they are likely violating the insider trading rules under the securities laws. If they do not disclose the information to plan participants, they may violate their ERISA fiduciary duties. Some courts have concluded that plan fiduciaries can remove themselves from this catch-22 by disclosing the non-public information to all investors and plan participants as soon as possible, eliminating company stock from the plan, or notifying the regulators of the specific dilemma. In addition, if the plan utilizes only independent fiduciaries and not company officers with respect to plan investments, those independent fiduciaries will likely not learn of the non-public information and therefore not be placed in this difficult situation. In any event, all communications by plan fiduciaries to participants should be prompt, accurate, clear, and consistent with disclosures to other company constituents. Clever spin or other vague or confusing communications should not be tolerated. Instead, the communications should be easy to understand and convey the whole truth. Even unsophisticated participants should be able to readily understand the disclosed information. Bad news should not be understated, and good news should not be overstated.

A new form of ERISA class-action lawsuit is emerging that increases focus on the potential liability of a company's officers and directors for failure to make adequate disclosures regarding the financial condition of the company. These claims look similar to claims under federal securities laws.

This new form of class-action lawsuit is being filed with growing frequency against directors and officers when the market price their company's stock drops significantly following the disclosure of surprising adverse information about the company. Historically, such a stock drop would often result in class actions filed on behalf of purchasers of the company's securities for some defined period before the surprising disclosure. Those class actions would allege that the company and its directors and officers, named as defendants, failed to disclose the adverse information sooner, thereby resulting in the artificial inflation of the market price of the company's securities during the alleged class period. The actions would allege that those who purchased securities at artificially inflated prices suffered damages and are entitled to recover the difference between what they actually paid for the securities and what the market price would have been if full and accurate information had been timely disclosed.

Securities class-action lawsuits are often filed following a company's surprising announcement of adverse information, particularly when the immediate stock drop following the disclosure of adverse information constitutes more than a 10% decline in the market price of the securities, the adverse information being disclosed is especially egregious or presumably was known or should have been known by insiders well before the disclosure (e.g., restatement of financial disclosures, dramatic and sudden decline in the company's financial performance or condition, etc.), or evidence exists that the defendants had the motive and opportunity to artificially inflate the company's stock price (e.g. insider trading, use of company stock to make company acquisitions, sale of company stock in a stock offering). Although ostensibly brought for the benefit of the injured shareholders, securities class actions frequently are instigated and prosecuted primarily by and for the benefit of the plaintiffs' lawyers.

As a result of the Private Securities Litigation Reform Act of 1995, more and more securities class-action lawsuits are being handled (and effectively controlled) by a small group of sophisticated and highly experienced plaintiff law firms, which are routinely retained as lead counsel by institutional investors serving as lead counsel. Plaintiff firms without institutional clients are shut out of the lucrative lead counsel role. This dynamic has caused some of those plaintiff law firms to explore other types of class-action lawsuits to recover large settlements in following a significant drop in a company's stock price, and thus recover large fee awards. A popular new type of class-action lawsuit now being filed by plaintiff law firms shut out of major securities litigation is brought under ERISA.

Primarily beginning with the Enron debacle, these class actions are brought on behalf of participants and beneficiaries of a company's retirement plan to the extent those plans own securities of the company. The complaints in these class actions contain the same factual allegations set forth in the securities class-action lawsuits (i.e., the defendants misrepresented or failed to disclose certain material information about the company or its financial performance or condition). Instead of alleging those misrepresentations or omissions constitute a violation of the securities laws, however, the new lawsuits allege the defendants breached their fiduciary duties under ERISA. As a result of the breaches, the plan participants and beneficiaries allegedly were allowed or induced to invest or maintain their plan assets in company stock at artificially high prices or otherwise suffered losses because their plan assets were invested in overpriced or ill-advised securities.

The claims asserted in these so-called tagalong class actions are summarized as follows:

- Claims against officers and directors for deceiving plan participants and beneficiaries by disclosing false and misleading information and failing to disclose material information about the company and its financial condition and performance, either in statements to the general public, to shareholders, or to employees

- Claims against plan fiduciaries (many of whom are also officers) for failing to disclose the adverse information to plan participants and beneficiaries, failing to disclose such information to other plan fiduciaries who were responsible for investing plan assets, and failing to correct misleading statements made by other officers and plan fiduciaries

- Claims against plan fiduciaries for retaining or investing in company stock in plan accounts, permitting participants to invest in company stock by continuing to include the stock as an authorized investment option in self-directed plans, failing to adequately diversify plan assets, and failing to investigate the suitability of plan investments

These ERISA tagalong class-action lawsuits are sufficiently new that there is not a meaningful body of case law addressing the propriety of the underlying legal theories. On their surface, however, these lawsuits, which typically name as defendants senior officers and the board of directors of the company as well as other designated plan fiduciaries, raise several concerns for the defendants.

Courts are split on whether to permit ERISA breach of fiduciary duty claims in similar circumstances. Some, like the Enron court, have rejected the existence of a conflict and refused to dismiss ERISA breach of fiduciary duty claims.[170] Others have dismissed ERISA claims based on a recognized conflict between federal securities law and ERISA fiduciary duties.[171]

PROHIBITED TRANSACTIONS UNDER ERISA

Under ERISA and the Internal Revenue Code, certain classes of transactions are prohibited between a plan and parties-in-interest. These transactions are prohibited regardless of the terms of the transaction and whether it provides economic or other benefits to the plan. In addition to these technically prohibited transactions, plan fiduciaries are also prohibited under ERISA from engaging in any transaction or conduct that would jeopardize their duty of loyalty to the plan. Plan fiduciaries and their advisors must be aware of these particular restrictions because even an inadvertent violation can subject the party-in-interest and the fiduciary to severe penalties.

Specifically, under ERISA section 406 a prohibited transaction occurs if a plan fiduciary causes the plan to enter into any of the following transactions with a party-in-interest:

- Sale, exchange, or lease of property
- Loan or extension of credit
- Transfer of plan assets or use of plan assets
- Acquisition of employer securities or employer real property in excess of certain limits

In addition to these specific prohibitions, ERISA focuses on self-dealing and conflict of interest by prohibiting a plan fiduciary from doing any of the following:

- Dealing with plan assets in the fiduciary's own interest
- Representing adverse interests in any transaction with the plan
- Receiving remuneration in any form from a party dealing with the plan in connection with a transaction involving plan assets

The penalties for violating these prohibited transaction provisions can be extreme. Under the Internal Revenue Code, the IRS can impose a penalty tax on the party-in-interest equal to 5% of the amount involved in the transaction for each year the transaction remains uncorrected. An additional tax of 100% can be imposed if the transaction is not corrected in a timely manner.

To the extent that a plan fiduciary engages in a prohibited transaction, the plan fiduciary is personally liable for making up any losses to the plan or for providing to the plan any profit earned through use of the plan assets. The DOL may also impose civil penalties on the plan fiduciary.

Party-In-Interest

A party-in-interest is defined under section 3(14) of ERISA to include any of the following:

1. Any fiduciary, administrator, trustee, counsel, or employee of the plan
2. Any person providing services to the plan
3. Any employer whose employees are covered by the plan, as well as any 50% owner of the employer

4. Any relative (spouse, ancestor, or lineal descendent) of the persons described in items 1, 2, and 3

5. Any employee organization that includes members who are covered by the plan

6. Any entity of which at least 50% is owned by any of the five categories just mentioned

7. Any officers, directors, or shareholders who hold 10% or more of shares, and employees of any person or company described in items 2, 3, 5, or 6

8. Partners of 10% or more of items 2, 3, 5, or 6

The purpose of the prohibited transaction rules is to prevent so-called insiders from using their influence over the plan to engage in a transaction under which they can personally benefit at the expense of the plan. Because of the relationship these persons have to the plan the opportunity for abuse is too great to allow any transactions with the plan except under certain narrow circumstances.

Statutory and Administrative Exemptions

In some instances ERISA specifically allows certain transactions that might otherwise have been prohibited, providing that the transactions meet the following conditions:

- Certain loans to participants and beneficiaries
- Necessary plan services for reasonable compensation
- Loans to employee stock ownership plans
- Ancillary services provided by a bank
- The acquisition or sale of qualifying employer securities[172]

All of these statutory exemptions are subject to comprehensive regulations and conditions. Interested readers are referred to the DOL's regulations on this subject.

In addition to statutory exemptions under ERISA, the DOL is permitted to issue administrative exemptions to permit specific transactions that are technically prohibited under section 406. In essence, the DOL is permitted to issue an administrative exemption if it is (1) administratively feasible, (2) in the best interest of the plan and its participants and beneficiaries, and (3) protective of the rights of participants and beneficiaries.[173] The administrative procedures and exemptions are complex and should only be undertaken with qualified ERISA counsel.

Finally, there are a number of class exemptions issued by the DOL that automatically provide relief to any party-in-interest and plan fiduciary that meet the specific criteria set forth in the exemption. These class exemptions cover a variety of common transactions and should be consulted with the assistance of qualified counsel. In summary, the prohibited transaction provisions are technical landmines. Plan fiduciaries must be extremely careful not to engage in such transactions regardless of their intentions and any benefits to the plan.

6

INVESTMENT MANAGEMENT FOR DEFINED CONTRIBUTION PLANS

Among the components of a defined contribution pension plan, investment management has generally received less attention than participant record keeping and communications. It appears that along with the shift from employer-directed to participant-directed plans came a diminished focus on one of the most important aspects of the plan—its investment options. Nonetheless, given the growing number of investment options available, better participant education and therefore greater investment sophistication, plus a recent influx of fiduciary breach lawsuits related to investments, the selection and monitoring of investments is gaining the attention of plan sponsors.

Companies have just begun to develop their own practices for managing fiduciary responsibilities in these plans. It is clear that the plan fiduciary has the same, if not greater, responsibilities in the selection and oversight of participant-directed plan investment managers as he or she does for any employer-directed plan. Throughout this chapter, five steps, as depicted in figure 6-1, function as a common theme: (1) analyze current position; (2) diversify or allocate assets or investment options; (3) formalize and document investment policy and procedures; (4) implement the policy; and (5) monitor and supervise the process and readjust when necessary.

Figure 6-1: The Investment Management Process

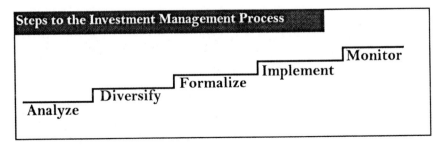

91

Giving participants investment choices imposes on plan fiduciaries the same daunting responsibility as overseeing the investment options in employer-directed plans. Although participants are ultimately responsible for their investment decisions, they have taken action against their employer for not offering a suitable range of investment options. As these plans mature and participants begin to receive distributions, those plan sponsors who engaged in a rigorous manager selection and review process should be protected from frivolous employee litigation.

This chapter explores and suggests standards for plan sponsors to follow as they select and monitor investment managers for their participant-directed pension plans. Although some of these practices may seem like a heavy burden to place on the plan sponsor, ERISA requires that "care, skill, prudence, and diligence" be used in the investment decision process.[174] Regardless of whether the plan seeks a full-service, bundled product, or investment management services alone, there are standards of prudence for proper management of plan assets.

KINDS OF INVESTMENT VEHICLES

At a minimum, plan sponsors should offer participants a range of investment options that has enough diversity in its risk and reward characteristics to satisfy the requirements of 404(c). Essentially, this means that the plan's investment options should be diverse enough to allow participants to construct their own portfolios covering unique asset classes. This risk-reward correlation is illustrated in figure 6-2. The objective is to put participants in a position where they can maximize their performance while minimizing risk through diversification of asset classes.

Figure 6-2: Risk and Reward Traits of Common Investment Vehicles

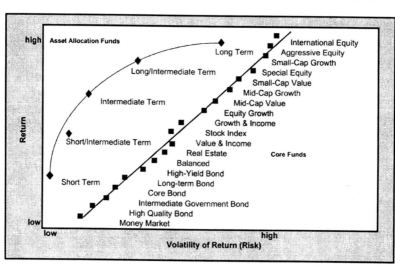

It is critical that plan sponsors retain a degree of oversight to ensure that the range of options does not become weighted in one investment style or another. For example, recent asset allocations are shown in figure 6-3. Fortunately, for plan sponsors there is a wide array of investment options available for pension plans, with more product development occurring as participant-directed plans gain in popularity and participants become investors that are more sophisticated.

Figure 6-3: Investment Allocation

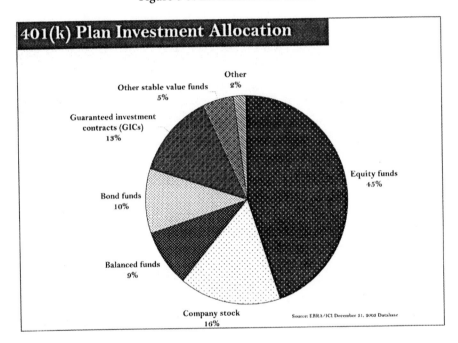

Mutual Funds

Mutual funds have become extremely popular as investment options in participant-directed 401(k) plans. In its August 2004 article "401(k) Plan Asset Allocations, Account Balances, and Loans Accounting in 2003" the Investment Company Institute (ICI) reported that mutual fund companies were the leading providers of investment management services for 401(k) plans. Several characteristics of mutual funds make them attractive as 401(k) plan options:

- Many plan participants understand mutual funds and may have invested in them outside their 401(k) plan. Participants take comfort in the fact that they can follow fund performance in the newspaper and generally feel familiar with the way these investments operate.

- Mutual funds range in investment objective from stable, fixed-income funds to aggressive growth funds, so plan sponsors can find mutual fund choices to suit virtually any participant population's investment needs.

- Many mutual fund companies offer "ready-mixed" asset allocation or "lifestyle" funds for participants who do not want to create their own investment strategy. These funds have become extremely popular because they allow participants who lack investment expertise to invest in all three asset classes, minimize their risk, and use more effective long-term investment strategies than they might create on their own.

- Mutual fund companies have developed record-keeping technology and shareholder communications to provide participants with a fair amount of regular information, including shareholder reports, performance figures, and updated prospectuses, which may help satisfy the "sufficient information" requirements of 404(c).

- The systems capability of many mutual fund vendors lends itself well to daily participant record keeping.[175]

The demand for mutual funds as investment options has increased significantly during the last ten years because their features are attractive to plan participants. According to the ICI, in 2003 401(k) plan assets in mutual funds were at $349 billion, which accounted for 45% of the total defined contribution market.

In cases where specific funds have been identified as under investigation by government agencies, fiduciaries should consider the nature of the alleged abuses, the potential economic impact of those abuses on the plan's investments, the steps taken by the fund to limit the potential for such abuses in the future, and any remedial action taken or contemplated to make investors whole. If such information has not been provided or is not otherwise available, a plan fiduciary should consider contacting the fund directly in an effort to obtain specific information. Fiduciaries of plans invested in such funds may ultimately have to decide whether to participate in settlements or lawsuits. In doing so, they will need to weigh the costs to the plan against the likelihood and amount of potential recoveries.

Bank Collective Funds

Another commonly used investment vehicle in defined contribution plans is the bank collective fund, which is exempt from registration requirements under federal securities law. These collective funds have relatively low internal operating costs and are not subject to some of the restrictions that are applicable to registered mutual funds. Thus, some people feel they offer investment flexibility and an enhanced ability to respond to immediate market pressures. The disadvantage of using collective funds is that their unit values are not normally listed in newspapers. Accordingly, participants tend to be less familiar and less comfortable with collective funds as investment vehicles in their accounts.

Insurance Company Separate Accounts

Insurance company separate accounts are most frequently used by small defined contribution plans. These investments are similar to mutual funds and collective funds in that they are commingled investment vehicles and generally well diversified. As with collective funds, separate accounts suffer a perception disadvantage because they are not listed in the newspaper. As a result, participants may be uncomfortable with a vehicle they do not understand. Furthermore, separate accounts normally are loaded with a variety of fees that can be difficult to identify and understand.

Separate Account Management

Plans with total assets over several million dollars often consider the separate account management services provided by many independent investment managers. The ICI reports that 40% of plans with more than four thousand participants or $50 million in assets use separate account management.[176] Under a separate account management arrangement, the investment manager would create a private fund for each investment category determined by the plan. A consultant or financial advisor can work with the plan sponsor to determine the most suitable separate accounts given plan parameters and the participant population. Like mutual funds, separate accounts can be created as asset allocation strategies where the investment manager spreads the assets among stocks, bonds, and cash. This type of account offers the benefits of diversification and asset allocation to participants who are uncomfortable mixing individual investment options to create an effective long-term allocation.

Separate account management offers the advantage of custom-tailored investment options so the plan fiduciaries and their advisors can specify with great clarity the investment objectives for each fund. The funds can be managed according to specific objectives set by the plan because they are not commingled with any other plans. In addition plan sponsors and their advisors can monitor these accounts in accordance with any custom-designed indexes or benchmarks they deem appropriate.

As with collective funds and insurance company separate accounts, the separate account unit values are not listed in the newspaper, which can be disconcerting to plan participants. In addition, separate account management can sometimes cause administrative difficulties with daily valuation and processing exchanges among other plan options.

Employer Stock

Many plan sponsors offer their company stock as an investment option for their defined contribution plans. Although employer stock is generally considered a more aggressive growth option, it can be attractive to participants because it allows them to have ownership in their organization. Moreover, service providers have developed both record-keeping services and technology to allow them to efficiently handle the administrative aspects of company stock as an investment option. Depending on the accounting methods used for company stock valuation, participants may or may not be able to track the performance in the newspaper. If the stock is valued using unit accounting, the unit value is not published in the newspaper; however, if the company stock is valued using share accounting, participants have a better chance of tracking performance on a daily basis.

Self-Directed Brokerage Account (SBA)

With the shift to a more dynamic, robust environment, the self-directed brokerage account has become a growing investment option in defined contribution plans. Plansponsor.com shows in its 2003 Defined Contribution Survey that approximately 22% of plans offer an SBA option. A SBA allows participants to invest in virtually any publicly traded asset instead of being limited to a group of pre-selected funds.

FINDING THE BEST INVESTMENT OPTIONS

Although all of the options discussed above have their advantages and disadvantages, there is not one perfect option. Instead, plan sponsors should consider how the features of the various options might meet the unique needs of their plan and participants. For example, the simplicity and acceptability of registered mutual funds might be appealing to a particular employee population. For other participants who require a focused investment strategy, tapping into a particular area of investment expertise through separate account management can provide more customized options. Generally, asset distribution in defined contribution plans is undergoing a shift from heavy concentration in fixed-income options to equity options. Given the decline in interest rates that occurred between 1994 and 2004, windows of outstanding stock market performance, and better participant education, plan sponsors have experienced increased demand for more investment options, particularly in the equity area. In the last year, more than half the plan sponsors who added investment options to their plans added growth and aggressive growth options. Applying the standards explained in the previous chapter, figure 6-4 illustrates the duties of a fiduciary to investment management.

Figure 6-4: Fiduciary Standards for Investment Management

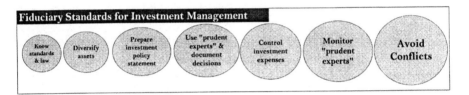

THE INVESTMENT POLICY STATEMENT

Just as a journey requires a roadmap, a defined contribution plan requires a clearly articulated set of directions for selecting and monitoring investment options. Plan sponsors can create and enforce these guidelines by establishing an investment policy statement. Unfortunately, although an investment policy statement is almost a perfunctory requirement in employer-directed plans, few participant-directed plan fiduciaries have thought it necessary in order to manage their fiduciary responsibilities. This is yet another sign of plan sponsors' misconceptions about their responsibilities in participant-directed plans.

From a fiduciary standpoint, there is no legal distinction between employer- and participant-directed plans. Just as plan fiduciaries have established investment policy statements in their employer-directed plans, they now must establish similar guidelines to govern the investment manager selection and monitoring process in their participant-directed plans. In fact, it is entirely likely that an investment policy statement is even more important in a participant-directed plan because the plan sponsors are in effect absolving themselves of day-to-day investment allocation decisions in participants' own accounts.

Section 401(b)(1) of ERISA requires that every employee benefit plan shall "provide a procedure for establishing and carrying out a funding policy and method consistent with the objectives of the plan and the requirements of this title."[177] Therefore plan sponsors must force discipline into the investment process by building a framework of investment options that can stand up to scrutiny at any time. The best way to do this is to create a clearly articulated policy with standards against which both the investment options and the managers can be measured.

Consider the possibilities when no investment policy statement is used. If either a disgruntled participant or the U.S. Department of Labor (DOL) were to raise a claim of imprudent selection and monitoring under ERISA, a court reviewing such a claim would want to see evidence of the fiduciary's conduct in the investment management process. Without a written investment policy statement, the investment selection process might appear haphazard. In contrast, the presence of an investment policy statement lends credence to the fiduciary's position that he or she has engaged in a through selection process, as evidenced by the fact that a written document was prepared to govern this systematic process. If an investment policy statement is not put in writing, it is not mutually understood, and the absence of understanding between the supervising fiduciaries and the investment professionals serving the trust is the most significant cause of not attaining the investment objectives.

As a practical matter, an investment policy statement is a written statement of the goals of the plan and the rules to be followed by the money managers to achieve those goals. Essentially the investment policy statement is the navigational chart that the plan sponsor establishes to first select and then guide the investment managers of the plan. The investment policy statement can also establish performance targets, risk parameters, communications objectives, and policies.

Establishing the Investment Policy Statement in a Participant-Directed Plan

Because the employees, not the plan sponsor, make the investment allocation decisions, the investment policy statement for the participant-directed plan will bear little resemblance to that of defined-benefit or even employer-directed defined contribution plans. Thus, the investment policy statement should focus on the steps necessary to ensure that participants' rights and interest are protected as specified under section 404(c) and relevant ERISA case law and regulations. Furthermore, the policy statement should emphasize the required actions of the plan fiduciaries to ensure that the participants are indeed in control of their assets.

Creating the investment policy statement should be a cooperative process, involving both the company's human resource and treasury professionals as well as the chosen investment manager. An interactive discussion about what options would be best for the plan, given its participant population and administrative parameters, should follow. Once created, the individuals responsible for its establishment should review this investment policy at least annually. Building an investment policy should involve creating a partnership between the plan sponsor and the investment manager. Plansponsor.com's 2003 Defined Contribution Survey indicated that 67.3% of plans have a written investment policy statement.

Step 1: Identify the Responsible Fiduciaries

The first step toward establishing the investment policy should be to determine who is responsible for the management of various aspects of the plan. The regulations issued under section 404(c) of ERISA inherently require a responsible fiduciary to designate investment managers or options, or both, under the plan. This fiduciary cannot have any affiliation with the investment management organization that is managing the assets. Thus, under normal circumstances the plan fiduciary will be a person who is employed by the plan sponsor. These regulations impose on the fiduciary the continuing obligation to assess the suitability of and prudently monitor the chose investment managers.

Step 2: Determine the Investment Options under the Plan

The process of selecting investment options for the plan should include the input of all plan fiduciaries as well as consultants or financial advisors. Before the actual selection of investment options can take place, there should be a formal adoption of the policy governing the range of investments offered under the plan.

The guiding light for the selection of investment options should be the section 404(c) regulations that require participants to be given a "broad range" of investment alternatives with varying risk and return characteristics. Nevertheless, in selecting options for the plan it is equally important to consider depth of investment knowledge of participants, risk tolerance of participants, size of plan, plan design features, cost considerations, and liquidity needs. Therefore, the investment policy should include the following directives:

- The range of options should include at least five or six vehicles that vary significantly in their reactions to market and economic conditions. An adequately broad range might include (1) a guaranteed investment contract (GIC) or money market fund, (2) a broad-based bond fund, (3) a conservative equity fund (domestic), (4) an international equity fund, (5) an aggressive equity fund, and (6) an asset allocation or lifestyle fund.

- Participants should have options with enough diversity in the risk and return characteristics such that they can make prudent and suitable investment decisions for their own portfolios.

- Participants should receive a reasonable opportunity to materially affect the potential returns as well as the ability to control risk in their account through diversification.

By incorporating these directives, plan fiduciaries can ensure that the plan offers an adequate range of investment options for participants, and at the same time they can identify categories and particular options to be offered under the plan.

Step 3: Set Investment Performance Criteria and Risk Parameters

Although many pension plan sponsors have not focused seriously on investment performance in their plans, establishing written investment performance objectives and risk parameters will help them conduct due diligence and careful monitoring. Plan sponsors should consider both quantitative and qualitative factors. Quantitative factors include (1) relative performance record versus designated benchmarks, similar advisors, risk/return measures, and track record quality; (2) consistency of investment style and discipline; and (3) consistency of performance through market cycles. Qualitative factors include (1) organization and fiscal strength, client services, compliance with legal requirements, operations and negative press; (2) qualification and consistency of investment management personnel; (3) clear and concise investment philosophy; and (4) trading capabilities with plan record keeper and trustee.

Establishing variable investment performance standards requires a sophisticated knowledge of capital markets and the relationship between investment returns and volatility. Most fiduciaries of pension plans benefit considerably by retaining a qualified consultant or financial advisor to help formulate performance standards and determine risk parameters.

Furthermore, when establishing target investment returns, plan sponsors must understand the relationship between investment returns and risk. Risk is generally defined by volatility—that is, the frequency and amount that an investment fluctuates (or deviates) from its average return. The more an investment deviates from that return, the more volatile (risky) it is, despite the fact that the investment might produce above-average returns.

Volatility is commonly measured through standard deviation, reflecting the range of price fluctuations likely for a particular investment. Most studies of standard deviation indicate that equities generally exhibit higher standard deviations than do bonds. Within the different varieties of equities, there is a wide range of standard deviations depending on industry groups, company particulars, and a variety of other market factors.

To establish investment performance standards in either absolute or relative terms, the investment policy must also clearly articulate appropriate risk parameters. The responsibility to quantify risk is virtually mandated under section 404(c), as noted earlier.

Step 4: Determine Performance Measurement Standards

Performance measurement standards should be made in conjunction with the establishment of performance objectives. Because most defined contribution pension plans today offer at least four investment options, the investment policy statement needs to identify the appropriate benchmarks for measuring investment performance in each respective category. Service providers, consultants, or financial advisors can work with plan sponsors to determine appropriate benchmarks for each asset category and, where appropriate, for individual options. Although performance measurement is discussed later in this chapter, for purposes of the investment policy statement there must be an identification of the indices that will be used as long-and short-term performance measurement standards.

The plan may adopt a variety of performance measurements. For instance, it may be appropriate to compare one stock portfolio to an index of growth stock portfolios. In a balanced fund, it may be appropriate to compare segments of the fund to referenced benchmarks on a nominal basis (for example, comparing the stock component to an index of relevant stock portfolios). Using indices appropriate for different segments of a fund will have more meaning than a single numeric comparison. In any event, there should be a consensus on which benchmark indices and what period will be used to measure investment performance for each fund.

Recent trends of DOL audits and participant scrutiny reflect a growing concern about fees. Although ERISA does not set a specific level for fees, it does require that fees charged to the plan are reasonable. Moreover, "reasonable" must be determined on a case-by-case basis. When evaluating fees plan sponsors should make informed decisions; remember fees are just one of several factors; assess the plan's performance over time for each investment option; look at the full value of services; consider all plan fees, not just fund expenses; and remember choosing lower fees does not necessarily mean a better-performing fund. An additional consideration related to fees is to remember that some investments, due to their nature, may have higher fees. In short, as long as expense ratios and fees are reasonable, the selection process should be guided by appropriate measures of performance versus risk, not by shaving a few points off the expense ratio.

Step 5: Determine Manager Termination Procedures

The investment policy statement must articulate the conditions that will lead to manager termination or other corrective action and the procedures to follow when these conditions exist. This is an extremely important matter because of the fiduciary liability risk associated with failing to take corrective measures when there is evidence of problems. As noted earlier, fiduciaries have an ongoing duty to assess the suitability of the designated investment managers and the further responsibility to take corrective measures when the suitability of any of the selected managers is in question.

Step 6: Establish Participant Control Parameters

Because participant-directed plans must allow participants to exercise control over their assets, it is appropriate to articulate the standards or parameters of control as a matter of investment policy. Following the DOL's regulations, the investment policy statement should dictate the following requirements pertaining to participant control:

- Participants should be given reasonable opportunity to give investment instructions to an identified plan fiduciary who is obliged to carry out these instructions.

- The plan may impose on the trust asset charges for reasonable expenses associated with the opportunity to exercise control, if participants are informed of this policy.

- Plan fiduciaries may decline to implement participant instructions under the conditions specified in the regulations.

- The plan may impose reasonable restrictions on the frequency of investment instructions, provided such restrictions are uniformly applied to all participants and provided that participants are given the ability to give instructions with such frequency as is appropriate given the volatility of the investment options as governed under the section 404(c) regulations.

- With respect to the three core investments constituting the broad selection of investment options under the plan, participants are given the ability to give investment instructions once every three months.[178]

To ensure that all plan fiduciaries fully understand the essence of participant control, the investment policy statement should indicate that participant control over assets is absent when (1) the participant is subjected to improper influence by the fiduciary or plan sponsor, (2) a plan fiduciary has concealed material nonpublic facts, or (3) the participant is legally incompetent and the plan fiduciary knows of this condition.[179]

Step 7: Establish Participant Communications Policies

The investment policy statement should include policies concerning communication of investment information because effective participant communication is integral to the success of a participant-directed pension plan. Where communications are deficient, fiduciary liability may result if it is determined that participants did not have control over their plan investments. Thus, as a means of limiting fiduciary liability, it is critical to include a participant communications policy to articulate the standards that will govern investment-related communications.

This statement should dictate, among other things, the methods and timing of communications, the nature of communication devices, and policies concerning the permissibility to render investment advice to participants. In the absence of a special prohibited transaction exception from the DOL, ERISA prohibits investment management organizations from giving investment advice to plan participants because of the potential for conflicts of interest.

THE FUND SELECTION PROCESS

In many ways, the defined contribution pension industry continues to be in its infancy with respect to the manager selection process. Consulting firms who have dominated the defined benefit investment manager search process have only begun to develop expertise in the area of participant-directed plan. As a result, decisions are often made based on who makes the best presentation, rather than on ability. With the multitude of investment managers and the growing complexity of the investment process, plan sponsors are beginning to recognize the need for independent expertise. The level of knowledge needed to select and monitor a 401(k) plan's investment options is normally beyond most plan sponsors' experience. In general, the process should include data gathering, quantitative screens to score and rank each product, due diligence research, and evaluation and rating of each product. Figure 6-5 provides an overview of the selection process.

Figure 6-5: The Selection Process

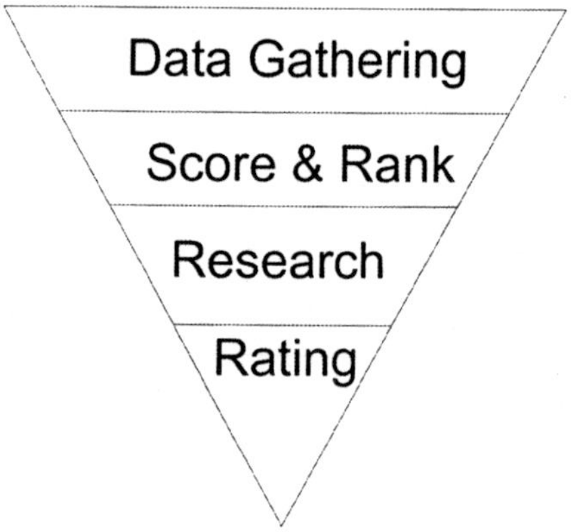

Data Gathering

Score & Rank

Research

Rating

Seek Outside Expertise: Hire a Consultant or Financial Advisor

A consultant or financial advisor's expertise can support plan sponsors in the fulfillment of their fiduciary responsibilities. More specifically, a consultant, financial advisor, or other advisor can assist the plan sponsor with the following:

- Establish investment policy statement
- Understand and determine appropriate investment management styles in the plan
- Understand and determine risk parameters
- Evaluate and select investment managers
- Monitor the performance and volatility of the funds
- Provide continuing due diligence
- Evaluate participant record-keeping capabilities
- Evaluate and customize participant communications programs

Establish Plan Asset Categories

The factors that will determine both asset category and individual investment option selection include depth of investment knowledge of participants, risk tolerance of participants, size of plan, plan design features, cost considerations, and liquidity needs. The partnership between the plan sponsor and service provider is critical to this selection process given the importance of input from the plan sponsor's treasury and human resources areas, and the need for the service provider to understand the plan's investment needs.

Most defined contribution pension plans today limit participants to several investment options that have been pre-selected by the plan fiduciaries. According to a survey conducted in 2003 by the Profit Sharing/401(k) Council of America (PSCA), 70% of plan sponsors offer ten or more mutual fund choices, with the average being sixteen.[180] The trend to increase the number of options beyond the traditional core investment categories is generally attributable to declining interest rates, good stock market performance, robust Internet technology, and better participant education programs.

In recent years, participants have asked for more help with their investment decisions. While investment education points the way, it does not give answers to participant questions about specific amounts in options. Providing investment advice through a third-party registered investment advisor may help participants make more informed and productive decisions.

Additionally, both media focus and plan sponsor concern about retirement risk (such as arriving at retirement without enough money on which to live) has put considerable emphasis on teaching participants to be investors rather than just savers. As such, it becomes even more critical for plan sponsors to provide a range of options that makes it possible for participants to create appropriate allocations based on their own needs.

Considering the pool of plan assets to be a pie, the asset allocation decisions will happen on two levels. First, the plan sponsor must determine the composition or ingredients of the pie. This requires a careful analysis of whether various asset categories and investment styles will effectively work together in numerous different allocations. Second, the participants will carve up the pie, making their own actual investment allocation decisions.

At a minimum, the plan's investment options should include at least one selection from the following categories:

- Stable value
- Fixed income

- Domestic stock (value and growth)
- International or foreign stock

Asset Allocation and Combining Investment Styles

Plan sponsors should choose investment options from each of the afore-mentioned categories because certain combinations of styles create more effective asset allocation than do others. For instance, if a plan were limited to three investment options consisting of a money market fund, a GIC fund, and employer stock, the plan participants would be hampered in their ability to maximize investment returns while reducing risk. Moreover, such a selection would not satisfy the broad selection criteria of section 404(c). Nevertheless, a participant who had access to aggressive growth, value, bond, and stable value investment options could create a more effective combination of investment styles, and therefore a more desirable allocation.

As an investment theory, asset allocation is a valid principle. Studies have shown that allocating assets among investment categories is far more impor-tant to investment returns than actually choosing the right stocks or bonds. In fact, over 90% of the movement in an investment portfolio is the result of strategic asset allocation (long-term exposure to a broad range of asset classes), whereas only 10% is the result of the actual stock selection.

In addition to strategic asset allocation, there is also tactical asset allocation, which refers to the movement of money between the asset classes, specifically, tactically shifting the asset mix. It is important not to confuse asset allocation with diversification. Diversification as a basic principle seeks to reduce risk and increase returns by spreading investments across asset categories that histori-cally have performed differently from one another.

The asset allocation strategy can create a serious dilemma for employees because many may be badly prepared to make these decisions. In a recent study of more than one thousand randomly selected plan participants, only 26% believed that they were well qualified to make investment decisions for them-selves.[181] Only 8% of sponsors believed that employees were well qualified to make their own investment decisions. Hence, employee communications and education programs are critical to participants' ability to make informed investment decisions. Suggestions for effective participant communications are described in Chapter 10.

Strategic asset allocation should be a long-term decision. Participants should be encouraged to ride out the inevitable ups and downs in the portfo-lio with the knowledge that in the long run they will do better than trying to time the market. Furthermore, participants must understand that passively maintained steady allocations will require periodic adjustments. For instance, if a participant were exercising asset allocation in her his or her portfolio with a 65% equity commitment, market appreciation or depreciation over time would change the percentage that the participant actually has invested in equities relative to the other categories. Thus, this participant would need to adjust the balance in his or her accounts in order to maintain a long-term strategic allocation of 65% equities.

For participants who simply do not wish to make their own asset allocation decisions, there are a growing number of asset allocation or lifestyle funds available as investment options. Because these funds are virtually tailor-made for plan participants—who generally have limited investment experience—plan sponsors should consider adding some type of asset allocation option to their plan. Asset allocation funds take all of the complex issues behind making investment decisions and boil them down to one simple strategy. In addition, these funds are created to target various investor strategies. Larger plans may also consider having an investment manager create a tailor-made asset allocation strategy as a separately managed account.

INVESTMENT MANAGER STYLES

There is more to successfully selecting investment managers in participant-directed plans than simply selecting equity, bond, and balanced mutual funds. Because there are a variety of styles in each asset category, plan sponsors must determine which investment styles would be appropriate for their plan. Once again, this task should precede the actual selection of investment managers. In fact, by making these decisions in advance, plan sponsors may save themselves considerable time by avoiding interviews with asset managers whose style is inappropriate to the plan's investment policy and objectives.

Active versus Passive Management

Because active investment management consistently outperforms market indices over time, most plan sponsors choose actively managed options over passively managed investments. Active managers essentially try to beat market returns by making intelligent buy-and-sell decisions based on their investment discipline and market and economic outlooks. In contrast, passive management attempts merely to mirror the investment returns in the market. The most common form of passive management is indexing, in which a basket of securities is purchased in an effort to precisely mirror a popular index such as the Standard and Poor's 500, Wilshire 5000, or Russell 2000. Indexing became extremely popular and successful during the 1980s, but index funds are generally valid only during sustained bull markets.

Value Managers and Contrarian Managers

Value managers look for stocks whose current market price is substantially less than what the managers believe the stocks' actual value should be. Value stocks are characterized by a low price-to-earnings ratio (which may result from investor disappointment) and often by high dividend yields. Typically, these are stocks of companies that the market has overlooked, whether because of a slump in business or lack of publicity. Generally, the market has low expectations for these stocks, which is why value managers can buy them at such low prices. Eventually (it is assumed), value stocks become attractive as expectations and trading activity rise.

Because value stocks can provide both current income and long-term capital appreciation, the value-management style is appropriate for plans that seek long-term total return. Value managers tend to perform better than the market when the market is trending down, while providing close-to-market returns in a rising equity market. During a market cycle, the objective of a value manager generally is to equal or exceed market returns with less risk.

To choose companies in which to invest, value managers focus on the following:

- Companies with anticipated growth in earnings per share, increasing dividends, or excess cash flow
- Medium to large capitalization stocks
- Companies with sound balance sheets
- Companies with a lower-than-market price-to-earnings multiple with a moderate to high dividend yield

Contrarian managers are an extreme form of value managers. Their focus is on the stocks of companies that are out of favor, so a contrarian manager purchases stocks that are priced much lower than their actual value. Generally, contrarian managers expect to perform well in down markets and should participate well in up markets.

Growth Managers

Generally taking a more aggressive approach than value management, growth management focuses on investments whose future potential for growth exceeds expectations for the market in general. Growth managers invest in the stocks of companies whose earnings are growing faster than the market average and are expected to continue to grow rapidly in the future. Generally, growth managers focus on the following:

- Companies with high current and expected earnings-per-share growth and momentum
- Small-to medium-sized companies with high-quality ratings and high financial advantage
- Companies with low dividend yields and high price-to-earnings ratios

As an investment style, growth management is a suitable choice for plans looking for long-term returns primarily through principal appreciation. Participants who use this type of option must be able to ride out the significant fluctuations in value typically associated with growth stocks in order to take advantage of higher potential returns.

Within the growth-management style, there is aggressive management that focuses on the following:

- Non-Standard and Poor's 500 and smaller capitalization companies with accelerating earnings per share
- Companies that are highly leveraged, have high price-to-earnings ratios, and low or no dividends

Aggressive growth funds are most suitable for investors with extremely high risk tolerance who are seeking appreciation. As an investment style, aggressive growth selections can perform well in up markets but generally do poorly in down markets. For this reason, it is important for participants who select this type of option to have a long-term investment period.

Asset Allocation/Balance Managers

Asset allocation or balanced managers function in part as both strategic and tactical asset allocators, shifting holdings among stocks, bonds, and cash depending on their evaluations of and predictions for economic and market conditions. In many respects, this management style, as discussed previously, offers investors one-stop shopping, and it is an option ideally suited for 401(k) plan participants. The asset allocation or balanced management style has the following characteristics:

- Global investment and economic perspectives
- Utilization of both growth and value styles, including small-and large-capitalization companies

- Strategically weighted investments in stocks, bonds, and cash
- Management capabilities within a variety of investment styles

As an investment category, asset allocation or balanced managers may incorporate different investment styles. For instance, some managers focus on value stocks within the general category of equities, whereas others might focus more heavily on growth companies. In either event, this type of option makes inherent sense in a participant-directed plan because a professional money manager makes the difficult asset allocation and market timing decisions.

Fixed-Income Managers

The fixed-income management style is more broad-based than the equity styles because these managers can focus on a variety of factors. For example, some fixed-income managers focus on short-term maturities, whereas others focus on the longer term. Other managers move up and down the yield curve depending on rates and projections.

Managers who move up and down the yield curve are trying to forecast interest rates and seek investment returns resulting from interest rate changes. For instance, such managers try to increase their exposure to long-term bonds when they expect interest rates to decrease. When the managers are correct, the long-term bonds they hold increase in value, and the managers may sell them in order to realize a gain in the portfolio. Conversely, these managers will attempt to purchase short-term bonds when interest rates are expected to rise. If the managers are correct, they are able to protect the portfolio from declining value. Furthermore, the managers are able to repurchase at higher yields as the short-term bonds mature.

Although focusing on interest rates can be extremely successful, other fixed-income managers believe that it is impossible to predict future interest rates. These managers buy bonds that have the same maturities, but they diversify the issuers between government and corporate bonds. Historically, the spread between government and corporate bonds tends to broaden in difficult economic periods and narrow during good times.

Another fixed-income management style involves purchasing high-yield bonds that are below the investment-grade level, commonly known as junk bonds. Although these investments can provide high yields, it is vital to communicate the downside, which is bond default risk to participants in pension plans.

GIC Managers

A guaranteed investment contract fund is a professionally managed, commingled pool of guaranteed interest contracts. GIC fund managers perform due diligence over the issuers of contracts, and then negotiate terms of the contracts. A good GIC manager will conduct rigorous evaluations of all issuers rather than relying solely on insurance company ratings to determine who will appear on the approved list. Normally a well-diversified, pooled GIC fund will hold no more than 10% of the portfolio with any one issuer. A well-managed GIC fund will consist of various maturity dates that range from one to five years.

Because these investments offer stability and yields comparable to intermediate-term bonds, a managed GIC fund is attractive as a conservative option for plan participants. Nevertheless, it is important to communicate to participants that although the intention of these investments is to maintain a stable value, there are no guarantees that participants will not lose money. Participants must understand that "guaranteed" refers to the rate promised by the insurance company and is not the same as the FDIC insurance.

Following Investment Style: "Fund Drift"

Once the sponsor has determined the management styles most appropriate for the employer's plan, it is imperative to find investment managers who follow his or her stated investment style. This concept, known as truth in labeling, refers to the idea that over time funds should strictly follow their stated objective, as expected for funds of their type.

Unfortunately not all mutual fund families line up. In theory, each mutual fund seeks to achieve a specific investment objective; therefore investors expect it to fall at a particular place on a spectrum of risk and reward. Many funds, however, do not fall where they are expected to because of deviations in management style. These funds do not adhere strictly to their objectives year to year and thus increase the likelihood that they do not meet their objectives.

This overlap can have a negative impact on individuals who truly want to diversify their assets, and it can be a problem for plan sponsors trying to meet their fiduciary obligations. Clearly, plan sponsors cannot meet their obligations to offer funds with materially different objectives if the facts are different from the promises.

A range of funds that follows the concept of truth in labeling will reflect more predictable, consistent risk and reward over time. This type of consistent, historical performance could help participants choose funds with more predictably diverse investment styles and will provide the benefit of true asset allocation. The plan's consultant or financial advisor can conduct a detailed style analysis necessary to address all fiduciary concerns.

GATHERING BASIC INFORMATION ABOUT CANDIDATES

The search for investment managers should entail a rigorous interview and discovery process, during which the plan sponsors must learn certain vital information before making the final selection. Again, hiring a consultant or financial advisor to help with this process can prove valuable to the plan sponsor because these individuals have such an in-depth understanding of management style, performance issues, and risk parameters.

The following list provides guidance for gathering information before conducting the actual provider interviews:

- History of the firm and background of key persons
- Minimum and maximum account sizes accepted, as well as total assets under management
- Breadth and depth of experience in portfolio management, research, marketing, trading, and operations
- Ownership of the company
- Investment philosophy and style(s)
- Structure of firm's decision-making process
- Source of research
- Credentials of key personnel
- Operational capabilities
- Fee[182]

The Manager Interview Process

Once the plan sponsor has eliminated the inappropriate candidates, it is proper for investment managers to conduct a presentation. The presentation may focus solely on investment management services or on all aspects of the plan if the sponsor is seeking a bundled, full-service provider.

During the service provider's (or investment manager's) presentation, plan sponsors should ask pointed questions with respect to the investment management of the plan. Try to get a sense for such factors as how investments are made; what investment philosophy or style the advisor uses; who establishes and monitors investment policy; and who determines what stocks, bonds, and so forth are purchased in a portfolio and how. Ask questions about the key personnel's (especially the project manager's) credentials, background and experience. Most important, understand the investment process that the manager will follow.

As with any selection process, there are certain pitfalls to avoid when a plan sponsor chooses an investment manager. Allowing corporate lending relationships to influence investment manager selection could pose some fiduciary risk. In addition, although past performance can provide some basis for investment manager evaluation, it should not be the sole reason for hiring a particular manager. Presentations of performance can vary dramatically by time periods shown, comparisons to benchmarks, and so on, so plan sponsors should be cautious about how much weight they give investment performance in their selection process. Finally, the fees associated with investment management services deserve careful scrutiny during the selection process simply because there are different fee disclosure requirements for the various kinds of investment management organizations. Fees are discussed in requirements for the various classes of investment management organizations. Fees are discussed in detail in Chapter 8.

Performance Evaluation and Investment Style Monitoring

As part of the general fiduciary responsibilities under ERISA, plan sponsors must arrange for periodic evaluations of both the investment performance and management style of the plan. Failure to objectively monitor the plan's investment options could result in the loss of any protections under section 404(c) for participant-directed plans.

By setting parameters for and monitoring both investment performance and management style, plan sponsors can hold their investment managers accountable to certain standards. It is imperative for plan sponsors to monitor investment style to determine whether the manager's investment options are adhering to truth in labeling and are in fact offering varying risk and return characteristics. For example, if a plan offers a value equity fund option that is described as pursuing both growth and income but actually invests in more volatile small-growth stocks to capture top performance, participants may be getting more volatility than they bargained for. In this case, the fund would not be following truth in labeling. Also, when a plan's investment options deviate from their stated investment management style, this may cause the total range of options to become too similar in their risk and return characteristics, which could jeopardize the plan's compliance with 404(c).

Therefore, investment option evaluations should include both a long-term performance review and performance attribution analysis, which will help detect any deviations in management style. As part of this review, plan sponsors should ask their investment manager what factors have contributed to a fund's performance, and they should question any deviations—good or bad—in the performance. Detecting management style deviation requires a considerable level of analysis. Many plan sponsors may not feel equipped to conduct such analysis, in which case they should retain an advisor or consultant to assist them with the evaluation process and ultimately ensure the integrity of their investment option selections.

Comparing Investment Performance

An important part of an advisor's role might be to help plan sponsors determine any benchmarks or indices that would be appropriate for monitoring investment performance. Some of the more common indices used for the equity or bond portions of a fund include the following:

- Standard & Poor's 500
- New York Stock Exchange Index
- Value Line Index
- Dow Jones Composite Index
- Wilshire Equity Style Index
- Lehman Brothers Government/Corporate Bond Index
- Morgan Stanley EAFE

The key to accurate tracking is to select an appropriate index with which to measure performance. In fact, no index is a truly perfect yardstick for measuring the performance of a given portfolio because funds are managed with objectives that generally differ from the index. Moreover, the market indices have no associated transaction costs, which creates a bias in their favor.

Still, the use of appropriate benchmarks can be useful in evaluating investment performance and detecting management style deviation. For example, a large-growth fund measured against a large growth index should show a correlation in performance explicitly. If one is up, the other should be up, and vice versa. If that same growth fund's performance moved in the opposite direction of the large growth index, this might indicate a deviation in management style; specifically, the fund manager might be buying something other than large growth stocks.

Another way to detect style deviation is to do a returns-based performance attribution, which compares portfolio returns to various style index returns and makes a judgment about the reasons for a fund's performance. A large capitalization fund manager who attributes a significant part of performance to value stocks has clearly drifted from the stated investment style and should be held accountable.

Calculating Rates of Return

Performance monitoring requires calculations of investment return. The rate of return is the percentage profit or gain achieved by holding an investment or portfolio for a particular time. In its simplest form, a rate of return is computed by subtracting the difference between the beginning and ending values and dividing this amount by the beginning value. The result is a decimal point return that can be converted to a percentage return by multiplying by 100.

For pension plans, this simple calculation becomes more complex because of the inflows (contributions) and outflows (distributions) of cash from the portfolio. If either a contribution or distribution is made during the period measured with the equation, the calculation will break down. Thus, to calculate performance for plan investment options some other rate-of-return calculation is necessary.

Time-Weighted versus Dollar-Weighted

There are two rate-of-return calculations designed to deal with inflows and outflows in a portfolio. The first is called a time-weighted rate of return, which is designed to eliminate the effects on the portfolio of the timing and magnitude of external cash flows. The other measure of return is called the dollar-weighted rate of return, which measures the impact of any inflows or outflows or assets. The time-weighted rate of return shows the value of one dollar invested in the portfolio for the entire period of measurement; the dollar-weighted rate of return shows an average return of all the dollars invested in a portfolio for the measurement period. The time-weighted rate of return is a more accurate measure of the investment manager's performance because the manager does not have control over the timing of contributions and withdrawals in the plan.

SUMMARY

Over time, as fiduciary standards for participant-directed plans evolve, there will be more scrutiny of the investment selection process that is followed by plan fiduciaries. To show that they have engaged in disciplined investment selection and monitoring, plan sponsors must take measures to put a structured process in place. By creating an investment policy statement, not only will plan sponsors have a credible set of written standards, but, more important, they also will have a system in place to carry out their fiduciary responsibilities. Not only must plan sponsors carefully select investments for their participants, they must monitor performance and ensure both the suitability of the individual options and the overall integrity of the plan's investments.

7

INVESTMENT MANAGEMENT FOR DEFINED BENEFIT PLANS

Don't put all your eggs in one basket.

Regrettably for employees and employers alike, defined benefits plans have lost their pinnacle status among pension plans to defined contribution plans, specifically 401(k) savings plans. In general, defined benefit plans cost employers less and provide a fixed benefit amount to employees. Having said that, defined benefit plans continue to comprise a substantial percentage of pension plan assets.

Similar to employer-directed plans described in Chapter 6, investment management of defined benefit plan assets requires that the fiduciary direct the investments. In contrast, however, a defined benefit plan introduces a new component—benefit liability. Figure 7-1 illustrates the interplay of all three components in managing defined benefit plan assets. As detailed in Chapter 3, the major difference between defined benefit and defined contribution plans is that the employer bears the risk paying certain benefits at a certain time. As such, the selecting and monitoring of investments in the defined contribution plan is supplemented by the factors of liability and fiduciary status. In managing a defined benefit pension plan portfolio the fiduciary must consider investment returns, investment risk, and plan liabilities.

Figure 7-1: Components in Defined Benefit Pension Asset Management

INVESTMENT RETURN

Investment return on stocks and bonds is the income (such as dividends and interest) and capital gains or losses, less fees and expenses. First, income and capital gains whether realized or unrealized must be combined to reflect the total return. Second, investment return must be measured net of fees and expenses because assets should be measured by what can be spent. All rates of return should be based on market value.

Measuring returns of a single asset is relatively straightforward. Conversely, in a pension fund investments have occurred over time and in a series of different asset classes—often including diverse funds within each asset class. Measuring a successful return in a portfolio of assets can be achieved by two methods—dollar-weighted return or time-weighted return. Each method is discussed in Chapter 6. Regardless of a single asset or entire portfolio, calculating rate of return merely requires applying the correct mathematics.

Determining whether a rate of return is good or not is a different matter.

INVESTMENT RISK

Risk is the probability of losing money or that the value of the investment will decrease. The higher the expected return, the higher the expected risk. The key to managing defined benefit assets is not to take as little risk as possible but instead to determine how much diversifiable risk can be taken.

Because it is the most measurable of all risks, the most widely used definition of risk is volatility, which measures how much asset values go up and down over time. Selected widespread categories of investment risk include the following:

- Risk vs. reward
- Market fluctuation risk
- Inflation risk
- Interest rate risk
- Other common risks

Risk versus Reward

One of the great truths of the investment world is that risk and reward go hand in hand. The greater the risk an investor is willing to undertake, the greater the potential reward. If an investor is willing to assume only a small amount of risk, the potential reward is also low. In an ideal world, there would be no risk in any investment. Unfortunately, such a risk-free investment does not exist.

There is more than one type of risk. An investor must understand each type of risk and use that knowledge to create a portfolio of investments that balances the level of risk assumed with the desired investment return.

Market Fluctuation Risk

In simple terms, market risk can be defined as the possibility that downward changes in the market price of an investment will result in a loss of principal for an investor. For many, market risk is most closely associated with the vicissitudes of the stock market.

Market risk exists for other investments as well. For example, the market price of bonds and other debt investments will move up and down in response to changes in the general level of interest rates. If interest rates rise, bond prices generally fall. If interest rates decline, bond prices generally rise. Tangible assets such as real estate and gold or collectibles such as art or stamps also face market risk.

Over time, a number of strategies have been developed to help reduce market risk:

- Invest only dollars that are not required to meet current needs. This helps avoid having to sell an asset when the market may be down.

- Develop a long-term approach. A longer time horizon allows an investor to ride out market vicissitudes.

- Diversify investments over a number of asset categories, such as stocks, bonds, or cash, and tangible investments such as real estate. Holding assets in different investment categories reduces the possibility that all investments will be down at the same time.

Inflation Risk

For many individuals, safety of principal is the primary goal when deciding where to place investment funds. Such investors frequently put much of their money in bank savings accounts, certificates of deposit (CDs), or T-Bills. While such investments can provide protection from market risk, they do not provide much protection from "inflation risk." An investor may hold the same number of dollars but over time those dollars buy less and less.

For example, consider a hypothetical investor who places $10,000 in a 10-year CD that earns 5.0% per year. The table below summarizes the effect of a 3.0% annual inflation rate on the purchasing power of these dollars.

End of Year	CD Value at End of Year (5%)	Purchasing Power at 3% Inflation Rate	"Real" Value of CD	"Loss" Due to Inflation
1	$10,500	97.09%	$10,194	$306
2	$11,025	94.26%	$10,392	$633
3	$11,576	91.51%	$10,594	$982
4	$12,155	88.85%	$10,800	$1,355
5	$12,763	86.26%	$11,009	$1,733
6	$13,401	83.75%	$11,223	$2,178
7	$14,071	81.31%	$11,441	$2,630
8	$14,775	78.94%	$11,663	$3,111
9	$15,513	76.64%	$11,890	$3,624
10	$16,289	74.41%	$12,121	$4,168

Over the 10-year period, inflation reduces the purchasing power of the investor's dollars by more than 25%. The impact of income taxes, ignored in this example, would further decrease the investor's net return.

While there are ways to shield the portfolio from inflation risk, most involve a higher level of market risk:

- Consider placing a portion of the assets in the stock market.

- Historically, tangible assets such as real estate or gold have tended to do well in periods of inflation.

Interest Rate Risk

The relationship between interest rates and the prices of fixed-rate securities, such as taxable and tax-free bonds, can expose the portfolio to risk. As interest rates fall, the prices of fixed-rate securities generally rise. Conversely, the prices of fixed-rate securities usually fall as interest rates rise. The investment management strategy can balance this risk by adjusting the term of the fixed-rate securities held. Again, the advice of a qualified investment manager can help optimize the portfolio's performance while protecting against the risk of rising interest rates.

Other Common Risks

In addition to market and inflation risk, there are a number of other common risks that each investor must be aware of:

- **Market risk for non-equity investments:** For example, the market price of bonds and other debt investments will move up and down in response to changes in the general level of interest rates. If interest rates rise, bond prices generally fall. If interest rates decline, bond prices generally rise. Tangible assets such as real estate and gold or collectibles such as art or stamps also face market risk.

- **Credit Risk:** This is also known as default risk and is the chance that the issuer of a bond or other debt-type instrument will not be able to carry out its contractual obligations. Keeping maturities short, diversifying investments among various companies, and investing in institutions and issues of the highest credit rating are common methods used to help control this type of risk.

- **Liquidity Risk:** Liquidity risk is the possibility that an investor will not be able to sell, or "liquidate," an asset without losing a part of the principal due to an imbalance between the number of buyers and sellers or because an asset is not "traded" often. Choosing investments traded on an active market and limiting investments to funds not needed for current expenses are approaches used to help lessen this risk.

- **Interest Rate Risk:** This is the risk that an increase in the general level of interest rates will cause the market value of existing investments to fall. Generally, this risk applies to bonds and other debt-type instruments, which move opposite to interest rates. As interest rates rise, bond prices tend to fall, and vice versa. One approach to reducing this risk is to "stagger" or "ladder" the maturities in the portfolio so that a portion of the portfolio matures periodically rather than all at the same time. Holding a security until maturity, at which time it is redeemable at full value, is also useful.

- **Tax Risk:** The possibility that a change in tax law at the federal, state, or local level will change the tax characteristics of an investment is known as tax risk. After such a legislative change, an investment may no longer meet an individual's needs. In some cases, new legislation has included a grandfather clause allowing current investors to continue under the old rules. Making an investment because it is a good investment rather than focusing on the tax benefits is an excellent way to help reduce this risk.

LIABILITIES

Unlike the assets of a defined contribution plan that belong constructively to its particular participants, a defined benefits plan has distinct liabilities called benefit obligations. The present value of those obligations to a participant is dependant on life expectancy. Actuaries are mathematicians who deal with this issue by weighing the dollars for each future month by the probability that a participant will be alive to receive the benefit. The law of large averages allows the actuary to predict the probabilities within a moderately narrow margin of error because a plan may have several thousand participants.

Measuring Liabilities

Computing pension liabilities is a two-step process. In the first step, the plan actuary estimates the payments that will be made to retirees each year in the future. The pension plan's actuary makes these estimates based on the plan's terms and estimates of how long current employees will work before retirement and how long they will receive benefits in retirement. Estimating the future stream of payments involves considerable judgment on the part of the actuary.

Step two, converting the value of future payments to today's dollars, is by comparison simple and mechanical. To convert payments in a future year to present dollars, the estimated payments are simply adjusted by the appropriate discount rate. Although some discounting schemes use the same discount rate to compute the present value of payments for all future years, it is no more difficult to compute the present value using different discount rates for each future year.

Choosing the right rate is the key to accurate pension discounting. The wrong rate leads to inaccurate estimates of liabilities that can be either too high or too low.

Pension Expense

Unlike accounting for defined contribution plans, which is straightforward, accounting for defined benefit plans is much more complicated because of two special problems. First, pension expense must be recognized at the time of employee service, not when benefits are paid to retired employees. Second, the costs are difficult to determine because they depend on the lifespan of the participants, changes in wage rates, and the rates of return earned on pension investments.

To compute pension expense, the services of an actuary will be required. The actuary will compute pension expense in three different ways. Each calculation is the amount the company would need to have in the plan today to be able to pay benefits to employees for service to date. This is also described as the present value of future benefits to be paid. The differences in the calculations result from assumptions about future employment:

- Vested benefit obligation (VBO) is what is owed if an employee is terminated immediately.

- Accumulated benefit obligation (ABO) is what is owed for service to date if the employee continues employment until the normal retirement age at the current wage rate.

- Projected benefit obligation (PBO) is what is owed for service to date if the employee continues employment until the normal retirement age and receives periodic adjustments in pay for increased experience and general inflation.

The most useful of the three calculations is the PBO because it represents the most realistic estimate of pension cost of a going concern. To calculate pension expense, six different amounts may need to be determined:

- Service Cost
- Amortization of Prior Service Cost
- Interest Cost
- Actual Return on Plan Assets
- Deferred Gain
- Excess Amortization of Deferred Gain or Loss

Therefore, the formula to calculate pension expense is as follows:
Pension Expense = S + P + I—R + D—E

While the first three amounts are based on the PBO, the last three amounts are based on the pension plan assets.

Service cost is the increase in PBO that results from employee service in the current period. Service cost is the primary component of pension expense. It represents the amount necessary for the company to set aside each year over the service life of an employee to fund promised benefits after retirement.

Prior service cost is the PBO that results from establishing or modifying a plan that gives employees credit for work performed before the date the plan was adopted. This cost should be amortized systematically over the average service time of the employees in order to conform to the matching principle— pension expense recognized at the time of service.

Interest cost is the increase in PBO that results from the passage of time. The PBO includes an interest rate assumption (or discount rate) for promised future benefits because PBO is a present value computation. As time passes, a company gets closer to the date benefits must be paid. Therefore, the present value increases.

Actual return on plan assets refers to the earnings or losses of the investments in the pension plan. This amount represents the change in value of assets available to pay benefits over the course of the year after adjusting for contributions and withdrawals. The value used is the market-related value of plan assets, not the historical cost of the asset.

Deferred gain is the portion of pension investment income or loss that is believed to be the result of short-term variations from the long-term expected rate of return on investments. The expected return is the market-related value on plan assets at the beginning of the year multiplied by the expected long-run rate of return on investments. To avoid significant fluctuations from year to year, the company usually defers the excess of the actual return on plan assets over the expected return in years the plans earns above-average returns and defers the excess of the expected returns over actual return in years the plan earns below-average returns.

Excess amortization of deferred prior pension gain is needed when the deferred gains or losses get too large. When net deferral exceeds 10% of the higher of the beginning PBO or beginning plan assets, the deferral amounts must be amortized over a period not exceeding the average service life of the employees.

Pension Contributions

An employer must fund a defined benefit pension plan even if the company has no profits in any given year. The annual funding calculation is made by an actuary, who must consider, among other things, the following factors:

- Life expectancy of participants and their beneficiaries
- Probability level of forfeitures
- Form of benefit payment
- Level of future compensation for the participants

The actuary's assumptions for the funding calculation must be reasonable overall. If conditions alter, such as a change in the plan's rate of return on investment, the actuary will need to adjust the plan's assumptions to consider actual performance.

During the 1980s, Congress restricted the amount of tax-deductible pension contributions that employers make. At the same time, the PBGC tightened the formula used to calculate minimum contributions, making it more conservative. The minimum and maximum contributions became tied to the 30-year Treasury bond rate.

Immunization

Immunization is a strategy whereby an investor—having an identifiable future financial obligation—invests a determinable amount of assets in a way that guarantees that the future value of the investment will precisely equal the value of the obligation when it comes due.

FUND MANAGEMENT PROCESS

With the components of defined benefit pension plan asset management fully vetted, the process of managing defined benefit pension funds can now be explored. The process includes several stages:

- Establishing and defining the investment objective
- Establishing a strategic asset allocation target
- Selecting desired benchmarks
- Developing an investment policy statement
- Developing an investment manager structure
- Selecting managers
- Monitoring performance and implementing change

Investment Objective

The overall mission of the pension fund must be consistent with its operating context. Remember from Chapter 5 that a fiduciary must adhere to the terms of the plan. In managing the assets of the pension fund, the fiduciary must consider the purpose under the plan's document. In most cases, the purpose of the plan is to provide secure long-term retirement benefits to its participants. To establish an investment objective, three interrelated elements must be defined for the plan being managed. They are time horizon, risk, and return.

Time Horizon

The time horizon is the average number of years until the plan needs the assets. This criterion determines how much risk can be assumed. For example, if the assets are needed in the near term, little risk can be assumed. On the other hand, if the assets are not needed for twenty years, a great deal of volatility is acceptable in between.

While defined benefit pension plans pay benefits to current retirees, much of the assets are intended to pay benefits many years from now. Therefore, other than the amount of current in-pay benefits, the assets can tolerate many cycles of vicissitudes because the average duration of benefit obligations is generally ten to fifteen years. As such, most defined benefit pension plan assets can focus on a rate of return over intervals of ten to twenty years. An extended time horizon offers an advantage because the range of returns narrows with time. Figure 7-2 reflects this normalization of returns over time.

Figure 7-2: Impact of Time Horizon on Investment Risk

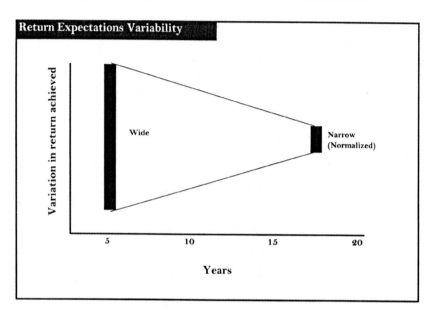

The foremost factor limiting investing a company's entire pension fund in high return, risky assets is the financial condition of the pension fund. A pension fund that does not have enough invested to cover its pension obligations is said to be underfunded, or to have a shortfall in invested assets, and companies are required to make this up through higher contributions. A pension fund that has more investments than necessary to cover its pension obligation is overfunded, or said to have a pension surplus. Companies with a pension surplus can reduce or suspend their contributions altogether. The financial condition of a pension plan depends on a number of factors:

- The demographic characteristics of the plan members have an enormous effect on the time horizon for investment. If the plan sponsor is a new company with relatively young employees, the eventual pensions are far in the future. This means if the value of the plan investments fluctuate considerably, there will not be a need for funds to be withdrawn at a low point when the investments' value is down considerably. A "young plan" can have a high weighting in riskier or more illiquid assets such as stocks, real estate and nontraditional investments. This is in contrast to a "mature plan" that has much older participants and actually is paying pensions to many retirees. These plans usually have more fixed income securities such as bonds and mortgages that fluctuate much less in price and provide a stable income source to pay pensions regularly.

- The financial state of the company itself is important. If a company is in a difficult financial situation, it will be more difficult to make large contributions to the pension fund to make up potential shortfalls from investment performance. This usually results in a more capital/risk-adverse approach and higher fixed income weighting.

- The historical investment performance of the fund's investment results for assets available at any time must be considered. A plan with poor historical investment performance will have generated a much lower rate of return and therefore will have fewer funds on hand to provide for pension obligations. Perversely, a "conservative" investment approach with a low equity weighting will result in low returns, which might lower the future risk tolerance of a plan.

Risk

Risk is difficult to handle in establishing the investment objectives of a defined benefit pension fund. In general, the lower the volatility the plan can endure, the lower the long-term rate of return the plan can seek to achieve, and vice versa.

Diversification

Diversification refers to spreading an investment over many asset classes and, within each asset class, over many individual assets. The old adage "Don't put all your eggs in one basket" applies. Indeed, prudently selecting how to spread a portfolio can actually increase the expected long-term returns while decreasing the portfolio's expected long-term risk/volatility. Altruist portfolios typically are extraordinarily diverse, often representing many thousands of stocks and bonds (indirectly through mutual funds).

Return

As discussed in the previous section on risks, the corresponding variable is return. Figure 7-3 demonstrates this compelling result by highlighting the highest performing asset class across multiple investment cycles. In other words, based on the ability of the plan to handle risk, the return can be targeted appropriately by creating the correct asset mix.

Figure 7-3: Asset Class Returns

Asset Class	1990	1991	1992	1993	1994	1995	1996	1997	1998	1999	2000	2001	2002
Cash	8.73%	7.42%	4.12%	3.51%	3.94%	7.11%	5.59%	5.72%	5.48%	4.24%	6.47%	4.84%	1.75%
Bonds	8.96%	16.00%	7.40%	9.75%	-2.92%	18.47%	3.63%	9.65%	8.69%	-0.82%	11.63%	8.44%	10.25%
Equity	-3.15%	30.45%	7.64%	10.07%	1.29%	37.57%	22.93%	33.34%	28.55%	21.03%	-9.09%	-11.86%	-22.08%
International Equity	-23.32%	12.48%	-11.85%	32.95%	8.06%	11.56%	6.37%	2.08%	20.24%	27.32%	-13.87%	-21.11%	-15.64%
International Bonds	12.70%	15.35%	4.50%	12.31%	1.56%	20.18%	5.12%	1.04%	15.33%	-5.24%	1.43%	-1.37%	19.59%
Real Estate	1.30%	-4.40%	-2.60%	0.50%	3.70%	7.80%	8.60%	10.90%	12.00%	13.10%	15.00%	4.10%	3.10%
Mortgages	10.72%	15.72%	6.96%	6.84%	-1.61%	16.80%	5.35%	9.49%	6.96%	1.86%	11.16%	8.22%	8.75%
GICs	9.12%	8.91%	8.70%	8.15%	7.52%	7.19%	6.73%	6.58%	6.57%	6.57%	6.56%	6.61%	6.33%
Private Equity								24.10%	19.80%	11.70%	79.40%	-3.40%	20.00%

The shaded areas represent the highest return asset class for that year.

Target Asset Allocation

The most important single investment decision made by a plan fiduciary is asset allocation. Asset allocation refers to the division of one's investment portfolio across the various asset classes. At the highest level, this refers to a split between stocks and bonds. Many more finely defined subasset allocations are also common. Developing a target asset allocation requires quantification of three critical characteristics of every asset class:

- **Expected return:** This refers to the compound annual net return expected over the next ten to twenty years.

- **Expected risk:** The probability of losing money—measured best by annual standard deviation—is the expected risk.

- **Expected correlations with every other asset class:** The lower the correlation between asset classes the more diverse the portfolio.

These characteristics are important because diversification enables the fiduciary to accomplish the basic investment objective—the highest net investment return within the acceptable annual volatility limit. The issue is that essentially riskless assets—such as U.S. Treasury bills—provide the lowest long-term returns. Comparatively, assets with the highest expected returns—such as start-up venture capital—are the most risky. By assembling a portfolio of asset classes that have a low correlation with each other, the portfolio can increase its expected return at any given level of expected volatility. The bottom line is the portfolio's aggregate volatility, not that of each asset or asset class.

The increase in the use of asset allocation theory since 1950 has significantly influenced the composition of assets in U.S. private pension funds. Figure 7-4 compares asset structure from 1950 to 2004.

Figure 7-4: Asset Allocation Mix of Private Pension Funds

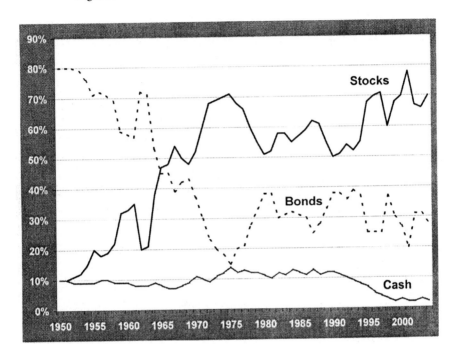

While stocks have historically been the better-performing asset class, they have also posted the highest one-year loss over the past fifty years. Figure 7-5 characterizes the performance of different asset mixes over the past fifty years. Determining the appropriate risk and return expectations are key components in the discovery process. Constructing and maintaining a portfolio with a stock and bond mix that provides desired positive potential within the tolerance level for a potential loss in any given year is optimal.

Figure 7-5: Determining the Right Asset Mix

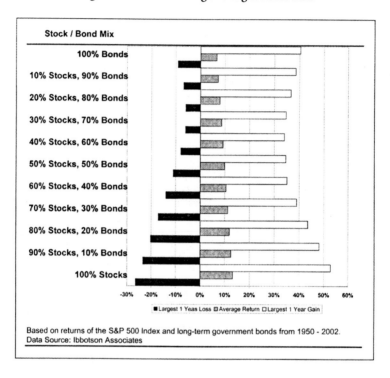

Based on returns of the S&P 500 Index and long-term government bonds from 1950 - 2002.
Data Source: Ibbotson Associates

Background

The following four factors contributed to the rise in popularity of asset allocation in defined benefit pension plans:

- Development of Modern Portfolio Theory in the 1950s and 1960s
- Decline of stock prices during the 1973–74 bear market
- Enactment of ERISA in 1974
- Expansion of more sophisticated financial markets

The roots of asset allocation theory began with the Capital Asset Pricing Model (CAPM). The CAPM theory revolves around the concept that there are essentially two classes of risk—diversifiable risk (or event-driven risk) and nondiversifiable risk (or market-driven risk). The premise is that investors would not subject themselves to a risk that could not be diversified away and there should be no expectation for additional return for accepting a diversifiable risk.

In 1952, Harry Markowitz revolutionized portfolio theory with his seminal work "Portfolio Selection."[183] In this paper and later in his 1959 book, *Portfolio Selection: Efficient Diversification of Investments*, Markowitz set forth a series of propositions that quantitatively addressed the issue of optimal asset allocation. The basic views were further developed by Sharpe, Fama, and others to become what is known today as Modern Portfolio Theory (MPT).[184]

Over the years, MPT has taken on many different names and shapes; however, it is still at the heart of the asset allocation decisions of almost every major investing institution. Classical MPT begins with Markowitz's premise that investing is a function of balancing risk and return. By definition, increasing risk increases return. Investors establish their utility function, or preference, for how much risk they will take to increase return.

In sum, MPT concludes that investors measure their tolerance for risk not by beta relative to the market but instead by standard deviation. The premise is the investors are willing to assume a certain amount of unpredictability in investment returns that is not necessarily related to market movements.

Two basic assumptions underlie the work done by Markowitz, which are as follows:

- Security returns are normally distributed
- Investors are risk averse

The first assumption is a statistically testable hypothesis that was later validated by Fama using rapidly advancing computer technology. The assumption proposes that the mean and variance of the return pattern are adequate to describe the distribution of future returns. Therefore, rational investors should only be concerned with the mean and variance of expected returns. In MPT the concern of the investor is with the return of the entire portfolio.

Appling the second assumption leads MPT to the solution. Risk aversion applied to the field of investments means investors prefer more return for a constant level of risk or less risk for a constant level of return. Under MPT an asset allocation is optimized by integrating and defining returns as expected return and representing risks as the historical variability of these returns.

In 1973 a sharp decline in stock prices resulted in the 1973–1974 bear market that impaired poorly diversified portfolios. Just before the onset of the bear market, over two-thirds of the assets in private pension funds were invested in stocks.[185] In many instances, the equity portion of the pension fund consisted solely of that company's own stock.

Of the four factors leading to the prevalence of asset allocation, ERISA is arguably the most important catalyst because it converted a promise by employers to employees into an irrevocable commitment and ensured that this commitment was monitored by various government agencies. ERISA established minimum standards for reporting and disclosure of information and placed restrictions on the investment practices of private pension funds. In general, ERISA encouraged a more prudent and more disciplined approach to investment management.

Similar to other trends in pension plans, the fourth factor arose from the development of more sophisticated financial markets and, in particular, the introduction of derivatives. A derivative is a synthetic security created from a plain vanilla long-term bond that has a variety of options attached to it that can add a higher degree of volatility than would otherwise be present in the underlying bond. A derivative security, for example, could have two, three, four, or five times the price volatility of a conventional bond.

Asset Classes

Similar to the assets classes discussed in Chapter 6, asset classes included in defined benefit investment management tend to be more complex and diverse because, unlike a participant-directed plan, the assets should always be managed by a professional advisor. Some of the more common asset classes are discussed next and by way of example are shown as percentage of total defined benefit investments in figure 7-6.

Figure 7-6: The Composition of Defined Benefit Portfolio Allocation

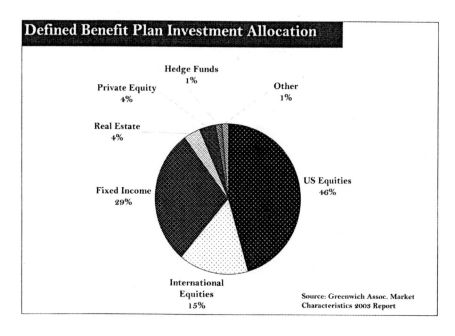

- **Cash:** Cash includes cash-equivalent securities (also called "near cash") such as savings accounts and deposits, CDs, Treasury bills, short-term investment funds, money market accounts, and money market mutual funds. Cash investments are the most liquid and least risky of the major asset classes because the maturity is short enough that no principle is lost. In most cases, the target allocation for cash equivalents should be zero because over the last seventy years cash has barely exceeded inflation. Many portfolios maintain cash equivalents to avoid selling a longer-term investment at an inopportune time when the need for cash arises. Over the long term, a portfolio will perform better by keeping zero cash and selling other securities as cash is needed.

- **Traditional Bonds:** Traditional investment-grade bonds come with a variety of maturities—typically one to thirty years—and various levels of credit risk. Bonds are riskier than cash equivalents; therefore, a higher long-term return is expected.

- **Long-Duration Bonds:** Replacing a traditional bond with a more volatile long-duration bond should be considered because the normal time horizon on benefit obligations is usually ten to fifteen years. Therefore, a bond with a longer duration hedges those obligations better than traditional bonds. A bond with a longer duration also provides more protection against declining interest rates.

- **Non-U.S. Bonds:** Foreign bonds tend to demonstrate a high correlation with U.S. bonds when properly hedged for foreign exchange risk. The key advantage of non-U.S. bonds is to not hedge—thereby providing more diversity from the volatility in foreign exchange values, which is uncorrelated with the volatility in bonds and equities.

- **High-Yield Bonds:** During good economic times, high-yield bonds can provide a portfolio with moderately higher returns than traditional bonds at approximately the same volatility. On the other hand, during weaker economic times more high-yield bonds default, which results in decreased prices.

- **Emerging-Markets Debt:** Emerging-markets debt returns are close to common stock territory. Emerging markets debt represent a good addition to a defined benefit portfolio if the volatility is acceptable because they can provide good returns and have a low correlation with more traditional bond assets.

- **Inflation Linked Bonds:** Mainly government bonds, this asset class promises a return adjusted above the inflation rate until maturity. As they gain more liquidity, they may play a greater role in asset allocation.

- **Larger U.S. Stocks:** This asset class has been the least volatile of any other stock class in the world and outperforms bonds by five percentage points and inflation by seven. Generally divided into multiple sub-classes—such as value and growth based on high earnings per share or low price to book value ratios—they should be included in an asset allocation for the benefit of diversity.

- **Small U.S. Stocks:** Small U.S. stocks are often treated as a separate asset class because they have periodically had slightly different returns than large stocks. In general, the volatility is higher than with large stocks. Nevertheless, the correlation between the two is low enough that when they are properly mixed with large stocks the aggregate portfolio volatility will decrease slightly. Similar to large stocks, diversification is enhanced because small stocks are divided into subclasses.

- **Non-U.S. Stocks:** Over the long-term the expected returns of non-U.S. stocks should not be materially different from U.S. stocks. Nevertheless, over shorter intervals the differences have been significant.[186] The foreign exchange risk is not reason to avoid including non-U.S. investments because—notwithstanding a significant percentage of assets being represented by non-U.S. investments—their inclusion improves the portfolio's diversity and increases its efficiency.

- **Emerging-Markets Stock:** The end of the cold war paved the way for the hasty proliferation of private enterprise across the world. This trend has given rise to a new asset class of emerging markets stocks that grow faster and therefore provide greater return.

- **Employer's Stock:** Often a plan sponsor considers the company's own stock in the pension plan portfolio's asset allocation. Unlike a defined contribution plan where the limitation is that of prudence, ERISA permits a maximum of 10% of a defined benefit portfolio to be made up of an employer's security. When reviewing employer stock as an investment option, consideration should be give to the following: (1) if the pension fund includes the employer's stock, the company loses the opportunity to diversify corporate risk; (2) a single stock will have a lower expected long-term rate of return than a market index fund because the market index fund is a more diversified portfolio; (3) concern that public investors will interpret a sale of employer stock from the pension portfolio as a loss of confidence in the company's future may deter such sale; (4) an inherent conflict of interest exists between the good of the pension portfolio and the good of the shareholders—although ERISA allows a fiduciary to wear both a fiduciary and corporate hat, recent positions by the Department of Labor (DOL) predicate an independent fiduciary where company stock is involved.

- **Real Estate:** Pension plan portfolios can invest in real estate in two ways—direct or securitized. The largest part of real estate allocation has historically been acquired by direct real estate investment. Additionally the introduction of manager style categories with real estate investing has provided an extensive array of opportunities for pension investors.

- **Venture Capital Funds:** Venture capital funds are among the more common alternative investment classes in pension portfolios. These funds are investments in private start-up companies. Although often an expensive investment class, the returns warrant such expense and risk.[187] Other than high fees, this class's shortcoming is volatile and potholed long-term returns.

- **Buy-In Funds:** Similar to venture capital funds, buy-in funds usually invest in start-up companies that are or have been profitable.

- **Buyout Funds:** A buyout fund purchases the whole company instead of providing a source of capital for the company.

- **Distressed Securities:** Distressed securities seek to invest in distressed assets at a substantial discount to fundamental value, where an advantage can be gained through superior credit judgment, expertise in the restructuring process, and substantial presence and experience in the below investment-grade credit markets. A well-managed distress fund can provide good returns and useful diversification to the defined benefit portfolio.

- **Natural Resources:** Natural resources, such as oil and gas properties, timberland, and farmland, provide one of the strongest diversification benefits. Natural resource investing in a pension plan portfolio can provide a great long-term advantage. Still, it may not be as appropriate with a short time horizon or where liquidity is necessary because many assets in this class are illiquid.

- **Absolute Return Funds:** Absolute return funds are liquid asset classes that focus on absolute returns or their returns relative to short-term interest rates, rather than their net internal rate of return over time. The prevalent liquid assets held in pension funds are arbitrage—such as merger and acquisition, convertible, or interest rate—and commodity futures—such as foreign exchange, grains, petroleum, or metals. Moreover, absolute return funds are a great diversifier in a pension portfolio because they are market neutral.

- **Hedge Funds:** The term "hedge fund" is an industry term not a legal one, therefore it is subject to some amount of interpretation. The term includes a multitude of skill-based investment strategies with a broad range of risk and return objectives. A common element is the use of investment and risk management skills to seek positive returns regardless of market direction.[188] A hedge fund is a pool of capital for accredited investors only and organized using the limited partnership legal structure with the general partner usually functioning as the money manager with a significantly high percentage of their own net worth invested in the fund. There are various types of investment companies known as hedge funds: legal structure, investment strategy, and investor pool. Hedge funds, unlike mutual funds, are not able to stand ready to buy and sell shares on any given date. Instead, they have two forms of liquidity constraints that they impose on investors: liquidity dates and lockup. Liquidity dates refer to pre-specified times of the year when an investor is allowed to redeem shares. Lockup refers to the initial amount of time an investor is required to keep his or her money in the fund before shares can be redeemed. Lockup therefore represents a commitment to keep the initial investment in a fund for a specified period. Additionally, high fees and expenses yielding not-necessarily-high returns and lack of transparency of the portfolio's composure are drawbacks.

Rebalancing

Rebalancing refers to periodically restoring a portfolio's asset allocation to its target proportions. Not rebalancing the portfolio generally causes the portfolio to naturally drift from the target allocation. This either increases or decreases the portfolio's risk profile, neither of which is desirable. Therefore, under ERISA's prudence rule, a fiduciary must review periodic rebalancing because failure to confront these decisions in a disciplined manner is a functional abandonment of the asset mix to the whims of the market.

There are several methods or reasons to rebalance. Some of the more common are described as follows:

- **Calendar Rebalancing:** The assets are rebalanced in accordance with the targeted asset allocation on a scheduled basis—examples could be monthly, quarterly, or annually.

- **Rebalance to an Allowed Range:** This method insures that the asset composition does not deviate from the extremes of the range prescribed in the targeted asset allocation. For example, consider a 50% targeted equity allocation, with a five-percentage point tolerance. This method would provide for a 1% sale when stocks reach 56% of assets.

- **Threshold Rebalancing:** This method assigns more weight to the wisdom of the original policy. Under this method, a deviation beyond the tolerance dictates a return all the way to the targeted asset allocation. Applied to the example described above, rather than a sale of 1% the sale would be 6%, thereby, returning the allocation for equity back to the original target of 50%.

- **Drifting Mix:** Although in theory this method of going with the flow would most likely provide high long-term returns, the volatility damage of increasing equities would diminish any respect for the investment policy statement, asset allocation, or the probable risk-aversion by any fiduciary.

Rebalancing sounds simple but it requires a great deal of discipline. The process of rebalancing requires selling those assets that recently have been the highest performing. While this may feel strange to novice investors, this discipline is what locks in the plan's gains and leverages on the portfolio's diversity.

Benchmark Portfolio

For each asset class consisting of a marketable security, an index should be used as the benchmark. If there is no rational basis for believing that the class will not outperform the benchmark, then the index should be used for that asset class.

Benchmarks are tools for measuring control states—what would have happened in the absence of a particular event. For example, the Standard and Poor's (S&P) 500 is frequently used as a benchmark for what would have happened in the absence of active management decisions.

A benchmark is calculated by applying the investment performance of the asset class benchmarks to the pension fund's asset allocation targets. The benchmark permits the fiduciary to compare the fund's actual performance to a passively managed proxy and to measure the contribution of active investment management and policy implementation.

In 1882, Charles Henry Dow, an American journalist, founded Dow Jones & Company with his partner Edward Jones. In 1884 with eleven stocks, most of them railroads (which were the first great national corporations), he averaged their closing prices to create the nation's first benchmark. He compared his average to placing sticks in the beach sand to determine, wave after successive wave, whether the tide was coming in or going out. If the average's peaks and troughs rose progressively higher, then a bull market prevailed. On the other hand, if the peaks and troughs dropped lower and lower, a bear market was in progress.

It appears naive today with myriad market indicators, but late in the nineteenth century it was like turning on a powerful new beacon that cut through the fog. The average provided a convenient benchmark for comparing individual stocks to the course of the market, for comparing the market with other indicators of economic conditions, or simply for conversation at the corner of Wall and Broad Streets about the market's direction.

The mechanics of the first stock averages were computed with paper and pencil: add up the prices and divide by the number of stocks. This application of grade-school arithmetic, while creative, is hardly worth remembering more than a century later. Nevertheless, the idea of using an index to differentiate the stock market's long-term trends from short-term fluctuations deserves a salute. Without the means for the ordinary investor to follow the broad market, today's age of financial democracy (in which millions of employees are actively directing the investment of their own future pension money and, as a result, are substantial corporate shareholders) would be unimaginable.

Following the introduction of the 12-stock Industrial Average in the spring of 1896, Mr. Dow, in the autumn of that year, dropped the last nonrailroad stocks in his original index, making it the 20-stock Railroad Average. The Utility Average came along in 1929 (more than a quarter-century after Mr. Dow's death at age fifty-one in 1902) and the Railroad Average was renamed the Transportation Average in 1970.

Originally the average was published irregularly, but daily publication in the *Wall Street Journal* began on October 7, 1896. In 1916 the industrial average expanded to twenty stocks; in 1928 the number was raised to thirty where it remains. In addition, in 1928 the newspaper's editors began calculating the average with a special divisor other than the number of stocks, which avoided distortions when constituent companies split their shares or when one stock was substituted for another. Through habit this index was still identified as an "average."

Nowadays, the Dow Jones Industrial Average indexes the value of thirty industrial stocks listed on the New York Stock Exchange and the NASDAQ stock exchange. All thirty are blue chip issues. Many have become household names: American Express, AT&T, Boeing, Coca-Cola, Eastman Kodak, General Electric, General Motors, Hewlett-Packard, IBM, Intel, Johnson & Johnson, McDonald's, Microsoft, Procter & Gamble, Walt Disney, and Wal-Mart.

Unlike other stock market indices, the Dow is not weighted by market capitalization (price times number of shares outstanding). Initially Charles Dow merely summed the prices and divided by the number of stocks to get a true average. Nevertheless, to preserve historical continuity, the divisor has been continually adjusted—most frequently to account for stock splits. By way of example, consider an averaged index composed of three stocks selling at $10, $20, and $30. The average price of these stocks would be $20 [(10 + 20 + 30)/3]. If, however, the $30 stock split 3-for-1, the average stock price would suddenly become $13.33 [(10 + 20 + 10)/3]. By changing the divisor from 3 to 2 to correct for the split, the average remains $10 [(10 + 20 + 10)/2]. Over the years, the divisor has become smaller and smaller. In 1986 it fell below 1 following a 2-for-1 stock split by Merck. Dividing by a number less than 1 is multiplication. Today, the Dow is not the only market indicator. There are a number of others that provide slightly different information.

McGraw Hill's Standard and Poor's unit introduced the S&P 500 Index in 1957, but the S&P indices date from 1926. (The S&P 90 introduced in 1928 was the first index weighted by market capitalization.) The Chicago Mercantile Exchange began trading a futures contract based on the S&P 500 in the early 1980s, and by the end of the decade the daily value this trade exceeded the daily value of all stocks traded on the floor of the New York Stock Exchange. The S&P 500 is intended to be made up the 500 biggest publicly traded companies in the United States based on market capitalization (in contrast to the FORTUNE 500, which are the 500 companies with largest sales revenue). Weighted by market cap, the S&P 500 Index comprises about three-quarters of total American capitalization. In 2001 forty of the S&P 500 stocks provided half of the index's total market cap. In 1999 nine of the S&P 500 stocks provided half of the index's total return. Most money managers treat the S&P 500 as a proxy for the U.S. stock market. Three-quarters of money in American index funds is tied to the S&P 500. Analysts using CAPM use the S&P 500 as a proxy for the stock market—and the standard for calculating beta (ß, market risk, where the S&P 500 has a beta equal to 1.00).

There are both objective and subjective standards for inclusion in the S&P 500 Index. To be included a company must be profitable, a criterion that has excluded Amazon.com. The prospective company must not be closely held (at least 50% of its stock should be public) and must have a large trading volume for its shares (no less than a third of its total shares). Although over a tenth of the companies listed on the NYSE are foreign (listed in the form of American Depository Receipts with underlying shares held overseas), these are excluded from the S&P 500. When Daimler-Benz acquired Chrysler in 1998, the new Daimler Chrysler was excluded from the S&P 500 because it was not based in the U.S. In July 2002 foreign companies that had formerly been grandfathered in the index for decades, such as Unilever (Netherlands) and Alcan (Canada), were removed. Schlumberger (headquartered in the U.S., but registered in the Antilles) and U.S. companies headquartered in Bermuda (such as Tyco) remained. Companies are usually removed from the index due to mergers, acquisitions, bankruptcy, or a significant drop in market cap. Companies removed from the S&P 500 suffer an average 12% loss between the announcement of removal and the actual removal, relative to the Wilshire 5000, but these losses mostly vanish within six months.

The subjective criteria are in the heads of the committee that meets monthly in New York City to review the stocks making up the S&P 500. The meetings are held in secret and minutes are not released to the public. Inclusion or exclusion of a stock from the index can have a dramatic effect on stock price because index funds typically buy more than 5% of a newly listed company's outstanding shares between the announced inclusion and the actual inclusion. An announcement is made at 5:15 PM (after market close) five days before inclusion/exclusion in the S&P 500. In the late 1990s, the S&P 500 committee showed a distinct bias toward the inclusion of technology stocks to reflect their "up-to-date" attunement with the New Economy—bringing tech stocks to roughly a quarter of the S&P 500's total value. Price/Earnings ratios (P/Es) were not a factor in making these inclusions, which resulted in the S&P 500's P/E average rising well above historic levels.

The ETF/UIT for the S&P 500 are traded on the AMEX under the symbol SPY, but the nickname "Spiders" comes from the name Standard and Poor Depositary Receipt (SPDR). Second in trading volume (nearly a third) only to the Cubes, Spiders were created over a half decade earlier in January 1993 and priced per share at one tenth the value of the S&P 500 Index.

The Russell 1000, Russell 2000, and Russell 3000 Indices were created in 1984 by the investment consulting firm Frank Russell Company of Tacoma, Washington. The Russell 3000 Index comprises the 3,000 largest American-domiciled publicly traded corporations rated by market capitalization as of May 31 each year. Unilever, Schlumberger, Seagrams, and all other foreign-domiciled companies are excluded. Also excluded are corporations whose share price is less than $1. The Russell 3000 Index is rebalanced annually on June 30, along with the Russell 1000 and the Russell 2000. The Russell 3000 Index represents about 98% of the total market cap of all American domiciled corporations. Unlike the Wilshire 5000, which attempts to include all the (more than 5,000) shares of publicly traded companies into an index, the Russell 3000 focuses on 3,000 frequently traded stocks as a way of creating a more accurate and readily-updated index.

The Russell 3000 is divided into the Russell 1000 and the Russell 2000. The Russell 1000 Index comprises the largest 1,000 companies in the Russell 3000, representing about 92% of the Russell 3000 market cap. The Russell 2000 Index comprises the 2,000 smallest companies in the Russell 3000, representing about 8% of the Russell 3000 market cap. Despite the large number of stocks in the Russell 2000, the index is no less vulnerable than the others are to a disproportionate influence from a few exceptional performers. In the June 30, 1999, to February 11, 2000, period the Russell 2000 advanced 17%, half of which was due to only thirteen stocks[189]

The Russell 2000 Index is far more widely watched and used than the Russell 3000 or Russell 1000. The Russell 2000 Index is widely accepted as representing the small cap portion of the U.S. stock market.

The ETF/UITs traded on the Russell 2000 are mostly iShares, creations of the San Francisco–based Barclay's Global Investors unit of the British bank Barclay's. Russell 2000 iShares trade on the AMEX under the symbols IWM, IWN, and IWO, which stand for total-market, value, and growth portions of the Russell 2000, respectively. Merrill Lynch has less widely traded ETFs for the Russell 2000, which are listed on the AMEX under the symbols RSM and RUM.

Market indexes are useful for gauging the performance of an investment portfolio over time. If the pension plan's portfolio substantially lags in a corresponding index, it may be time for a change in strategy. The fiduciary should be sure to select an appropriate index as the benchmark. For example, comparing a small-cap stock portfolio to the Dow Jones Industrial Average may not be meaningful. Conversely, comparing it to the Russell 2000 Index, a popular measure of the stock price performance of small companies, would be a more appropriate benchmark.

Since their emergence as investment tools, benchmarks have played a significant role in managing pension plan assets. In today's defined benefit pension plan asset management environment, benchmarking functions on three levels. Fundamentally, benchmarks offer a means for passively investing in an asset class inexpensively through the purchase of an index fund. The emergence of index funds has become a massive business for many investment management providers and has become a major force in today's financial markets. Additionally, the explosion of benchmarked index funds has provided great insight into the behavior of various asset classes under contradictory market conditions.

Second, benchmarks offer a means of measuring active managers to determine the value added. A carefully selected benchmark is critical in measuring the manager's ability. Instead of using beta return, which is the return of an asset class, managers should be measured on alpha return, which is performance generated by a manager's skill.

Finally, benchmarks offer a means to control active risk within the investment process. Active risk is the risk a manger takes by holding a set of assets that differ in number and amount from the benchmark. As a manager's portfolio begins to differ from the benchmark, the manager's return and volatility begins to differ from the benchmark. This difference creates active risk or tracking error. The more the portfolio differs, the more risk relative to the benchmark the manager is taking. Therefore, the benchmark becomes a risk control device because many managers will not allow their portfolio to drift too far from the benchmark.

Selecting the appropriate benchmark is difficult, not only because of the numerous roles a benchmark plays in the portfolio management process but also because of the various masters a typical plan sponsor might serve. In reality, a plan sponsor must juggle the demands of multiple constituents and multiple periods.

First, the fund's guiding principle might be to preserve the long-term value of the pension fund. In other words, lose no money. Managing a pension portfolio to generate a return that exceeds the rate of inflation with low or no volatility involves a different set of benchmarks than a relative return rate. In this case, a low-risk real return benchmark would reflect the portfolio's risk-free basis.

Alternatively, a benchmark that targeted the plan's liabilities would consist of a portfolio of long maturity bonds that would produce the necessary cash flows at the proper times to fund the liabilities as payments are due.

Third, a policy benchmark is designed to measure how well the portfolio is doing relative to a passively managed portfolio of assets. This approach seeks the generation of a return higher than the assumed rate in order to maintain contribution rates at a relatively stable and affordable rate.

The typical pension plan is faced with the reality that there is no single benchmark that perfectly fits every objective. Unfortunately, for fiduciaries it seems that they must establish several benchmarks in order to do their best to serve all masters at various points in time. A well-constructed, prudent benchmarking policy should reflect all the facts and circumstances of a pension plan.

Investment Policy Statement

More than any other activity, a well-drafted investment policy statement helps a plan fiduciary to not only set the course for the pension plan but also to keep it on track. One of the most critical elements in keeping a pension plan in compliance and demonstrating prudence is the consistent evaluation of the merits of the investments offered through the plan.

Unlike investment policy statements for defined contribution plans, such statements are practically universal for defined benefit plans. While the content and rationale will differ from the defined contribution plan ISP discussed in Chapter 6, the overall structure—mission statement, policy specifics, and policy monitoring procedures—will be present. These elements are tailored to the aspects of the defined benefit plan's objectives regarding liabilities, time horizons, returns, and risk.

Investment Management Structure

Once the plan's objective, asset allocation, and policy are established, an investment manager for each asset class must be selected. A pension plan's fiduciaries can manage the portfolio through one of four methods: (1) index funds, (2) in-house management, (3) outside management, or (4) any combination of the first three.

- **Index funds:** An index fund should be the investment vehicle of choice unless an actively managed fund can be found that will outperform the index. Although an index fund can provide useful diversification, its composition is different from being an optimal risk/return/time horizon model.

- **In-house management:** In most cases, in-house management will be active management because it is hard to justify in-house management of index funds when the outside manager fees are low. While some companies believe they hire the best and the brightest, realistically they cannot retain that personnel forever. Moreover, when performance does decline an in-house manager will be fired—put on the street—unlike an outside manager who will still have a job, just not on a certain account.

- **Outside management:** For the fiduciary, the decision to structure using outside management creates more decisions. Specifically, he or she must select the outside manager. The following section discusses consideration for selecting an investment manager.

Unfortunately, for fiduciaries the establishment of a manger structure is not as precise or well defined as asset allocation, benchmarks, or the selection process. Modeling and implementing a manager structure is less precise. In general, a portfolio consists of a passive core layer that provides diversification by manager strategy and improves the overall efficiency of risk profile and costs. Next, an active core layer generates long-term performance with moderate downside risk. Finally, an active satellite layer serves as a more aggressive (or conservative, if necessary) layer with greater volatility to achieve performance that is more closely aligned with long-term needs.

The optimal number and composition will vary greatly based on the characteristics of each the pension fund. Figure 7-7 illustrates a prudent method of reviewing the efficiencies of a manager structure.

Figure 7-7: Cost-Benefit Analysis of Management Structure

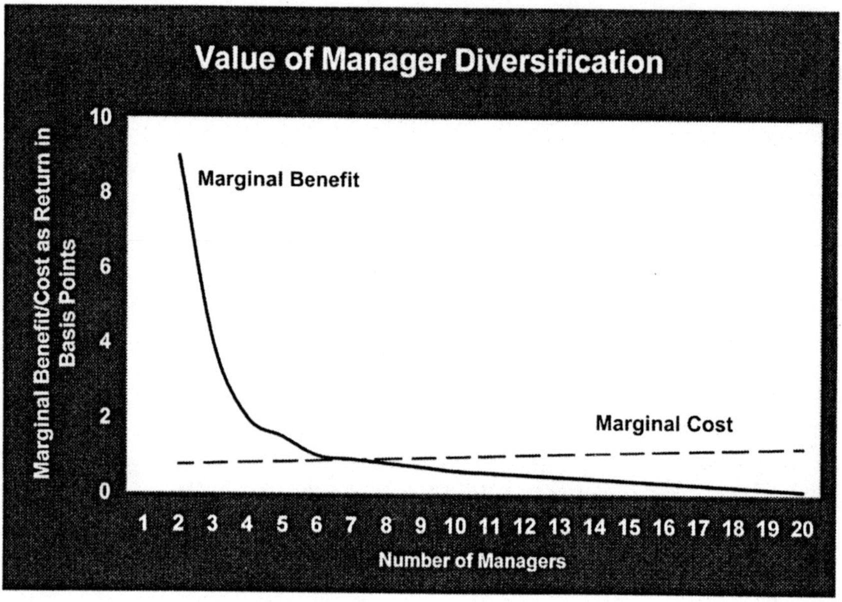

Value of Manager Diversification

Selecting an Investment Manager

After the plan's fiduciary has determined the management structure, he or she must develop a procedure for selecting the investment manager. The following elements must be documented and set forth in the records of the pension plan:

- The fiduciary should carefully document procedures by which competent investment managers will be identified.

- The fiduciary should obtain sufficient information from identified candidates to enable them to prudently choose the investment manager. That information, with appropriate supporting documentation, should include, but not necessarily be limited to, the information listed below:

o The candidate's qualifications as an investment manager pursuant to ERISA § 3(38)

o The candidate's business structure and affiliations

o The candidate's financial condition and capitalization

o A description of the investment style that the candidate proposes to use

o A description of the investment process that the candidate will follow

o The identity, experience, and qualification of the professionals who will be involved in handling the pension trust's account

o Information regarding any relevant litigation or enforcement actions that have been initiated within a reasonable relevant period against the investment professionals who would have responsibility for this pension plan's account

o A description of the experience and performance record of the candidate and his or her investment professionals, including experience managing other tax-exempt and employee benefit plan assets

o Identification of any affiliated broker/dealer that the proposed investment manager has and proposes to use, and, if such an organization is to be used, identification of the sorts of transactions for which the affiliates would be used and a description of the manager's financial arrangement with that broker/dealer

o Description of the procedures that the manager would employ to comply with ERISA's prohibited transaction restrictions, including a statement of whether the proposed management firm is a qualified professional asset manager (QPAM)

o Information about whether the candidate has the bonding required by ERISA

o A statement regarding the proposed manager's fiduciary liability or other insurance that would protect the interests of the plan in the event of a breach of fiduciary duty

o The proposed fee structure

o A list of client references

o A statement regarding the total amount of assets under the proposed investment manager's control

o Any other appropriate and relevant information

The information provided should be verified by reliable independent sources. Inquiries should be made to the DOL and the Securities and Exchange Commission about any enforcement actions that have been initiated within a relevant period with respect to the proposed investment manager, his or her officers or directors, or other investment professionals who will have responsibility for the plan's account.

The fiduciary should review the information provided by the candidates and the information obtained in the verification process and then select an investment manager(s) based on this information and any other information the fiduciary deems relevant.

After selecting the investment manager and consulting with legal counsel, the fiduciary should enter into an appropriate investment management program. This agreement should carefully document the relationship between the parties. It must set forth the terms and conditions of the investment manager's engagement and the right of the pension plan to terminate that manager should it wish to do so. The investment guidelines are an important part of this agreement and should be attached to it.

Managing Investment Managers

After the selection process, careful consideration must be exercised in the continued management and monitoring of fund managers. A prudent fiduciary should enter into written agreements with manager and advisors. This agreement, while somewhat standardized for most components of each relationship, allows for specifics in any relationship. Moreover, exhibits to the agreement may include objectives of the account and a detailed fee schedule.

Establishing Objectives of the Account

The objectives of the account should elucidate the goals, benchmarks, and constraints for the account in addition to anything about the account that differs from the overall standard language of the manager agreement. Furthermore, the account's purpose for the overall portfolio should be included in the objectives. For example, although ERISA requires diversification of the portfolio, unless a manager's objective includes the parameters of diversification and the portion of the total portfolio he or she is managing, the account may or may not need to be diversified. Moreover, unless the appointing fiduciary is an investment expert, the fewer constraints, the better able the manager is to use his or her resources and creativity.

Monitoring Results

Once the fiduciary has selected the plan's investment manager, he or she has a continuing obligation to monitor both the investment manager and the investments. The fiduciary should undertake all the actions listed below on a regular basis to ensure that the investment manager is performing his or her duties in accordance with ERISA and the investment guidelines established by the plan. In addition, because real estate is an illiquid investment, the fiduciary should review that the investment manager is doing his or her job effectively

Unless the fiduciary appointing a manager is an expert, he or she should not micromanage the work of the manager. Under ERISA, a fiduciary is permitted to appoint qualified experts and rely on their expertise—of course with prudent monitoring. Efforts to monitor at a macro level leave the fiduciary with the following options regarding the investment manager relationship: accept the status quo, terminate the manager, modify the objectives, take money away from the manager, or give more money to the manager.

Required Monitoring Actions

- Review at least quarterly the portfolio of each investment manager for compliance with investment guidelines.

- Promptly review each investment manager's quarterly report and generally compare that report in material respects to information provided by the plan's custodial trustee, including the custodial trustee's statement of transactions.

- Review at least quarterly the valuation basis for assts under each investment manager's control.

- Compute quarterly rates of return for each investment manager on an overall basis by asset class and, if investments are in more than one sector, by sector.

- Compare quarterly investment results of each investment manager with appropriate indices or benchmarks.

- Verify at least quarterly each investment manager's fee computation.

- Review at least annually the plan's cash management and short-term investment procedures and performance as well as the overall performance of the plan's custodial trustee(s).

- Meet with each investment manager at least annually. Meetings should include a review of investment performance and any significant changes in corporate or capital structure, investment style, brokerage affiliation or practices, investment process, and professional staff.

- Establish procedures for communicating information regarding investments and investment managers among the trustees, the plan's staff, and the plan's service providers (including but not limited to the plan's attorneys, actuaries, and custodial trustees). Review these procedures at least annually.

Performance

While some plan sponsors rely on a trustee to calculate performance against a standard, the fiduciary is ultimately responsible for monitoring performance. The fiduciary's role is to sift out evidence of skill or lack thereof among managers. In the previous discussion on benchmarks, it was demonstrated that in a defined benefit pension plan one benchmark generally does not suffice. Moreover, a single benchmark in most cases is not adequate even within a single asset class because of multiple goals and parties owed a duty. In most plans, each asset class manager is measured across a matrix of at least three benchmarks. It is the fiduciary's role to establish the benchmark(s) and appropriately apply them to each asset class. Additionally, the manager's performance using alpha and beta is essential to fully understanding the performance.

Composition

The composition of an account should be monitored by tracking the shifts in key aggregate characteristics. A quarterly analysis should be conducted on each manager's portfolio. The quarterly analyses from multiple quarters when trended will demonstrate any shift in the portfolio's overall composition. The industry standard for assessing a portfolio's composition was developed by Barr Rosenberg and is known as the BARRA factors. These factors include variability in markets, success, size, trading activity, growth, earnings to price, book to price, earning variability, and yield.

Organization

Turnover in a management organization is common and regardless of the manager's past performance, organizational changes can have significant impact on the fund's or manager's future performance. In any management agreement, the manager should be required to disclose any organizational changes to the fiduciary committee. A common approach is to require each manager to present in person to the fiduciary committee not only a summation of the economic and historical perspective of the account, but also an assessment of the plan's investment strategy—an overview of the stability or lack thereof within the organization. Moreover, at least every three years the visit should be at the manager's location in order to meet other key people working on the plan's account. After each meeting the fiduciary committee should record in the committee's documentation file a summary of the visit, a detailed evaluation of the manager, and any concerns regarding the manager or the organization.

PURCHASING COMMERCIAL ANNUITIES

In 1995 the DOL issued ERISA Interpretive Bulletin 95-1 to address concerns about plan fiduciaries who had purchased benefit distribution annuities from insurers who had invested a substantial portion of their assets in high-yield securities known as junk bonds. These obligations offer higher rates of return than investment-grade securities because of the greater risk of default presented by non-investment-grade securities. Several insurers who had invested heavily in junk bonds were later forced out of business when the once-booming market for junk bonds collapsed in the early 1990s.

DOL Interpretive Bulletin 95-1 (IB 95-1) clarifies that the process of selecting an annuity provider for benefit distribution is a fiduciary act that is governed by the fiduciary standards of ERISA. This includes a fiduciary's duty to act prudently and solely in the interest of the plan's participants and beneficiaries. The bulletin provides that plan fiduciaries must take steps that are designed to procure the safest annuity available unless it would be in the interest of the participants and beneficiaries not to do so.

Interpretive Bulletin 95-1 also provides factors that should be considered when determining a provider's creditworthiness and claims-paying ability, as follows:

(a) The quality and diversification of the annuity provider's investment portfolios
(b) The size of the insurer relative to the proposed contract
(c) The level of the insurer's capital and surplus
(d) The lines of business of the annuity provider and other indications of an insurer's exposure to liability
(e) The structure of the annuity contract and the guarantees supporting the annuities, such as the use of separate accounts
(f) The availability of additional protection through state guaranty associations and the extent of their guarantees

If a fiduciary does not have the expertise required to evaluate these factors, a qualified, independent expert must advise the fiduciary. The bulletin provides that there are situations where it may be in the interest of participants and beneficiaries to purchase an annuity other than the safest available one—for example, if one annuity is only marginally safer but much more expensive than a competing annuity. Increased costs or other considerations, however, can never justify placing participants and beneficiaries at risk by purchasing an unsafe annuity.

In Adv. Op. 2002-14A, the DOL affirms that the general fiduciary principles set forth in IB 95-1 concerning selection of annuity providers are equally applicable to defined benefit and defined contribution plans. Accordingly, a defined contribution plan fiduciary in evaluating the claims-paying ability and creditworthiness of an annuity provider should take into account the six factors set forth in IB 95-1.

In addition, in response to the insurance companies' more specific questions, Adv. Op. 2002-14A states that a plan fiduciary, when considering the availability of additional protection through state guaranty associations, should determine:

- Whether the provider and annuity product are covered by state guarantees

- The extent of those guarantees, in terms of amounts (e.g., percentage limits on guarantees) and individuals covered (e.g., residents as opposed to nonresidents of a state)

- Whether there are facts calling into question the ability of a state guaranty association to meet its obligations.

The DOL states that if the fiduciary has sufficient expertise or knowledge to evaluate the claims-paying ability and creditworthiness of an annuity provider, including the factors set forth in the IB, the fiduciary is not required to engage a qualified, independent expert to evaluate such factors. The DOL points out that, for purposes of the IB, "independent" means independent of the annuity provider.

Concerning IB 95-1's section on costs, the DOL confirms that a defined contribution plan fiduciary may consider the costs and benefits to the participant of competing annuity products. Nevertheless, the DOL also confirms that a lower cost cannot justify the purchase of an unsafe annuity even when it would pay a higher benefit amount to the participant.

The DOL also addresses IB 95-1's section requiring special care and independent advice in reversion situations where the fiduciaries' interest in the employer creates a conflict of interest in selecting annuity providers. The DOL states that in the absence of any possibility of funds reverting to a plan sponsor in connection with the termination of a defined contribution plan IB 95-1's conflict-of-interest section would not apply to such plans.

8

PLAN FEES AND EXPENSES

You can only spend what you have left after expenses

Recently the U.S. Department of Labor (DOL) has focused increasing attention and audit-enforcement activities on assessing whether pension plans are properly allocating plan expenses. In response to the questions that arose during these audits, the DOL issued guidance.

The plan fiduciary is responsible for understanding and monitoring the fees and expenses charged against the assets of the plan. If a fee or expense is charged to the plan, the fiduciary must insure that such charge is: (1) a plan expense, (2) reasonable, and (3) properly allocated.[190] Moreover, such fees must be disclosed in the plan's summary plan description.

OVERVIEW OF FEES AND EXPENSES

Most plan sponsors receive a breakdown of some of the fees paid by the plan and receive in-depth disclosures as to an individual fund's expense ratio. Most plan sponsors and fiduciaries, however, are unaware of the extent and effect of the fees in a pension plan. The mere presence of fees is not always indicative of a poor plan—there is a difference between value and price. However, a pension plan fiduciary should be aware of the extent of all fees to properly judge the value versus the price. A pension plan generally includes the following fees.

Plan Expenses

There are obviously costs associated with administering the plan. The plan may hire accountants, third-party administrators, investment advisors, custodians, trustees, and lawyers. Additionally, the plan may offer extra services to employees such as education or investment advice. These extra expenses may be paid directly from the plan or from the general assets of the plan sponsor. Usually these expenses account for less than 10% of the total expenses of the plan.

Investment Expenses

The bulk of a plan's expenses will come from investment expenses. These fees are more difficult to understand because they are often deducted as a percentage of assets from the plan or directly from the fund, and at times include additional fees that the plan participant will never see as the investment advisor directly collects these fees. Fees in this area vary greatly and can be as much as two or three times as expensive depending on the particular platform.

To determine where fees come from, a fiduciary should first work with a comprehensive fee disclosure worksheet. The Revere Coalition, a consortium of independent fee-only retirement plan consulting firms, recently published an excellent fee disclosure form.[191] Some categories to be aware of include:

- **Hard-Dollar Fees:** These expenses are generally easy to determine. Simply look at the plan and determine how much vendors are charging participants on a per-participant basis or in aggregate. These are generally the expenses charged by investment money managers and investment advisors.

- **12b-1 Fees:** This is a hot area these days. 12b-1 fees are charged based on an SEC rule allowing investors to receive savings through certain economies of scale. Many registered investment advisors capture these 12b-1 fees for the plan, offsetting their own costs to the plan.

- **Revenue Sharing Fees:** These fees might include sub-transfer agent fees, commission or finders fees, share class fees, and many other fees paid to the fund or out of the fund to the service providers or money management companies. Revenue-sharing fees are a significant source of a fund's expenses and often the most difficult to determine.

Soft-dollar fees are difficult to discern and determine because they are generally deducted from the investment return of the fund and not expressly listed as a direct expense for the participant. These expenses are usually disclosed in the prospectus, but some of the revenue-sharing fees are extremely difficult to find and the analysis should be undertaken by an expert professional. Once the total fees are understood, a plan can consider the lost opportunity cost due to the plan's expenses.

PERMISSIBLE PLAN EXPENSE

Plan expenses are distinguished from settlor expenses because plan expenses relate solely to the management or administration of the plan. In traditional trust law vernacular, a settlor is the party who designs, establishes, and funds a trust, while the fiduciary administers the trust in accordance with the terms adopted by the settlor. The DOL has adopted this terminology for ERISA plans. Thus, an employer setting the terms of its employee benefit plan is a settlor, but an employer administering the plan is a fiduciary.

The following list of fees and expenses may be charged to a pension plan:[192]

- Accountant fees
- Actuarial fees
- Appraisal fees
- Annual valuations of trust assets
- Independent appraisal of employer stock in a plan
- Attorney fees
- Investment advisory and management fees
- Third-party administrator fees
- Trustee and custodian fees
- Required bonding
- QDRO and QMCSO determination
- Claim processing and payment
- Check writing
- Distribution processing
- Hardship
- Calculating of benefit
- Reporting and disclosure
- Costs of amending a plan for a required regulatory change
- Costs of implementing a plan termination
- Determination letter expenses for initial qualification of a plan

On the other hand, the following list of fees and expenses may not be charged to a pension plan and thus are the responsibility of the employer (these are also known as settlor expenses).[193]

- Plan design and implementation of plan costs
- Legal costs for corporate issues involved in establishing a plan

- Amending a plan for a business reason (and not a required regulatory amendment)
- Employer decisions regarding amending a plan (for example, for an allocation or benefit formula change)
- Plan termination costs other than those resulting from the implementation of the termination
- Costs associated with bringing a plan back into compliance under EPCRS
- Excise taxes and cost of preparation of Form 5330 to pay excise taxes

REASONABLENESS OF FEE OR EXPENSE

While ERISA does not set a specific level for fees, it does require that fees charged to a plan be "reasonable." The plan fiduciary is therefore responsible for determining whether an expense is reasonable. Held to a high standard of care and diligence, the fiduciary must make the determination based solely on the interests of the plan's participants and their beneficiaries. Among other things, this means that employers must ensure that fees paid to service providers and other plan expenses are reasonable in light of the level and quality of service provided. In general, the fiduciary must consider if paying the expense is prudent and the expense is in the sole interest of the plan's participants and beneficiaries. The fiduciary should be mindful of the importance of using prudent judgment in determining whether an expense is a reasonable one.

The plan fiduciary must make the following determinations before purchasing goods or services with plan assets:[194]

- The plan document does not prohibit the payment of the expense.
- The goods or services (and related expense) are related to the fiduciary's administration of the plan and not to settlor decisions.
- The expenditure is a prudent one and the amount is reasonable.
- If the service provider is a party in interest, the service arrangement meets the conditions of an ERISA exemption.
- If the services are provided by a plan fiduciary, the amount paid to the fiduciary from the plan is limited to the fiduciary's direct expenses.

ALLOCATION METHOD

In 2003 the DOL surprised many practitioners by reversing its 1994 position on the allocation of QDRO fees. After reviewing ERISA, the DOL concluded "plan sponsors and fiduciaries have considerable discretion in determining, as a matter of plan design or a matter of plan administration, how plan expenses will be allocated among participants and beneficiaries."[195] There are two primary issues regarding the allocation of expenses that can properly be charged to a defined contribution plan:[196]

- The allocation of expenses on a pro rata rather than per capita basis
- The extent to which plan expenses may properly be charged to an individual account rather than the plan as a whole

First, a pro rata allocation is based on a proportional share of plan assets. For example, if participant A's account balance comprises 10% of all plan assets, his account would bear 10% of the expense allocation. In the alternative, a per capita allocation is allocated equally to each participant, regardless of account values.

The DOL stated that when the plan document specifically provides the allocation method to be used, fiduciaries must follow the prescribed method. Failure to do so would be an unauthorized alteration of plan benefits. Absent specific plan provisions, fiduciaries must follow a method that is prudent and solely in the interest of all participants. The method chosen must have a rational basis with some reasonable relationship to the services provided or available to an individual account.

The DOL's language on this issue is actually quite general and few concrete examples are given. A per capita allocation may be appropriate with certain fixed administrative expenses, such as record keeping, legal, auditing, annual reporting, or claims processing. Investment management fees would more likely qualify for the pro rata basis because the DOL's rationale is "with regard to services which provide investment advice to individual participants, a fiduciary may be able to justify the allocation of such expenses on either a pro rata or per capita basis and without regard to actual utilization of the services by particular individual accounts."[197] The guidelines for the proper allocation method appear to be broad and open to interpretation. Prudence and reasonableness should be the primary concerns.

Second, the DOL provides guidance on charging specific fees to a participant's account. Recent interpretations differ from the above discussion on allocating expenses among all participants. The DOL, referring to its 1994 position on QDRO determination fees, concluded that "neither the analyses or conclusions set forth in that opinion are legally compelled by the language of the statute [ERISA]."[198] The DOL noted that ERISA places few constraints on how expenses are allocated among participants, and therefore the same principles applicable to determining the method for allocating expenses among all participants should apply to permissible allocation of specific expenses to individuals rather than the plan as a whole.

On this subject, the DOL did provide specific examples of expenses, to the extent they are reasonable, that can be charged to an individual account. The examples are as follows:[199]

- Hardship withdrawals
- Calculation of benefits payable under various distribution options
- Qualifying a domestic relations order
- Benefit distributions, including periodic check writing expenses
- Administrative expenses for accounts of separated vested participants

Regarding the last item, the DOL stated that it would be reasonable for fiduciaries to charge administrative expenses against accounts of terminated participants even if the plan sponsor pays such expenses for active participants. Initially, the IRS expressed concerns that only charging the former participants and beneficiaries for expenses could lead to a significant detriment.[200] The IRS concluded in 2004 that fees imposed on the former plan participants and beneficiaries would be analogous to fees charged in the marketplace had the assets been held in an IRA.

OBLIGATIONS REGARDING "FLOAT"

Service providers to pension plans often receive some investment earnings on funds in transit. "Float" is the short-term interest earned on such funds. The DOL's long-standing position is that any float earned on plan assets is considered part of the plan's earnings. Service providers may retain the float as part of their compensation; however, they must fully disclose the arrangement to the plan sponsor. Moreover, because it is a fee of the plan, to satisfy ERISA's fiduciary standards plan fiduciaries must (1) review service providers and arrangements for the treatment of float, (2) determine how the float is generated, and (3) evaluate the role and amount of float in the overall compensation to the provider.[201]

9

ADMINISTRATION AND COMPLIANCE

RECURRING FIDUCIARY DECISIONS IN PENSION PLANS

The fiduciaries of a pension plan, as the fiduciaries of any other employee benefit plan, are subject to all of the fiduciary standards referred to in the previous chapters. The application of these standards to situations that frequently confront pension plan fiduciaries is described in this section.

Bundled versus Unbundled Programs

Banks, brokerage houses, insurance companies, mutual fund companies, and others now offer a wide assortment of packaged or bundled pension programs that include a plan document, an investment program, and, occasionally, plan administration services. These bundled programs are available to large and small employers alike and often are marketed and purchased like many other financial products—with little or no thought given to the fiduciary responsibility provisions of ERISA. The employer that blithely purchases a pension program with the same amount of diligence applied to the purchase of an auto insurance policy, however, may be making a grave mistake.

When an employer purchases a particular bundled pension plan, the employer actually is making a series of decisions, several of which are subject to ERISA's fiduciary standards. By adopting a bundled program, the employer either is establishing a new plan or modifying an existing program. ERISA's fiduciary standards do not apply to the decision to adopt or amend a plan. At the same time, in choosing a bundled program the employer also is selecting the related investment program. This decision (as well as certain other decisions that are intertwined with the selection of a particular bundled program) clearly is subject to ERISA's fiduciary standards, including the prudent man rule.

Monitoring Performance

Once the trustee, investment manager or investment funds are initially selected, the fiduciary must monitor their performance. At least annually and preferably quarterly, investment performance should be reviewed against standard market indices. Periodically, performance should be compared with the performance of competing programs by following an approach similar to the one used in making the initial selection. Once again, professional assistance may be necessary depending on the experience of the fiduciary.

Expenses

Fees and expenses are discussed in detail in Chapter 8. In part because fees and expenses are currently of ominous concern with the U.S. Department of Labor (DOL), they are highlighted again here. Expenses associated with investment options and various administration programs available for pension plans can have a significant impact on the rate of return experienced by plan participants. In order to satisfy the prudent man rule, plan fiduciaries who are charged with the responsibility of selecting these products have an obligation to carefully identify all of the charges that will be incurred by the plan and assure that the charges are reasonable in light of the services provided and other available alternatives.

Negative Elections

Prompted in part by a recent favorable ruling from the IRS, some employers are adding negative election (also known as automatic enrollment) features to their defined contribution plans. With a negative election program, a prospective plan participant is notified that a certain percentage of his compensation (e.g., 3%) will be withheld and contributed to a plan on his behalf unless he elects otherwise. While these arrangements are acceptable from an Internal Revenue Code perspective, they do place some added burdens on the plan fiduciaries.

With a negative election program, those who participate automatically likely will fail to issue any investment directions. Accordingly, plan fiduciaries will be responsible for the investment of the contributions made by these participants. If the fiduciaries invest the contributions in an investment option that declines in value, the inadvertent participant may well be unhappy and assert a claim.

In order for a negative election program to pass muster under Revenue Ruling 98-30, plan participants must have an effective opportunity to elect to receive the contributions in cash, which necessarily means that the participants must receive an advance communication from the employer or some plan fiduciary. Of course, these communications must be accurate in order to satisfy the fiduciary's duty to avoid misinforming a plan participant.

Conversions

A number of issues arise when an employer or another plan fiduciary decides to convert from one bundled product or one set of investment alternatives to another. Naturally, in selecting the new bundled plan or investment package the responsible plan fiduciary must analyze the underlying investment alternatives and comply with the general fiduciary standards described above, including, most important, the prudent man rule.[202] If the conversion also involves a switch in plan administrative service providers, this selection too must pass muster under the prudent man rule, the executive benefit rule, and the other fiduciary standards.

The plan fiduciary also should consider the impact of any blackout periods on plan participants. Typically, whenever a plan converts from one set of investment funds to another, participants are precluded from taking any action (such as taking a loan from the plan or transferring amounts from one fund to another) for a period of time that is generally referred to as the "blackout period." A blackout period is inevitable and deciding to convert to a program that includes a reasonable blackout period cannot be, in and of itself, a breach of the fiduciary standards. The plan fiduciaries nonetheless should consider the impact of the blackout period on the plan participants and make every effort to minimize its length. Moreover, the plan fiduciaries should make sure that the rules that will apply during the blackout period are carefully and accurately communicated to the plan participants well in advance of the commencement of the blackout period so the participants to take action before the period begins.

Sarbanes-Oxley Act Notice

The DOL has finalized, with some changes, requirements for blackout notices to plan participants as required by the Sarbanes-Oxley Act[203]. The guidance addresses the required contents and timing of the notice and includes a model notice.

Blackout Notice Requirements—In General

A blackout is defined generally as a temporary suspension, limitation, or restriction of participants' or beneficiaries' rights otherwise available under the plan to diversify or direct investments, or obtain a loan or distribution. Plan administrators must meet the notice requirements whenever a blackout will last for three consecutive business days or more.

Contents of Notice

Concerning the contents of the notice, the guidance indicates the following:

- The notice must describe the reasons for the blackout period and the participants' and beneficiaries' rights that will be suspended, limited, or restricted.

- The notice must indicate the blackout period's projected duration. Previous guidance had required plan administrators to identify the expected start and end dates. Under the final guidance plan administrators may instead identify the calendar week during which the blackout period will begin and end, provided that during such weeks information about whether the blackout period has begun or ended is readily available without charge, such as via a toll-free number or Web site, and the notice describes how to access the information.

- In the case of investments affected, the notice must state that participants and beneficiaries should evaluate the appropriateness of their current investment decisions in light of their inability to direct or diversify their assets during the blackout period.

- The notice must provide the name, address, and phone number of the plan administrator or other contact responsible for answering participants' questions about the blackout.

Timing of Notice

If plan administrators do not issue notice of the blackout period at least thirty days before it begins, in most cases the notice must explain the delay. The notice may not be issued more than sixty days before the blackout, although plan administrators may provide supplemental communication to participants before then.

The thirty-day advance notice requirement does not apply under three circumstances:

- When deferring the blackout period for thirty days after giving the notice would violate ERISA's fiduciary standards (e.g., if the plan fiduciary immediately suspends investment in employer stock because the employer has filed for bankruptcy)
- When the events prompting the blackout were unforeseeable or beyond the plan administrator's control
- When the blackout period applies only to one or more participants or beneficiaries solely in connection with their becoming, or ceasing to be, participants or beneficiaries of the plan as a result of a merger, acquisition, divestiture, or similar transaction involving the plan or plan sponsor

In each of these circumstances, the plan administrator must furnish the notice to all affected participants and beneficiaries as soon as reasonably possible under the circumstances unless such notice in advance of the termination of the blackout period is impracticable.

Updated Notice

If the duration of a blackout period changes after notice is provided, the administrator must issue an updated notice to all affected participants and beneficiaries explaining the reasons for the change and identifying all material changes to the previous notice. The administrator must furnish the updated notice as soon as reasonably possible unless such notice in advance of the termination of the blackout period is impracticable.

Exclusions from Blackout Period Definition

A blackout period does not include a suspension, limitation, or restriction under the following conditions:

- Results from application of the securities laws
- Is a regularly scheduled suspension, limitation, or restriction under the plan (or change thereto), provided it has been disclosed to affected plan participants and beneficiaries through at least one of the following methods:
  - The summary plan description
  - A summary of material modifications
  - Materials describing specific investment alternatives under the plan and limits thereon or any changes thereto

- o Participation or enrollment forms for any other documents and instruments under which the plan was established or operates that have been furnished to such participants and beneficiaries
- Occurs due to a qualified domestic relations order or a pending determination of whether a domestic relations order already filed with the plan (or reasonably anticipated to be filed) is a qualified order
- Occurs due to a participant's action or inaction, or because of an action or claim by a party unrelated to the plan involving a participant's account

Penalties

The penalty for violations is $100 per participant per day, which means that a plan with one thousand participants that has a fourteen-day blackout period but fails to give timely notice may be penalized $1.4 million.

Given the enormity of the potential penalty amounts, employers—even those not planning a blackout period—should review their plan operations, keeping in mind the exclusion from the blackout period definition for any regularly scheduled suspension, limitation, or restriction already adequately disclosed to affected plan participants and beneficiaries. If adequate disclosure has not been made, employers should do so as soon as possible.

Notice to Issuer of Employer Securities

Plan administrators also must furnish notice to the issuer of any employer securities held by the plan and subject to the blackout period. If the duration of the blackout period specified in the notice changes, the plan administrator must furnish an updated notice to the employer. Notice to the agent for service of legal process for the employer will constitute notice to the employer unless the employer informs the plan administrator that someone else should receive notice. If the employer designates the plan administrator as the person to receive notice, the employer will be deemed to have received notice when the notice is furnished to affected participants and beneficiaries.

This notice to the employer relates to another provision in Sarbanes-Oxley that bans company insiders from buying or selling certain employer stock during certain blackout periods, even stock held outside the plan. To facilitate this ban, under commission rules the employer must provide notice to the affected executives and the Securities and Exchange Commission.

Mapping

If participants are allowed to direct the investment of their accounts between and among various investment funds, the conversion from the old investment alternatives to the new can be a challenge. One alternative is to collect new investment instructions from all of the participants. This approach, however, can be problematic. Because of inertia alone, many participants may fail to return the new investment instructions and the result may be an unacceptable extension of the "blackout period."

An alternative approach that is favored by many, if not most, employers and service providers is a technique called "mapping." With mapping, each of the displaced investment options is compared to the new options. When the conversion takes place, amounts are then automatically transferred or mapped from the displaced option to the most comparable new option.

Although mapping may be the most administratively acceptable approach, it may deprive plan fiduciaries of any protection under section 404(c) following the completion of the conversion. Based on the regulations issued by the Department of Labor under ERISA section 404(c), many advisors believe that 404(c) relief is only available if the participant has exercised actual control over the investment of his or her account. With mapping, the participant never actually selects the new fund. Instead, the participant selected the displaced fund from which the participant's account was transferred.

If the mapping concept is carefully explained to participants in ample time for them to make investment fund changes before the blackout period begins, it may be possible to argue that the mapping process results in a "silent direction" by the participant to transfer his or her account to the mapped successor funds. Whether this "silent direction" argument will be successful is unclear.

Voting and Tender Decisions

The voting of any employer securities held by a pension plan and decisions concerning the tender of securities also can prove troublesome. If plan fiduciaries are responsible for voting and tendering employer securities, they must observe all of the fiduciary standards described above. Plan fiduciaries who also serve as officers or directors of the plan sponsor must be particularly mindful of the prudent man and exclusive benefit rules as well as the conflict-of-interest prohibitions of ERISA section 406(b).

If the voting and tender decisions are passed through to the plan participants, fiduciaries should carefully consider the positions taken by the DOL in a series of advisory opinions. Plan fiduciaries also should consider the special employer security provisions described in Section II H 5 (Complying with the 404(c) Regulations—Employer Securities).

The DOL initially took the position that plan fiduciaries may not automatically follow the directions of participants with regard to the voting or tender of shares allocated to the participants' account. In an April 30, 1984, letter regarding the Profit Sharing Retirement Income Plan for the Employees of Carter Hawley Hale Stores, Inc., the DOL advised the trustee of the plan that it could accept the participants' directions only if the trustee concluded that the participants had exercised independent discretion, had received complete and accurate information, and had not been subject to coercion by the employer[204].

In 1995, the DOL changed its stance a bit. In a letter to Ian D. Lanoff, the DOL rephrased its position with respect to a fiduciary's acceptance of participant directions.[205] According to the Lanoff letter, a fiduciary must follow a participant's directions unless the fiduciary is able to "articulate well-founded reasons why doing so would give rise to a violation of titles I or IV …for example, the prudence requirement of title I."[206]

Identification of Any Designated Investment Managers

The following list provides an explanation of how to give investment instructions, any limits or restrictions on giving instructions, and any restrictions on the exercise of voting, tender, or similar rights.

- A description of any transaction fees or expenses that are charged to the participant's account
- Immediately following an investment in an investment alternative subject to the Securities Act of 1933 (such as a mutual fund or other publicly traded investment), a copy of the most recent prospectus, unless the prospectus was furnished immediately before the participant's investment
- Subsequent to an investment, materials provided to the plan relating to the exercise of voting, tender, or similar rights, to the extent such rights are passed along to participants.
- A description of the information available on request and the name, address, and phone number of the plan fiduciary responsible for providing that information.

As noted above, certain information must be provided only on request. Information that is required to be provided on request includes:

- A description of the annual operating expenses borne by investment alternatives, such as investment management fees

- Copies of any prospectuses, financial statements and reports, and other information furnished to the plan relating to an investment alternative

- A listing of assets that make up the portfolio of an investment alterative that holds plan assets, the value of such assets, and, in the case of such assets that are fixed-rate investment, contracts issued by a bank, savings and loan association, or insurance company; the name of the issuer of the contract; the term of the contract; and the rate of return on the contract

- Information concerning the value of shares or units in investment alternatives available to participants, as well as information concerning the past and current investment performance of the alternative

- Information concerning the value of shares or units in investment alternatives held in the account of the participant

Employer Securities

In the case of a plan that offers an investment alternative that is designed to permit a participant to directly or indirectly invest in an employer security, section 404(c) relief is conditioned on the following requirements in addition to those set forth above:

The employer securities must, among other things, constitute "qualifying employer securities" (as defined in ERISA section 407(d)(5)), be publicly traded on a national exchange or other generally recognized market, and be traded with sufficient frequency and in sufficient volume to assure that directions to buy and sell may be acted upon promptly.

The plan must establish procedures intended to ensure the confidentiality of information relating to participant transactions involving employer securities, including the exercise of voting, tender, and similar rights. These procedures must be put in writing and distributed to all participants and beneficiaries. Additionally, the plan must designate a plan fiduciary who is responsible for ensuring the adequacy of the procedures and for monitoring compliance with the procedures. The participants and beneficiaries must be given the name of the fiduciary so designated. Finally, the plan must appoint an independent fiduciary to carry out any activities that the designated plan fiduciary determines involve a potential for undue employer influence on participants with respect to their rights as shareholders.

Voting, tender, and similar rights relating to employer securities must be passed through to the participants, as must information provided to shareholders generally. The fiduciaries of a plan that otherwise meets the requirements of section 404(c) will not lose the protection of section 404(c) merely because an employer security investment alternative fails to meet the conditions for section 404(c) relief. Yet plan fiduciaries will not be relieved of liability for employer security investments, even if the investments are participant directed, unless the requirements for section 404(c) relief are satisfied with respect to the investments.

Default Investments

A frequently encountered problem is how to deal with a participant who has not given any investment instructions. A common approach is to specifically state in the plan document that if a participant does not provide investment instructions, the participant's accounts will be invested in the most risk-free investment alternative available, such as a money market fund. Under the regulations, a plan fiduciary is not relieved of any liability for investing a participant's account unless the participant actually exercises control over the investment of the account. As a result, many advisors have assumed that these "default" investment provisions are ineffective and have cautioned plan fiduciaries to prudently invest the accounts of any participants who have not given specific instructions. In light of the Eleventh Circuit's decision in *Herman v. NationsBank Trust Company*, this position may be unnecessarily conservative.[207]

The NationsBank case arose out of competing tender offers for the stock of Polaroid. Shamrock Acquisitions made one of the tender offers, and the other was a self-tender by Polaroid. NationsBank described both of the tender offers in a letter to plan participants, who were asked to instruct NationsBank regarding the tender of the shares allocated to them. The letter also informed the plan participants that a failure to respond would be treated as a "silent direction" not to tender the shares allocated to them.

In the Eleventh Circuit, the DOL argued that NationsBank could not rely on the plan's silent direction provision to support its failure to tender the nonvoted shares. Although the court noted the deference that should be given to the DOL, it nevertheless rejected their position. According to the Eleventh Circuit, as long as participants are clearly advised that the failure to issue any directions will be treated as a silent direction to not tender the stock, the trustee may honor the silent direction.

Based on *NationsBank*, a colorable argument can be made that a participant's failure to issue explicit instructions is a silent direction to invest the participant's account in the plan's default investment option. Whether this argument will be successful is unclear.

Nonetheless, assuming a more conservative view, under ERISA a plan sponsor, or a delegated committee or named fiduciary, retains full fiduciary responsibility for investing plan assets for which participants have not provided investment instructions. Fiduciaries are expected to invest as prudent and experience investors would—not as an inexperienced participant might. Under ERISA, retirement plans are not required to invest in "safe" assets, and fiduciaries are permitted to invest in assts that may experience short-term losses in pursuit of long-term returns.

Today, most fiduciaries select a fixed-dollar investment option as a default fund. Even so, selecting a fixed-dollar investment option as a default fund is inconsistent with two prudent investment principles underlying current participant education programs. First, the existence of a positive equity risk premium contravenes the principle that within various asset classes higher volatility is warranted by higher long-term returns. Although future performance could dramatically differ from the past, ERISA case law emphasizes that plan fiduciaries are not held to a standard of certainty in the future outcome of their investment decisions. Instead, ERISA requires that fiduciaries have well-reasoned and thoughtful processes for evaluating potential risks and returns and that they pursue an investment program that is diversified and prudent. Second, variations in an individual's risk-taking ability based on age draws to the principle that younger individuals are able to assume greater equity market risk than older individuals.

Fiduciaries selecting a default fund should: (1) evaluate the objectives of the pension plan; (2) determine which investment principles underlie their notion of a "prudent investor"; (3) select a fund or funds consistent with this analysis; and (4) document their decision-making process and conclusions. Additionally, fiduciaries should seek to reconcile the investment principles of their participant education programs with their own choice of a default fund.

Disregarding Directions

Generally, in order for the regulations to be satisfied, the plan must provide that a participant's instructions will be honored by the plan fiduciaries.[208] Nevertheless, fiduciaries are allowed to disregard the participant's instructions in certain limited circumstances. Compliance with the regulations is a challenge for any plan that allows participants to direct the investment of their accounts. Although the addition of an open-option feature does not significantly increase the compliance burden, the risks of noncompliance may become more significant.

The fiduciary of the more typical or traditional participant-directed plan can limit the risk of noncompliance with the regulations somewhat by carefully selecting the investment options offered to its employees. If the investment options are selected with care, the risk of substantial, sustained losses is diminished significantly, and this diminished risk in turn lessens the likelihood of participant suits and the importance of compliance with the regulations.

With an open-option program, every participant is given the opportunity to invest in virtually anything. This added flexibility increases the chance of poor decisions, significant losses, and the likelihood that plan fiduciaries will be the subject of a suit by a disgruntled participant. In order to provide the plan fiduciaries with the necessary protection, strict compliance with the regulations is well worth the effort.

KEEPING PLANS IN COMPLIANCE

A qualified pension plan can provide many benefits to employees as well as the sponsoring employer. Employees are ultimately provided with income to help sustain their lifestyle in their post-retirement years. Employers are given a tax deduction for contributions made to the plan, which helps them provide a valuable fringe benefit and boost employee morale.

When Congress passed ERISA, it provided much-needed protection for workers' retirement benefits. That law, as well as applicable sections of the Internal Revenue Code, established a host of administrative rules that must be followed in order for a plan to maintain its qualified status and avoid excise taxes and fiduciary penalties. A summary of the ongoing compliance requirements for qualified plans follows.

Nondiscrimination Testing

One of the basic requirements of a qualified plan is that it does not discriminate in favor of employees who are considered highly compensated employees (HCEs).[209] Generally, an active HCE includes any employee who during the current year and preceding year fulfilled any of the following criteria:[210]

1. An officer

2. A shareholder owning (directly or through related individuals such as spouses and lineal ascendants of descendants) more than 5% of the voting power or value of the employer

3. Any person who during the preceding year was an employee who received compensation of at least $90,000

4. A spouse or dependent of any of the foregoing

Each of these alternative definitions of HCE is the subject of extensive regulations. The determination of who is an HCE in any given year is the responsibility of the plan administrator working with the employer. For the purposes of this chapter, it is useful to understand that HCEs are the class of employees in favor of whom the plan may not discriminate. Non-highly compensated employees (NHCEs) include any employees who are not highly compensated under the previous definitions.

Coverage Requirements

The first area of possible discrimination involves the coverage requirements of Internal Revenue Code section 410(b).[211] This comes into play when a plan is established for only a portion of the employer's staff and not the entire company. Testing is done on an annual basis to insure that the percentage of the company's NHCEs covered under the plan is at least 70% of the company's HCEs that are covered. Alternatively, the plan can pass a more complicated "average benefits test" that illustrates that the benefits provided do not discriminate in favor of the HCEs.

Employer Contributions

Money purchase pension plans and profit sharing plans contain a formula for allocating employer contributions, although in profit sharing plans contributions are often discretionary (optional) from year to year. Such contribution allocations must not violate nondiscrimination rules. While the formula established under the plan generally must prohibit discrimination, certain facts and circumstances need to be considered each year. For example, a plan may require employment on the last day of the plan year to be eligible to share in the contribution, as well as completion of up to 1,000 hours of service. Nevertheless, if a significant number of employees who worked over 500 hours are eliminated from the allocation because of these rules, the plan may be considered discriminatory. This could result in having to include some of the otherwise ineligible participants in the allocation.

401(k) Plans

Plans that allow salary deferrals, matching contributions, and other employee contributions must test these contributions for discrimination at the end of each plan year (except safe-harbor 401(k) plans). The ADP (actual deferral percentage) and ACP (actual contribution percentage) tests compare contributions made on behalf of the HCEs with contributions made on behalf of the NHCEs. Generally, the HCEs are allowed an average percentage that is somewhat larger than the average for the NHCEs. The differential varies depending on the NHCE contribution level.

Plans that do not pass the ADP or ACP test, or both, usually satisfy the test(s) through corrective distributions, although other methods are available such as making additional employer contributions. A failed test must be corrected within twelve months of the end of the plan year. Yet corrective distributions made more than two and a half months after the plan year-end will be subject to a 10% excise tax.

Contribution and Benefit Limitations

Internal Revenue Code section 415 provides the maximum benefit and annual additions limitations for each participant.[212] For plan years beginning in 2005, the maximum annual retirement benefit that can be provided in a defined benefit pension plan is $170,000.[213] In defined contribution plans, the maximum annual additions (i.e., total contribution and forfeiture allocations) are the lesser of 100% of a participant's compensation or $42,000.[214] For benefit and contribution calculation purposes, the maximum compensation that can be utilized is $210,000.[215]

The maximum salary deferral for 2005 is $14,000.[216] If permitted by the plan, those age fifty and older can defer an additional $4,000 as a catch-up contribution.[217] In Simple 401(k) plans, the maximum deferral is $10,000, and the catch-up limit is $2,000.[218]

The plan administrator must make sure that these limits are not exceeded. Excess annual additions must be distributed to the participant, reallocated, or transferred to a suspense account in accordance with the plan provisions. Excess deferrals must be distributed by April 15 following the calendar year of the excess.[219] It is the employee's responsibility, if he or she participated in salary deferral plans of more than one employer, to notify such employers of any excess because the deferral limit includes all plans in which an employee participated during the calendar year.

Top-Heavy Testing

Each retirement plan must be tested annually to determine if it is "top heavy."[220] A plan is considered top heavy if key employees (generally owners and highly paid officers) have more than 60% of the total account balances (defined contribution plans) or present value of accrued benefits (defined benefit plans) of all plan participants.[221] The determination date for the calculation of top heavy status is the last day of the previous plan year.[222]

If a plan is determined to be top heavy, the employer must provide certain minimum contributions or benefits and meet one of the enhanced vesting schedules.[223]

Reporting Requirements

Form 5500 Annual Report—Most plan sponsors must file an annual report, Form 5500, with the Department of Labor by the end of the seventh month following the plan year-end. The deadline may be extended an additional two and a half months by filing an extension. If the owner of the company is the only participant, the plan is exempt from filing a Form 5500 until total assets of all plans of the employer exceed $100,000.

Plans with one hundred or more participants at the beginning of the year (large plans) are required to attach an accountant's audit report to Form 5500. An exception applies for plans with no more than 120 participants that were able to file as a small plan the previous year. Small plans are only exempt from the audit requirement if 95% of the assets are "qualifying plan assets" or if a fidelity bond is purchased for nonqualifying assets and a notice requirement is satisfied in the summary annual report (see below). Qualifying plan assets include assets held or issued by a registered investment company or financial institution, qualifying employer securities, participant loans, and participant-directed investments. Additionally, ERISA requires plan fiduciaries to obtain a surety bond for at least 10% of the value of plan assets. The amount of the bond in force must be reported on Form 5500.

Form 1099-R—Distributions from qualified plans are required to be reported to the IRS on Form 1099-R with a copy furnished to the participant. This is true even if the distribution is nontaxable, as in the case of a direct rollover to an IRA or other qualified plan. Form 1099-R must also be filed for a defaulted loan treated as a distribution. The deadline for furnishing the participant's copy is January 31 following the calendar year of distribution.

PBGC Premiums—Defined benefit plans that are subject to the federal government's PBGC insurance program must pay the required annual premium accompanied by the appropriate PBGC forms. The deadline varies depending on the size of the plan and its funding status.

Participant Notifications

Certain information must be provided to participants throughout the year. Here is a list of the necessary notifications:

- **Summary Annual Report:** A summary of Form 5500 must be provided to each participant within two months of the 5500 filing deadline (including extensions).

- **Summary Plan Description (SPD):** This document, which summarizes the plan provisions, should be provided to new participants within ninety days of their plan entry date. The SPD should be updated every five years if the plan has been amended, or every ten years if no amendments have been adopted.

- **Summary of Material Modifications:** When a plan amendment results in a material modification of one or more plan provisions, an explanation of the amendment must be provided to participants within 210 days of the end of the plan year in which the amendment was adopted.

- **Benefit Statements:** Most plans provide benefit statements to participants at least once a year and if not are required to do so upon request. Pension plans must automatically provide a benefit statement when a participant terminates employment or has experienced a one-year break in service within 180 days of the close of the plan year in which such termination or service break occurred.

- **Safe-Harbor Notice:** 401(k) plan sponsors who elected to make safe-harbor contributions to avoid ADP and ACP testing must give out a safe-harbor notice within a reasonable time before the start of the plan year. A notice distributed between thirty and ninety days before the first day of the plan year will automatically be considered timely.

- **Distribution Forms:** Participants who are entitled to a distribution of their benefits should be provided with appropriate distribution forms as well as tax and rollover information. Plans that contain annuity distribution options must also furnish a notice explaining spousal rights and comparing equivalent values of optional forms of benefits.

- **Qualified Pre-retirement Survivor Annuity (QPSA) Forms:** Plans that offer annuity distribution options must provide a written explanation of the QPSA and a waiver form to each participant between the ages of thirty-two and thirty-five. Where the QPSA first becomes available after age 35 (as with participants hired after that age), the materials must be provided within one year of applicability. Participants who terminate employment before age thirty-five should be notified within one year of separation.

- **Investment Information:** Many plans today, particularly 401(k) plans, allow participants to direct the investments in their accounts. In order for plan fiduciaries to limit their liability for poor investment results in such accounts, ERISA section 404(c) requires that participants be given the opportunity to exercise control over their accounts. Consequently, they must be furnished with sufficient information about the investments available to them under the plan. Prospectuses and other reports about available investments must be provided on a regular basis (and upon request), and statements showing account balances and activity should be provided at least once every three months.

- **Blackout Notice:** When investment direction, loans, or distributions will be unavailable to participants, as in the case of the transfer of plan assets from one custodian to another, a blackout notice must be provided between thirty and sixty days before the blackout period begins.

SUMMARY

There are numerous administrative procedures and reporting requirements that must be followed throughout the year to keep a qualified retirement plan in compliance with ERISA and the Internal Revenue Code. Failure to comply can result in fines, excise taxes, and even plan disqualification. A properly administered plan can be a valuable fringe benefit for employers and employees.

10

COMMUNICATIONS

It is cheaper to communicate than litigate.

Recognized as one of the most important elements in pension plan management, participant communications have received tremendous attention during the last few years. Participant communications are vital because, very simply, if participants are going to direct their own retirement investments, they must learn how to do it. Only effective participant communications programs will help them learn to make sound investment decisions that will improve their chances for financial security. In addition, it is up to plan sponsors and fiduciaries to make sure their participants receive and understand this education.

Although the shift of investment control to participants and ERISA section 404(c) both mandate more attention being paid to participant communications, plan sponsors feel a genuine sense of responsibility to give participants tools to plan for their retirement. The commitment to participant communications is not just a matter of liability, but a genuine feeling on the part of the plan sponsor that it is the right thing to do. This sense of responsibility, along with growing media focus on the problem of inadequate retirement income, has driven the need to develop communications programs that go beyond minimum standards and legal requirements. Still, it is important to review the minimum communications standards under ERISA as the foundation of any participant communications program.

MINIMUM COMMUNICATIONS STANDARDS UNDER ERISA

Except for the section 404(c) regulations and the communications requirements implicit within that section, ERISA contains few explicit participant communications requirements. Instead, as we will discuss later in the chapter, ERISA's participant communications standards as they relate to the fiduciary's responsibilities will continue to evolve under ERISA case law. These cases eventually will dictate minimum standards for participant communications.

Summary Plan Descriptions

ERISA's statutory provisions require that participants receive a summary plan description (SPD), a booklet that describes the plan's provisions and the participants' rights and obligations in simple language. ERISA section 104(b) requires that each participant received an SPD no later than 90 days after first becoming a participant in the plan or within 120 days after the plan begins or within 120 days after the plan first becomes subject to ERISA's reporting and disclosure requirements. For a new plan requiring IRS approval, the 120-day period begins the day after the IRS issues its approval. In the event that the plan is adopted retroactively, the 120-day period would run from the time the plan is adopted. Not only must plan participants receive the SPD, but also the U.S. Department of Labor (DOL) must receive one at the same time.

After the first SPD is provided to participants, the plan must provide an updated SPD every five years thereafter, including all plan amendments that have occurred within the five-year period. An SPD provides little in the way of usable information to plan participants and most participants tend to ignore it. Rather, the SPD is a legally required communication that must contain certain information. Some plan sponsors use the SPD as a catalyst to describe all elements of the plan, transforming this otherwise-dry document into a viable communications piece. Nevertheless, as a legally required communication the SPD must contain the following information:

- Plan name
- Employer name and address
- Employer identification number (EIN)
- Type of plan (for example, defined contribution)
- Type of administration
- Name, address, and telephone number of the plan administrator
- Identity of designated agent for the service of legal process (and the address of such person)
- Eligibility requirements
- Statement describing joint or survivor benefits
- Statement and descriptions of vesting provisions
- Identification of trustee (including title and address)
- Statement of whether the plan is maintained pursuant to any collective bargaining agreements and when copies of those agreements may be obtained

- Statement of whether the plan is covered by termination insurance from the Pension Benefit Guaranty Corporation (not applicable in defined contribution plans)
- The plan's fiscal year
- Sources of contributions and the methods used to calculate the amount of contributions
- Plan termination provisions
- Participant claim and remedy procedures
- Statement of ERISA rights of participants

The information that participants legally must receive is administrative and generally concerns technical and operational elements of the plan, such as who the responsible parties are and how the participant should seek remedy if his or her rights have been violated contrary to ERISA. Although this information is important, employees do not generally review SPDs because they are difficult to understand and do not seem to provide information that is relevant in the early enrollment stages of the plan.

The information contained in the SPD must be written in a manner that can be understood by the average plan participant. If there are a sufficient number of participants who have a first language other than English, they must receive with their SPD a written notice in that language to inform them of assistance available to help them understand the plan.

Summary Description of Material Modifications

In addition to the required initial SPD filing, any change in the plan that constitutes a "material modification" must be communicated to participants in a summary description of material modifications (SMM). The SMM must be provided to participants and the DOL within 210 days after the close of the plan year in which the material modification is adopted. In essence, a material modification is one that changes any of the information that was required in the SPD.

Summary Annual Report

The summary annual report (SAR) provides participants and beneficiaries an annual statement summarizing the latest annual report (Form 5500). A SAR must be furnished on or before the last day of the ninth month following the close of a plan year in the same manner as applicable to the SPD.

Participant Benefit Statements

ERISA section 105 requires that plan participants be able to obtain a benefit statement once per year. The industry standard for most pension plans is to provide quarterly participant benefit statements.

RELATIONSHIP OF PARTICIPANT COMMUNICATIONS, FIDUCIARY RESPONSIBILITY, AND SECTION 404(C)

In addition to the legally mandated participant communications just discussed, there is an evolving standard for participant communications concerning the investment component of defined contribution plans. Participants need a certain amount of investment education in order to truly take control of the investments in their own accounts for purposes of section 404(c).

One of the objectives of giving participants control over their own investments is to allow plan fiduciaries to transfer the responsibility (and potential liability) for investment allocation from themselves to individual plan participants. Having control over their investments is a function of the participants' ability to invest in a broad selection of investment vehicles and make changes periodically. Such control also requires that plan participants receive sufficient information about the plan's investment options to enable them to make informed decisions.

Potential Liability

Under section 404(c), little protection is available if the fiduciary has not given participants sufficient information to enable them to make prudent investment decisions. As discussed in Chapter 5, these requirements provide both participants and the DOL an effective enforcement tool by which to impose liability on plan fiduciaries for imprudent investments. Rather than argue that the plan fiduciary was imprudent in his or her investment selection or monitoring, participants will simply argue that they did not receive sufficient information to make a prudent investment decision. As a result, the section 404(c) regulations put an enormous premium on participant communications.

This is a difficult, if not an impossible, standard. As described earlier, the section 404(c) protections require that in any given case where a plan fiduciary is claiming protection from a participant's own investment decisions, the fiduciary must show that the participant in fact exercised independent control over the investments in his or her account. In other words, it does not appear to be enough for plan participants to receive generic investment information about the investment options in the plan. Rather, it must be shown in each instance that the participant who is challenging the plan fiduciary actually was in control over the investments in his or her account. Whether this occurs depends on a number of elements:

- Whether the participant received the minimum required disclosures under the 404(c) regulation
- The sophistication of the participant
- The method in which the plan investments were communicated to the participant
- The ability for the participant to gain more information about the investments if needed

Development of a Standard

As described earlier in Chapter 5, the section 404(c) regulations mandate minimum disclosure requirements for participant-directed plans. Although these requirements are significant, they are merely the beginning of a standard that will develop over time in the courts, just as all other fiduciary standards have evolved under ERISA. The reason these standards do not exist today is that participant-directed plans are still a relatively new development in the area of retirement plans. The DOL's regulations and future advisory opinions will provide a basis to which courts may turn in setting standards, but they will not be binding on the courts as definitive statements of law. As a result, the courts are likely to look at other areas of the law where the protection of individual investors' rights is paramount.

Plan fiduciaries and their advisors should establish their own standards of prudence for participant communications because no minimum standard for adequate communications exists today. Fiduciaries need to consider the practical implications of ERISA's primary purpose: to protect plan participants. In fact, both ERISA and section 404(c) were enacted to protect plan participants, not plan fiduciaries.

Accordingly, plan sponsors should approach participant communications from a standard of reasonableness. Applying common sense and taking into account all investment-related information made available to plan participants, the plan fiduciary should be comfortable that an average participant receives enough information to make a prudent investment decision. If this does not occur, the plan fiduciary must do more to inform and educate plan participants if the plan is going to continue safely as a participant-directed plan.

INVESTMENT ADVICE VERSUS EDUCATION

At the inception of pension plans and even ERISA, sponsors provided participants with basic plan information, much as described under the compliance and communications sections of this book. The evolution of investment related communications is illustrated in figure 10-1. Anything more was reserved as a perquisite for executives. As the workforce became more investment savvy, demand for a higher level of service evolved.

Figure 10-1: Evolution of Investment Advice

Crossing the line between investment education and advice has been a major concern of pension professionals trying to help plan participants make better investment decisions. A study conducted by the Profit Sharing/401k Council of America found that 51.9% of respondents provide investment advice.[224] Of those that do not, the three most frequently cited reasons that potentially deter employers from making advice available were:

1. Fiduciary concern about liability for advice that results in a loss, even if the advisor is competent and there is no conflict of interest (cited by 93.1% of respondents)

2. Fiduciary concern about ability to select competent advice provided under ERISA prudent man standard (cited by 91.1% of respondents)

3. Fiduciary concern about ability to monitor advice provided under ERISA prudent man standard (cited by 90.2% of respondents)[225]

In 1996, the DOL released its interpretive bulletin distinguishing between investment advice and investment information in participant-directed retirement plans.[226] With this interpretive bulletin, the DOL has tackled a particularly thorny issue for pension professionals and plan sponsors, specifically, identifying at what point investment education would be considered investment advice. This subtle distinction is critical and illustrated in figure 10-2. It allows people involved with pension plan investment communications to avoid inadvertently becoming plan fiduciaries and, as a result, engaging in prohibited transactions under ERISA. By defining precisely which type of information and materials would not be considered investment advice, the bulletin provides important safeguards for pension professionals who can now communicate to participants with certainty that they are not acting as fiduciaries. It also brings closure to a gaping hole in the regulatory structure governing participant-directed plans.

Figure 10-2: The Line between Education and Advice

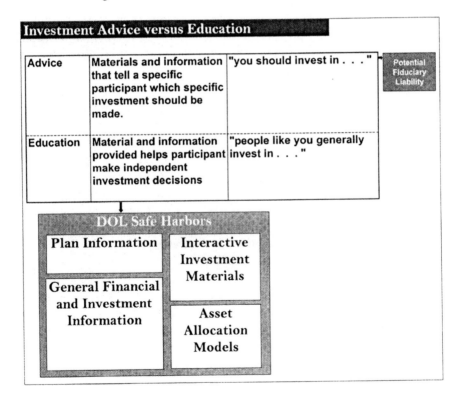

Both the DOL's approach to distinguishing investment advice from education and the historical factors that drove the need for such clarification will shape the future impact of this bulletin. First, the DOL clarified the applicability of ERISA section 3(21)(A)(ii), relating to the definition of a fiduciary under ERISA with respect to providing investment education materials. As noted in Chapter 4, a person is considered a fiduciary for a pension plan to the extend that he or she offers "investment advice" for a "fee or other compensation, direct or indirect."[227] Specifically, the regulations define as fiduciaries those people who, among other things, provide advice on a regular basis "pursuant to a mutual agreement or understanding" that the advice will serve as the primary basis for a plan fiduciary's investment decisions.[228]

The DOL's interpretive bulletin clarifies the scope of this fiduciary definition to include those people who provide investment advice to participants. Pension industry professionals have long recognized this regulation could be used to confer fiduciary status on people involved in plan communications, and the lack of clear distinction between what constitutes advice has been an area of great concern. This is because much of the investment education information that is used in the pension industry might be construed under ERISA section 3(21) to be advice, and the people providing it could in the absence of clear guidelines be deemed fiduciaries.

Given the potential liabilities associated with fiduciary status, pension professionals must know how far they can take education and still avoid this designation. Most pension professionals do not want their activities construed as advisory for a number of reasons. First, if they were inadvertently deemed investment advisors by virtue of their education activities, pension professionals would have to register as investment advisors with the SEC. In this regard, the SEC has indicated that employers who provide investment information of the type indicated in the DOL's interpretive bulletin would not be subject to registration or regulation under the Investment Advisers Act of 1940.[229]

Next, the communicator's education efforts might become prohibited transactions under ERISA section 406 if he or she is inadvertently deemed a fiduciary. As discussed earlier in Chapter 5, this section bars fiduciaries from engaging in certain transactions with a plan or its participants when there is a potential conflict of interest. The most obvious example in the pension industry would be when a mutual fund company is deemed to be providing advice to plan participants with respect to investments in that company's own funds. Generally, it would be considered a prohibited transaction for an entity to advise participants to invest in funds for which that entity or an affiliate earns management fees. As such, mutual fund service providers must take great care to ensure that their communications activities are purely educational rather than advisory in nature.

The fear of liability associated with participant communications has weighed heavily on the minds of plan sponsors and service providers for quite some time. Lacking a real definition of "sufficient information," plan sponsors developed real fears over potential litigation by participants who had poor investment performance in their retirement portfolio. As a result, most pension professionals took the approach that more is better, even if they were not sure that their communications materials truly met the sufficient information requirement. Nevertheless, while 404(c) may have raised participant education to a higher priority level, it created greater concerns over liabilities associated with such aggressive participant education programs. No one really knew where to draw the line between investment education and advice, and thus avoid liability and fiduciary status. This is where the DOL finally stepped in.

Recognizing that absent clarification on this issue, professional communicators might limit their investment education programs, the DOL knew that more substantive standards were mandatory. Limited investment education was not an option given participants' general inability to make effective investment choices. As such, plan sponsors needed some structure to help drive their efforts to push participants up the investment learning curve.

The DOL's interpretive bulletin drawing a line between education and advice represents a long-awaited answer to the call for regulatory guidance on participant communications.[230] Spurred by both the explosion in participant education programs and the confusion over participant-directed plans, the DOL's bulletin offers much-needed standards for those who want to create effective participant communications. Furthermore, given the breadth of information that falls outside the definition of investment advice, the DOL's guidance will have a mostly positive impact on the business of participant communications.

Taking Advantage of the Safe Harbors

The DOL's bulletin points out "safe harbors" or categories of information and materials that would not be considered investment advice.[231] These safe harbors include plan information, general financial and investment information, asset allocation models, and interactive investment models. Within each safe harbor, the DOL describes the characteristics of information and materials that would not be advisory in nature.

Plan Information

Plan information may include the benefits of both plan participation and increasing plan contributions, the impact of pre-retirement withdrawals on retirement income, and the terms and operation of the plan. Descriptions of plan investment options, including investment objectives, risk and return characteristics, historical return information, and all information required by section 404(c) and prospectuses, are also included in this safe harbor.

General Financial/Investment Information

Under this safe harbor, general financial and investment concepts such as risk and return, diversification philosophy, dollar cost averaging, compounded return, and tax deferral are all considered appropriate. In addition, these communications may include historic differences in rates of return among asset classes, methods for estimating future retirement income needs, and ways to determine investment time horizons and risk tolerance.

Asset Allocation Models

The fact that the DOL considers asset allocation models outside the realm of advisory is good news for professional communicators. Considered one of the most effective ways to teach participants how to create their own retirement portfolios, asset allocation models have previously been considered close to the line of offering advice. Under this safe harbor, though, communicators may use models of asset allocation portfolios of hypothetical individuals with different time horizons and risk profiles. Of all the safe harbors, asset allocation models are susceptible to broad and subjective interpretation; therefore, they should be used with caution because, in general, the concept is contrary to the current law. In order to avoid the characterization of this material as "advice," several precautions must be observed:

- All of the models must be based on generally accepted investment theories that recognize the historic returns of various asset classes
- The material facts and assumptions must be stated
- If the model matches one of the plan's investment alternatives with a particular asset class, and other similar investment alternatives also are available, the model must be accompanied by a statement that apprises the participants that other similar investment alternatives are available and advises them how to obtain information on the other alternatives

- A statement must accompany the models stating that in applying any particular asset allocation model to the participants' circumstances they should consider other assets, income, and investments

Interactive Investment Materials

Another type of communication considered potentially advisory was interactive material that required input from the participants. However, allowing considerable flexibility in its guidance, the DOL does not consider these communications advisory provided they adhere to certain standards. This safe harbor allows questionnaires, worksheets, software, and similar materials that give participants a way to estimate future retirement income needs and assess the impact of different asset allocations on retirement income. These materials must be based on generally accepted investment theories and should include all material facts.

In addition, there must be an objective correlation between asset allocations generated by the material and information and data supplied by a participant. Moreover, if the asset allocation generated by the materials identifies an investment option available under the plan, the materials must identify all other plan options with similar risk and return characteristics.

It is important to note that the safe harbors described above represent examples of the types of information and material that would not constitute investment advice when provided to plan participants. The DOL suggests careful consideration of the facts and circumstances involved in each element of an investment education program to determine whether it would be considered advisory.

The Bulletin's Effect on Communications

Clearly, given the breadth of information and materials that fall outside of investment advice, the DOL's guidance will have a mostly positive impact on participant communications and those involved in providing educational programs. The bulletin is an affirmation of what the best people in the industry have been doing to teach participants to make more appropriate investment decisions. Asset allocation models and interactive communication pieces have proven to be the most effective ways to influence participant investment behavior. Furthermore, the DOL's guidance means a win for professional communicators, who will now have a clear understanding of what they can and cannot do without liability.

For large service providers, there will be little difficulty adhering to the DOL's standards given that the types of materials and information contained in the safe harbors are common elements of their educational programs. As such, it will be simple for large service providers to structure their investment education programs to meet the criteria established by the DOL.

For brokers, financial advisors, and similar intermediaries, however, the DOL's guidance may require careful scrutiny and evaluation of their current educational activities. Because many of these individuals have placed themselves in advisory roles to participants, it is now clear according to the bulletin that these people could be considered fiduciaries and, as a result, be subject to considerable restrictions.

Recent Trends

In the aftermath of recent corporate collapses where employees experienced significant pension losses, there is congressional pressure for sponsors to provide investment advice. Additionally, as employees become more sophisticated in financial planning their demands for more than mere investment education will pressure plan sponsors.

Understanding the desire to offer investment advice above education should be a carefully deliberated fiduciary decision. In fulfilling his or her duties, it is recommended that the fiduciary investigate the background and credentials of a prospective investment advice service provider before making advice available to participants. While there are no specific guidelines under ERISA for monitoring investment service providers, some experts suggest that in addition to action toward any co-fiduciary, fiduciaries should:

- Determine whether the advice is given in a timely manner
- Be diligent in monitoring changes in advisory personnel
- Be comfortable with the style of investment advice given, and be satisfied that the results are appropriate for the characteristics of the participant population

Employers are not liable for acts of investment advisors. DOL Interpretive Bulletin 96-1 indicated that in ERISA section 404(c) plans the person designated to provide investment advice would not be liable for loss that is directly the result of the participant's exercise of control. As with any selection of a service provider, however, the plan fiduciary is still responsible for the prudent selection and periodic monitoring of the designated advisor.

Providing Advice

The crux of the issue is thus simple: If an employer advises a participant on how to invest his pension assets, the employer may take on fiduciary responsibility for the provision of such advice but would not have such fiduciary responsibility if the employer merely educates the employee so that the employee can make his or her own investment decisions. "The risk involved when giving advice to plan participants is probably no greater than for any other fiduciary action or decision that a company makes concerning the plan," says David Wray, president of the Profit Sharing/401k Council of America. "Knowing this, the employer can provide advice to participants while acting responsibly to keep fiduciary risk to the company manageable. Remember that ERISA requires prudent decision-making, not [a] successful outcome," noted Wray.

Not Providing Advice

Many assume that by not providing advice they can avoid any liability because ERISA does not require a plan to provide investment advice. This may not be the case. Fred Reish of the law firm Reish Luftman & Reicher has noted:

> DOL regulations under section 404(c) specifically state that fiduciaries have no duty to provide investment advice to participants under a 404(c) plan. However, there may be an additional duty under the "circumstances then prevailing." For example, if the plan sponsor knows the workforce is unsophisticated about investing, what would a knowledgeable and prudent person do in a similar situation? While we are not aware of any case law or regulatory pronouncement that would impose a requirement for providing investment advice to participants, under the general prudence rule an argument could be made that the plan fiduciaries cannot fulfill their duty to act prudently if they do not make investment advice available.[232]

Additionally, the DOL holds the position that it is a participant-by-participant assessment. "We understand that some employers may be reluctant to provide advice out of concern that such activities give rise to fiduciary liability," noted the U.S. Labor Department's Leslie Kramerich in a major address at the American Society of Pension Actuaries Conference in Los Angeles. She outlined several salient points that answer specific concerns voiced by the plan community about investment advice, including the following:

- **Many employees need investment advice.** Many employees are not schooled in the complexities of investment management, risk/return strategies, asset allocation, and diversification principles, yet often have the responsibility for making investment decisions in their pension plans.

- **Investment education is an important tool.** When the DOL issued Interpretive Bulletin 96-1, it distinguished a variety of investment-related investment education activities from the fiduciary act of providing investment advice. It made clear that designating a person to provide investment advice to participants would not, in and of itself, give rise to liability for losses resulting from the individual participant's investment decisions.

- **Investment education may not be enough for some employees.** Many employees may not wish to assume responsibility for making such decisions and may need professional advice. A plan may pay reasonable expenses in providing such investment advice to the plan's participants.

- **Employers are not liable for acts of investment advisors.** DOL Interpretive Bulletin 96-1 indicated that in ERISA section 404(c) plans, the person designated to provide investment advice would not be liable for loss that is directly the result of the participant's exercise of control. As with any selection of a service provider, however, the plan fiduciary is still responsible for the prudent selection and periodic monitoring of the designated advisor.

- **Prudent selection of an investment advisor limits the employer's liability.** The rules applying to the prudent selection of one or more investment advisors for plan participants are similar to those applying to selecting any plan service provider. Responsible plan fiduciaries must engage in an objective process to elicit information necessary to assess the provider's qualifications, quality of services offered, and reasonableness of fees charged for the service. The process also should be designed to avoid self-dealing, conflicts of interest, or other improper influence.

- **Monitoring of investment advisors.** In monitoring investment advisors, the DOL anticipates that fiduciaries will periodically review, among other things, any changes in the information that served as the basis for the initial selection of the investment advisor, utilization of the services by the participants, and comments and complaints of participants.

Assessing Participants' Need for Investment Advice

A number of companies use a three-tiered profile to describe the different types of investors within its plans. They are the do-it-yourselfer, interested-but-need-some-help, and do-it-for-me. In deciding what level of investment communication to provide, fiduciaries must determine the investment profile and specific needs of the participant population. Although any classification works, the three-tiered profile suffices for most.

First, the do-it-yourselfer participant is an experienced investor who prefers to make his or her own investment decisions. To satisfy these participants, the plan should provide a solid array of diverse funds and general information—such as, those required for compliance with 404(c). Chapter 5 provides detail on those types of communications.

Second, the interested-but-need-some-help participant wants to be involved but needs support. They are interested in investment education or advice programs, such as workshops. Most participants match this profile

Third, the do-it-for-me participant does not have the time, inclination, or educational background to become an involved investor. Generally, they prefer to have someone else give advice or manage the account. In many organizations, many participants in this profile are not satisfied.

In order to profile plan participants, plan sponsors can use surveys, focus groups, informal employee feedback, or statistics from the record keeper. Once the participant base has been profiled, the sponsors may decide the level of support needed.

Liability in the Selection and Monitoring of an Advice Provider

As with any decision to hire a service provider for a plan, the designation of a person or firm to provide investment advice to plan participants and beneficiaries is an exercise of discretionary authority or control. This requires that the fiduciaries making the designation must act prudently and solely in the interest of the plan participants and beneficiaries, both in selecting the person or firm and in continuing the relationship. Thus, when a plan sponsor decides to provide investment advice to its participants, the plan sponsor must make the selection in a prudent manner and must periodically monitor the performance of the investment advisor. "The plan sponsor, through its designated officers, must make that decision in accordance with ERISA's fiduciary standards, that is, 'with the care, skill, prudence, and diligence under the circumstances then prevailing that a prudent man acting in a like capacity and familiar with such matters would use in the conduct of an enterprise of a like character and with like arms.'"233

The selection of a financial advisor should employ the same due diligence process and same level of prudence as for other plan fiduciary activities. Plan sponsors should consider using a formal request for proposal (RFP) to ensure that advisors are evaluated prudently and consistently and that the process is documented. The following are suggestions about what to address in an RFP:

- Organizational overview
- Program objectives
- Instructions for responding to the RFP
- Respondent's background and qualifications
- Detail of services to be provided
- Fees

A well-designed investment advice program that properly matches the plan participant's needs with preferred solutions can both help the plan be more successful, assist participant retirement needs, and, when properly designed and implemented, reduce fiduciary exposure.

IDENTIFYING COMMUNICATIONS PROBLEMS

Although 404(c) gives plan sponsors good reason to focus on effective participant communications, their own sense of responsibility to their employees also plays an important role. In any case, both factors should motivate plan sponsors to identify communications problems and take measures to resolve them.

Communications problems manifest most obviously when participants say that they do not understand the materials. In spite of this, plan sponsors should recognize several other symptoms of communications problems.

Low Participation

A common reason for lack of participation is failure to understand the plan. If the communications program fails to adequately explain the plan and its investment options to the employee population, eligible employees simply will not get involved. Furthermore, if the communications program is not targeted to the appropriate levels (both investment sophistication and education) for the employee population, it will also be ineffective and will result in low participation. The communications materials, much like advertisements, must target their message to the audience. If the employee population is relatively young and uninterested in saving for retirement, it is imperative to create communications materials that will appeal to this group.

Demographic issues such as a multicultural employee population may also influence the effectiveness of a communications campaign and result in low participation. If much of the employee population does not speak English, employees have little chance of understanding communications about the plan and therefore are not likely to participate. Plan sponsors with a multicultural workforce face additional communications challenges, which we will discuss later in the chapter, if they are going to increase the participation level of this type of employee population.

Poor Investment Allocations

If a plan's participant population directs more than 50% of their assets into guaranteed investments and cash equivalents, undoubtedly there has been a failure to communicate the risk and reward characteristics of the other investment options, as well as the importance of diversification. Participants who do not understand concepts such as inflation risk and the value of long-term investments in equities will often invest in the most conservative options simply by default or out of fear. Given effective communications about their investment options, participants can make appropriate decisions about allocating their retirement assets.

Participant Questions

One of the best ways to learn what participants find confusing or overwhelming is to listen carefully to the kinds of questions they ask. The more general and infrequent the questions, the less participants truly understand about their pension plans and their investment options. Participants who ask few questions probably do not understand the plan enough to look for more details. In addition, if participants ask many questions about the same issue—for example, what is asset allocation—that can give plan sponsors clues about areas in need of further clarification and education. Service providers can be helpful to plan sponsors in identifying communication problems by sharing data from the telephone service lines. If telephone calls to representatives reflect regular occurrences of certain questions (perhaps about an investment option, for example), the service provider can alert the plan sponsor to a possible need for better communication on this particular topic. Employee meetings also give the plan sponsor an opportunity to identify communication needs by listening to the types of questions asked during or after the presentation.

Although it is important to recognize communication problems, it is equally important to identify their cause in order to take appropriate steps. Some of the most common causes of communication problems are outlined in the following sections.

Participant Communications Lack Stated Objectives

A study on employee communications stated, "[I]f an organization is to disseminate information effectively about its benefit package to the employees, then these communication efforts must be mutually reinforcing and designed to achieve a specific goal."[234] In other words, the organization must use a strategic communication plan. Interestingly, this study concluded that most plan sponsors do not develop their communications programs according to any written objectives, which is why many such programs fail. Without a set goal, communications materials lack focus and often try to cover too many concepts in one piece, which results in information overload for the participants. As we will see later in this chapter, setting goals and objectives for the communications program is paramount to its success and ultimate benefit to the participants.

Participant Communications Are Treated as a One-Time Event or Campaign

Much like an advertising campaign that assumes people will only change their behavior after absorbing the same message several times, a communications program must deliver messages to participants on a regular, ongoing basis. The program should be a process rather than an event in order to give participants the opportunity to absorb the material in stages and have the chance to ask questions along the way. Treating communications as a single event that occurs early in the introduction of the plan results in participants not fully understanding their plan; therefore, they may choose not to participate. Only an ongoing process rather than a one-time event will help participants become educated investors who can make prudent decisions about directing their retirement savings plans.

Participant Communications Are Too Generic

When communications are too broad and generic, participants do not absorb the concepts because the material does not feel relevant to their particular situation. Whether the communications medium is print, slides, or video, employees simply do not related well to generic examples. Instead, eligible employees need to see how participation will influence their own situation. For example, participants need to understand how much it will cost them in real dollars out of their take-home pay to participate in the plan at different contribution levels. They should also be aware of how much their employer will match their contributions so that they can see the direct impact on their own saving levels. The tone and content of communications must be appropriate for the employee population—some employees will not pay much attention to a highly sophisticated discussion of investment concepts.

Service providers have recognized the need for customized participant communications and have responded by producing innovative communications programs that can be tailored to individual plan specifics. Many service providers have created modular communications materials that enable plan sponsors to select certain kinds of material and create a customized program for their participants. Modular communications materials come in all sorts of media including print, video, and slide presentations. Plan sponsors can choose modules that focus on basic investment concepts, plan provisions, or the benefits of tax-savings associated with participating in a pension plan. The point is that service providers have created a way for plan sponsors to tailor their communications program to meet the needs of their specific employee population.

Many of the communications materials offered by service providers can be customized with the plan sponsor's logo, which often makes the plan feel more familiar to the participants. Furthermore, service providers should consider employee demographics such as education levels and ethnicity to create effective materials that present concepts either graphically or in alternative languages. There is a significant trend toward customization of participant communications simply because more targeted materials can have a greater impact on participation.

Too Much Emphasis on Print Materials

The most commonly used medium for participant communications is still print, but the most effective programs use a multimedia approach instead. Employees do not like to read written employee benefit communications because the concepts can be complex and print materials are a one-way communication that do not allow for questions and answers. In addition, a recent study noted that more than 27 million U.S. employees are functionally illiterate, so plan sponsors must use other media to communicate plan details to participants. Colorful graphics, posters, and attention-getting devices used to get employees interested in the plan can often be much more effective in raising participation levels than can printed materials.

A multimedia approach not only gives participants several opportunities to digest information about their plan but also offers plan sponsors a chance to encourage participants to learn more. Furthermore, the multimedia approach is essential for an organization that has a multicultural workforce. This type of employee population may not absorb printed plan information because of a language barrier, so plan sponsors must present plan details and investment concepts in some visual manner that enables their employees to understand the plan and have the opportunity to ask questions. Studies have shown that some media are more effective for communicating a message to the various ethnic groups. For example, certain cultures might respond better to oral communication than to printed materials. Others may be more oriented toward saving. Thus, communication efforts must be tailored accordingly.

Assessing the cause of communications problems will help sponsors develop better programs. Communications programs must be evaluated on a regular basis and modified accordingly. By using participant surveys, reviewing telephone inquiries, or soliciting some other type of participant feedback, plan sponsors can evaluate the impact of the communications program and determine the topics on which participants need further education.

PARTICIPANT NEEDS

One of the best ways to head off communications problems before they occur is to truly understand what participants need for education and information about their pension plan. By doing some front-end analysis of the employee population, including demographics and investment sophistication levels, plan sponsors can get a good sense of how to construct a communications program that will have the greatest value for their employees.

As a rule of thumb, participants need real guidance and considerable handholding as they take control of their retirement investments. The trouble is that most plan sponsors are wary of providing this level of assistance because of fiduciary concerns—they cannot be seen as giving advice. Section 404(c) and its corresponding regulations attempt to absolve plan fiduciaries of any responsibility for participants' own investment allocations under certain conditions. Moreover, a fiduciary has no obligation to advise participants specifically with respect to their investments in a participant-directed plan, nor should this occur. Fortunately, as discussed earlier in this chapter, the DOL has clarified the distinction between information and advice so plan sponsors can avoid inadvertently crossing this line.

Yet many plan sponsors now offer their participants access to outside financial advisors to help them put their total financial picture in context in addition to determining suitable investments for their plans. From a liability management perspective, plan sponsor concerns have changed significantly following the shift of investment control to participants. Plan sponsors were once concerned with the risk of giving bad advice concerning the investment of participant's retirement plan assets; now they must contend with the risk of not providing enough guidance. Plan sponsors now fear that participants who encounter pool investment performance in their plan accounts could take action against their employers for not giving them enough information to invest wisely. As discussed earlier, the courts will determine the standards for this type of action.

Therefore, the challenge for plan sponsors is to create a communications program that provides enough guidance for participants to comfortably direct their own participant-directed plan investments without crossing the line of providing advice—no small task. The real key is to help participants feel comfortable making choices on their own. An effective communications program will provide the tools for participants to become educated investors, rather than apprehensive savers.

The Needs of a Multicultural Workforce

One of the toughest parts of making sure employees have the tools and information to make sound investment decisions is dealing with a multicultural workforce. For ethnically diverse employees, simply providing information is not enough; plan sponsors must ensure that these employees actually understand the materials. Fortunately, there are practical solutions for communicating investment information to a multicultural workforce. Recognizing the growth of multicultural employee populations and their clients' need for effective communications, a few leading companies provide a variety of services such as multilingual investment education materials, prospectuses, and enrollment meetings. In addition, desktop publishing systems allow plan sponsors to produce multilingual versions of employee newsletters without adding significant cost or resources.

Although removing the language barrier may help the communications effort, diversity experts caution plan sponsors to be sensitive to dialects, such as Mexican Spanish versus Puerto Rican Spanish, and to be sensitive to the education levels of the participants. Too often organizations assume their employees have a much lower education level than is actually the case simply because they do not understand English.

Choice of medium also plays a critical role in communicating effectively with a multicultural workforce. By using posters to capture ideas simply and videos with colorful graphic presentations, plan sponsors can deliver one message that will reach several cultures. Communications experts also suggest that multilingual enrollment meetings improve the level of understanding because they give participants a chance to ask questions and receive answers in their native language. Multilingual enrollment meetings also give plan sponsors an opportunity to assess their participants' level of understanding and to get a sense of where they might need further education.

Designing an Effective Communications Campaign

Designing a communications campaign should be much like building a house. It requires careful planning, a detailed schedule, and an assembly of key players (communications professionals) who will be involved in the process. It is important for an effective communications program to have goals and objectives set before construction begins.

It helps to think of a communications program as having three major elements: the message, the method, and the medium. First, the message refers simply to whatever points sponsors want to get across to the participants. Items to consider are what the sponsor want participants to learn or gain from a communications program or what the participant should take away from the message communication. Next is the method, which refers to the manner in which the program will be constructed, including one-time communications (enrollment meetings) and ongoing elements (newsletters and quarterly statements). Finally, there is the medium, or how these messages will be communicated to the employees, whether it is in print, audio, video, or another format such as the Internet. More often than not, the communications medium will be a combination of these methods.

Before each of these elements is discussed in more detail, it is important to review the necessity of assembling resources and setting a schedule for a communications program. The determination of who will actually create and implement the communications program must be resolved. In keeping with the general trend toward outsourcing many plan administration functions, most plan sponsors seek outside assistance for their communications programs. The larger service providers usually offer a comprehensive communications program as part of their bundled service package. These programs include various elements such as printed brochures, enrollment meeting slide presentations, videos, posters, streaming video, Web applications, and a variety of ongoing communications materials.

Some of these elements may be standard, off-the-shelf pieces, but most contain good, basic information about pension plans in general as well as important investment concepts. In addition, many service providers offer custom communications programs, in which they tailor materials to the plan sponsor's employee population, plan provisions, and specific investment options. Custom communications campaigns are most effective because they take a targeted approach toward educating the plan sponsor's employees, taking into account demographics, investment sophistication levels, and general corporate culture.

Plan sponsors seeking a custom communications approach for a smaller plan can take advantage of the expertise of a financial advisor associated with their pension plan. Uniquely qualified to educate individuals about investing, some advisors spend much of their time distilling difficult investment concepts down to a layperson's terms. Furthermore, a financial advisor who is working directly on other plan administration issues will be familiar with the employee population, plan provisions, and any particular challenges the plan faces, so he or she can offer extremely valuable assistance in participant communications.

Clearly, plan sponsors gain access to valuable resources and expertise by outsourcing their communications programs, given that both large service providers and financial advisors understand participants' education needs. Many plan sponsors simply lack the expertise necessary to determine what is sufficient investment information for participants and how to present it most effectively. By taking advantage of external resources for communications programs, plan sponsors can make sure that they will meet their participants' education needs and fulfill their fiduciary responsibilities.

Once plan sponsors have assembled key players and determined the resources for their communications program, implementers must develop a detailed, realistic schedule for implementing the program. It is important to consider major plan milestones when putting together a schedule for the communications program. For example, if plan sponsors are switching service providers, they must build their communications program around milestones such as when plan assets move to the new provider, when new telephone and Internet services become available, and when participants can start switching among new investment options. These events will influence a communications program schedule because it is vitally important to let participants know when each milestone occurs and what steps they need to take with their own plan accounts.

Keeping participants informed and educated before any major plan events take place is essential to maintaining the integrity and credibility of the plan. The more up-front understanding participants have of their plan's provisions and operations, the more likely they are to take advantage of its benefits.

Participants are more likely to understand these benefits if the communications program takes into account the three elements discussed previously: the message, method, and medium.

The Message

Determining the message to communicate is much the same as setting the goals and objectives of the communications program. The question of the motivating need to communicate must be addressed. In other words, an assessment of what participants should gain from the program is necessary. Not all communications programs set out to achieve the same goals and having a clear understanding of the motivation or issue behind the need to communicate helps create an effective message. For example, some programs are designed to introduce a new plan, in which case they will focus heavily on messages about plan benefits, tax savings, and the need to plan for retirement. On the other hand, a communications program geared toward increasing diversification might contain more messages about the advantages of investing in stocks, the value of taking a long-term approach, the need to understand inflation risk, and the benefits of asset allocation.

Although each plan and employee population has different communications needs, there are some basic messages that should be part of every communications program:

The need to save—Explaining the need to start preparing for retirement early is one of the most critical messages in a communications program because it motivates employees to participate in the plan. Media coverage of the United States' savings crisis along with concerns about reaching retirement without enough money to live on should be strong motivators for employees to take advantage of their retirement savings plan. In addition, disappearing Social Security benefits, longer life expectancies, and the rising cost of living are key messages for employees who do not pay enough attention to their retirement needs. Though these messages may sound like fear tactics, they have proven to have significant impact in helping employees understand the consequences of not saving for retirement. From a liability and simple responsibility standpoint, plan sponsors who have consistently communicated these messages can take comfort in the fact that they have made an effort to help their employees provide for a more secure future.

The benefits of a pension plan—Once motivated, employees need to understand how to use the tools available to them, one of the most valuable being their pension plan. From the beginning, the communications program should stress the benefits of participating in a pension plan: tax savings, a convenient and disciplined savings plan that helps employees save before they spend through salary reduction, and the possibility of extra savings through employer matching contributions. It is important for participants to realize that by using a tax-advantage retirement savings plan, they are actually keeping more money in their own pocket and thus can truly afford to save some money despite the fact that they may have a limited budget.

Introducing participants to the concept of tax-deferred earnings and the power of compounding can also help motivate them to participate in their plan. This concept helps people recognize the potential to build up more money in their plan than they could with a regular taxable savings account.

Selecting investments/asset allocation—Every communications program should include basic investment education so that employees understand how to choose the most suitable investments for their individual needs. Most employees are unsophisticated investors who feel so overwhelmed by industry jargon and information overload that they simply choose the most conservative investments by default. Investment education does not have to be complicated and should target the lowest sophistication level while maintaining the interest level of those who may be more financially discerning. Well-educated people do not necessarily know a lot about the fundamentals of investing. The entire employee population should have access to basic investment information, including a discussion of the various asset classes, risk and reward characteristics of each type of investment, risk tolerance and time horizon considerations, and the value of taking a long-term approach to investing for retirement.

Effective communications help employees understand risk and their own tolerance for it. Participants must learn about the different types of risk associated with investing and how they feel about taking risk. They should also be asked to consider their time horizons for investing, which is one of the most critical factors in helping them decide on their own asset allocation. Many participants do not understand the concept of investing for the long term and that if they have several years until retirement they should probably consider some investments in equities.

Only by seeing the advantages of investing more aggressively and diversifying their plan investments where applicable will participants actually change their behavior and choose investments that are more suitable. Part of this motivation should come from communicating clearly the difference between taking market and investment risk versus inflation risk. Once participants realize that by investing too conservatively their savings will not grow fast enough to keep up with inflation, they usually have more incentive to allocate their assets accordingly.

The Method

Although this may seem like a lot of information for employees to absorb, the method of delivery is just as important as the messages in a communications program. Some of these messages are more appropriate in an up-front, more elaborate presentation, such as an employee meeting, whereas others are best delivered on an ongoing basis. Educating an employee population should take into account the fact that employees do not necessarily absorb the message the first time they hear it, and in some cases they must receive it several times before they truly understand and can act on the information. In addition, using ongoing communications to supplement employees' initial introduction to the plan, its benefits, and options avoids overwhelming employees with so much information that they simply tune out and do nothing.

Ongoing communications are suitable for reinforcing certain investment concepts such as the need to invest for the long-term rather than reacting to short-term vicissitudes in the market, as well as for delivering performance information. In fact, participants should receive performance information at least on a quarterly basis, preferably with their statements. Providing a summary of market conditions with the performance data helps participants understand why their investments performed in a certain manner because the market data sets a context for the performance statistics.

Access to a toll-free telephone number for customer service is considered an ongoing communication because employees can speak with well-trained representatives who can discuss investment option suitability. For other ongoing communications, it makes sense to schedule and deliver materials in whatever way has the biggest impact on participants. For example, if a plan intends to add new investment options within the next three to six months, it might make sense to use a statement stuffer or back slip in the participants' quarterly statements to describe the new investment options soon to be available.

The Medium

The medium used for participant communications can have a huge impact on the program's effectiveness. Communications professionals agree that the most successful communications programs take a multimedia approach, using a variety of media to deliver different messages. Participants are typically busy people who are bombarded with hundreds of messages a day, so plan sponsors must creatively use different media to focus their participants' attention on the plan. Several service providers who understand the importance of participant communications have devoted substantial effort and resources toward making multimedia communications programs available to plan sponsors, including print, video, audio, and computer software.

For the initial introduction to the plan, employee meetings with either slides or laptop computer presentations are most effective because they allow the presenter to tailor the meetings to the audience. In most cases, these enrollment meetings can be customized to reflect a particular plan's provisions and investment options. During the course of the meeting, employees should have the opportunity to ask questions, which not only helps them better understand the material but helps the plan's sponsor see areas that might need further education.

Enrollment meeting presentations, whether by slide or video, are usually supplemented by print materials so that employees have another resource to refer to either during or after the presentation. By using both media, the presentation is more effective because it is not necessary to pack all of the details into the video, which can make it overwhelming and less interesting. Another way to make the greatest use of an enrollment meeting is to send employees printed plan information beforehand. This way, employees have a chance to review the material so that the concepts presented during the meeting will not seem as foreign.

Meetings are also an effective medium for reenrollment, to introduce investment options, or to communicate any other major plan changes. It is a good idea to consider reenrollment if any of the following events have occurred:

- Significant levels of new hires
- Merger or acquisition of a new division
- Significant numbers of newly eligible employees
- Unusual reductions in plan participation percentages
- Changes in ownership of the plan sponsor

During the communications planning stages, some plan sponsors decide that whenever plan participation drops below a specified percentage, such as 75%, they will do a reenrollment communications campaign. This is a good way to focus on a major communications effort on a regular basis.

In terms of other ongoing communications, some elements of the program are best delivered through attention-grabbing devices such as posters, tabletop displays, or bulletin boards. Using colorful graphics and short, punchy messages, these media can direct employees' attention to upcoming meetings about the plan, new investment options, or ways to get more information. Finally, information like performance statistics is usually best delivered through print media such as quarterly statement stuffers, employee newsletters, or performance highlight sheets, which allow employees to take the time to understand financial statistics.

The key to selecting the most effective media is to consider what will have the greatest impact on an employee population. If employees are likely to read a benefits newsletter, then that might be one of the best ways to communicate with them. Alternatively, if they gather around bulletin boards in hallways, this might be a good place for an attention-getting message about the plan. The point is to consider employee behavior during selection of media for a participant communications program.

Of course, certain media are effective with one employee population but not another. Computer software to assist in retirement investment planning can be highly effective for employees who are comfortable learning in this manner. These programs, which are available from large service providers, take an employee through a systematic process of figuring out how much money he or she needs to save to maintain a certain standard of living during retirement and what investments might be most appropriate to help achieve his or her goals.

Innovative technology provide a means for plan sponsors and service providers to achieve one of their most critical goals with respect to participant communications—on-demand information. As participants become more accustomed to directing their retirement investments, they will need more education and information resources to manage their accounts effectively. Additionally, in keeping with a trend toward total benefits outsourcing, eventually participant communications will encompass all employee benefit information. The goal is for participants to use one resource to get all of their benefits information. Therefore, although sufficient information has been top priority for participant communications over the past few years, "integrated information" will be the buzzword and the challenge through this century.

11

MANAGING FIDUCIARY RESPONSIBILITY

Bad facts make bad law.

ERISA was enacted to promote secure retirement benefits for participants and help protect their interest in pension plans. Acting in the best interest of participants, making careful and prudent decisions, following the terms of the plan documents, and diversifying plan assts are critical to satisfying ERISA's standards and managing fiduciary responsibilities. As indicated in this book, managing fiduciary responsibility is no easy task.

As in most cases, the laws, governance, and precedent surrounding ERISA are in large part results of reactionary behavior—in many incidences behavior motivated by bad facts. This book in no way should be interpreted as implying that ERISA is bad law. Certain court holdings based on bad facts, however, are undoubtedly reactionary and generally bad law. Nonetheless, this chapter discusses three critical aspects that will help reduce fiduciary risks through the creation of good facts around the fiduciary role—considerations before accepting an appointment as a fiduciary, continuing management of fiduciary responsibilities, and addressing mistakes.

CONSIDERATIONS BEFORE ACCEPTING AN ASSIGNMENT AS A FIDUCIARY

ERISA's fiduciary duties have been called the highest known to the law.[235] Yet those duties are not nearly as high as best practices. Think of imprudence as the basement, ERISA prudence as the floor, and best practices as the attic. Then consider putting the plan's fiduciary office in the attic. That has several advantages: Plan fiduciaries will be well above ERISA's legal "floor" and have the personal satisfaction of a job well done. More important, a fiduciary and sponsor will help participants become financially secure for their retirement years.

Fiduciary litigation by plan participants against employers has become front-page news. The officers of Enron, WorldCom, Lucent, and others were named as defendants in lawsuits filed by class-action attorneys on behalf of plan participants. Some corporate officers and fiduciaries are in jeopardy of losing much, if not all, of their personal net worth because ERISA imposes personal liability on fiduciaries of pension plans.

A well-intended fiduciary's focus should begin as a prospective fiduciary. Upon receipt of an appointment invitation to a fiduciary role, the prospective fiduciary should begin by ensuring that the basic structure and processes are in place for good governance and effective fiduciary decision making.

My grandfather taught me a lot in life; his philosophy on woodworking applies to ERISA's fiduciary duties as well—measure twice, cut once. With expanded legislation, recent corporate scandals, and increased litigation against corporations and their management, my grandfather's precautions are relevant now more than ever because current events have severely heightened the risks facing fiduciaries.

In today's business world, few individuals are willing to put personal assets on the line in order to sit on a fiduciary committee. That is because public and private trustees face a myriad of increasing risks when accepting a fiduciary role, which makes it is critical to establish and adhere to certain precautions. The first and most critical is to understand what is being accepted and the infrastructure that solicited the appointment and will support the fiduciary role. In other words, anything worth doing is worth doing right. The minimum steps a potential fiduciary should take before accepting the role are as follows:

- Establish responsibilities delegated by the employer
- Ensure adequate protection
- Identify fiduciaries
- Secure proper fidelity bond
- Review the plan document and trust agreement
- Evaluate personal loyalties
- Engage outside ERISA counsel for the plan
- Review the existing due diligence file

Establish Responsibilities Delegated by Employer

Recent cases emphasize the importance of carefully delineating who the plan fiduciaries are and the extent of their responsibility.[236] The members of the plan sponsor's board of directors are usually fiduciaries under ERISA because, in most cases, they are ultimately responsible for the selection and retention of other plan fiduciaries; therefore their delegations—either through resolutions, adoption of plans, or execution of agreements—should be researched and documented.

Furthermore, a potential fiduciary should review the plan document and trust agreement regarding named fiduciaries and procedures to appoint named fiduciaries. Next, he or she should review provisions specifying the authority of various plan fiduciaries and clarify as appropriate. In Enron, the court conceded that a person is a fiduciary only with respect to those aspects of the plan over which he exercises authority and control.[237] Thus, it is wise to clearly understand the extent of the fiduciaries' authority.

Ensure Adequate Protection

While fiduciaries cannot totally insulate themselves from liability, the risk can be mitigated with insurance. Fiduciary liability insurance can be purchased to cover liability or losses resulting from a fiduciary's acts or failure to act.[238] In today's environment, fiduciary coverage extends to protect directors, officers, sponsoring organizations, plans, and employees against the expansive range of claims they can face under ERISA litigation. After finding an individual personally liable for losses in a benefit plan, the Ninth Circuit Court of Appeal held that "While we are not unsympathetic to his burden, we note that fiduciaries may be insured for this type of liability. It would appear that prudent fiduciaries would have their plan or employers secure such insurance."[239]

Many carriers have become more conservative or have exited the market because of the increase in and uncertainty of ERISA litigation and the severity of recent losses. Moreover, such policies typically do not cover fraud or deceptive practices. Other coverage that should be considered are directors and officers (D&O) coverage and errors and omission (E&O) insurance.

While acquiring fiduciary liability insurance can protect the plan against loses, it does not protect the fiduciary for breach of duty.[240] Some suggestions for reviewing and selecting fiduciary insurance policies are as follows:[241]

- The policy should define wrongful acts
- The deductible should apply to a single act or interrelated acts, not each claim for an act
- The policy must include a waiver of recourse provision to personally cover fiduciaries (note: the premium for this portion cannot be paid from plan assets)
- The policy should include a severability clause to prevent dishonesty of one fiduciary

- The policy should be supplemented by a separate policy for defense costs or include a defense outside the limit of liability endorsement
- The policy should include defense costs for allegations of discrimination and other claims generally excluded from indemnity coverage
- The policy should include an endorsement to pay DOL or IRS penalties, taxes, fines, or sanctions levied for breach of fiduciary responsibility

Additionally, an employer may indemnify plan fiduciaries from any liability incurred in implementing their duties—although this is limited in some states with respect to corporate officers. Typically, employers provide indemnification for fiduciaries who incur personal liability for their actions in the administration of a plan. Although most indemnity plans cover simple negligence, most do not cover liability that arises from a fiduciary's gross negligence or intentional misconduct.

Potential fiduciaries should review the fiduciary insurance policies and directors and officers insurance policies to ensure that the employer and its officers and directors who serve as fiduciaries under ERISA are adequately protected. Fiduciaries should also request separate indemnification for serving in a fiduciary role.

Identify Fiduciaries

With assistance of ERISA counsel, all fiduciaries should identify other fiduciaries of a plan. As discussed in detail in previous chapters, a fiduciary is anyone who (1) exercises discretionary control over the management of the plan, (2) has any discretionary authority or responsibility regarding plan administration, or (3) offers investment advice regarding the plan assets and derives compensation from it.[242] Additionally, fiduciaries should ensure that all other identified plan fiduciaries are aware of and understand (1) their identification as a fiduciary, (2) their responsibilities, and (3) their duties as a co-fiduciary to monitor.

In addition to the identification of all other fiduciaries, it is essential that the process of appointment has been proper. Such items to review and document for each fiduciary appointment are listed below:

- Acceptance obtained
- Desires and intentions communicated
- Contingencies for naming successors, should a primary fiduciary become unable or unwilling to fulfill responsibilities

As part of the process of identification of all plan fiduciaries, it is necessary to recognize all operations of the plan and know which are fiduciary decisions versus non-fiduciary decisions because the determination of a fiduciary is generally based on the facts and circumstances of each case. ERISA and DOL recognize that not every decision affecting an employee benefit plan is a fiduciary decision. For example, a plan sponsor's decision to establish, amend, or terminate a plan is not a fiduciary decision; therefore, it need not be made solely in the interest of the plan participants.

The good news is that the law has traditionally distinguished between fiduciary functions for which an officer or director may be held personally liable and "corporate" functions for which no personal liability is attached under ERISA. Accordingly, not every act by an officer or director affecting a benefit plan is a fiduciary act. As one court has stated: "[f]iduciary status …is not an all or nothing concept …. [A] court must ask whether a person is a fiduciary with respect to the particular activity in question."[243] The bad news is that the courts have not drawn a clear line as to where corporate functions end and fiduciary functions begin.

Moreover, a fiduciary being appointed to a committee role should consider the committee composition. Particularly if the plan holds employer stock, it may be advisable to exclude senior executive officers who may have inside information relevant to the company stock investment from the plan committee.

Part and parcel of the review of committee members, a potential fiduciary should review the entire plan's operation and administration for an effective fiduciary structure. Figure 11-1 highlights six measures used to assess the effectiveness of a fiduciary structure.

Figure 11-1: Elements to Review in a Fiduciary Structure

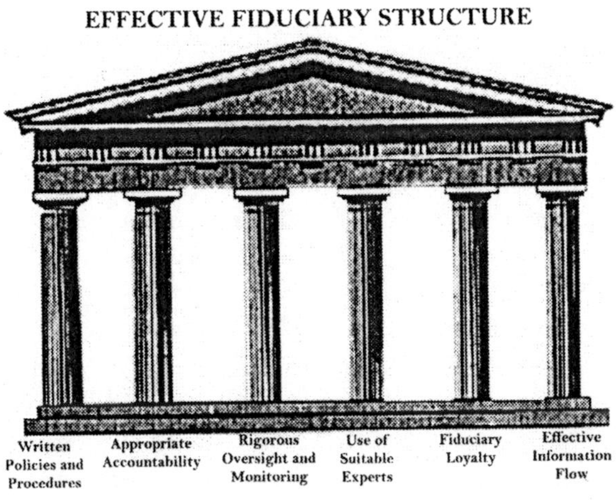

EFFECTIVE FIDUCIARY STRUCTURE

| Written Policies and Procedures | Appropriate Accountability | Rigorous Oversight and Monitoring | Use of Suitable Experts | Fiduciary Loyalty | Effective Information Flow |

- **Written Policies and Procedures:** Maintaining current written policies and procedures for the plan—not just for investments but also for plan administration and communications, ethics, and conflict of interest issues—assist fiduciaries to better manage their ongoing obligations. At a minimum, written records that should be maintained include fiduciary committee minutes, participant communications, internal memorandums regarding fiduciary functions or activities, and plan vendor contracts.

- **Appropriate Accountability:** Maintaining fiduciary committee charter, written delegations, charting roles, and responsibility ensure accountability.

- **Rigorous Oversight and Monitoring:** Periodically overseeing performance of fiduciaries and service providers and regular monitoring of plan compliance and operations facilitate satisfaction of the duty to monitor.

- **Use of Suitable Experts:** Understanding that when a fiduciary or fiduciary committee lacks knowledge in an area, a qualified expert should be sought to provide this service demonstrates the fiduciary's ability to act with familiarity in such matters.

- **Fiduciary Loyalty:** Understanding when and where potential or perceived conflicts exist is essential for a fiduciary to discharge his or her duties for the exclusive benefit of the participants.

- **Effective Information Flow:** Ensuring an effective flow of timely and relevant information among decision makers, third-party administrators and service providers, consultants, counsel, and advisors is necessary to meet the obligations of prudence.

Secure Proper Fidelity Bond

ERISA requires that every plan fiduciary and every person who "handles funds or other property" of a plan be bonded.[244] The purpose of ERISA's bonding requirement is to protect plans against loss due to fraud or dishonesty by plan fiduciaries and others who handle plan funds, whether directly or through cooperation of others. This type of bond is commonly referred to as a fidelity bond. The bond must be for at least 10% of the amount of funds handled in the preceding plan year but generally must be for no less than $1,000 and no more than $500,000.

In addition to the review of the bond before accepting an appointment as a fiduciary, the bond requirement, as discussed below, should be a part of an annual fiduciary audit. In light of this requirement, all fiduciaries, therefore, must be able to be bonded. When reviewing the other fiduciaries of a plan, this requirement should be considered.

Review the Plan Document and Trust Agreement

In addition to reviewing the plan documents to ensure proper appointment of fiduciaries, potential fiduciaries should review the plan document and trust agreement for inconsistencies with administrative practices. Inconsistencies between plan documents and administrative practices can lead to widespread benefit calculation errors, misleading disclosures, costly remedies to operational defects, and potential challenges to the plan's tax-qualified status. If these inconsistencies have occured over a substantial period, plan fiduciaries may lose of have lost the ability to use approved corrective measures.

Evaluate Personal Loyalties

While the company and the plan's counsel can assist with the duty of prudence, the duty of loyalty is, in large part, a personal assessment. If there is doubt or suspicion that loyalties may be compromised or a conflict may exist, a potential fiduciary should consult his or her personal attorney before accepting the assignment. Although relatively few in number, criminal sanctions have been issued against a colorful array of people involved with employee benefit plans over the years. Plan fiduciaries have been convicted of criminal charges. The crimes involving retirement plans in most incidences have involved an individual's personal misdoings or negligence.

Engage Outside ERISA Counsel for the Plan

In the eyes of ERISA, a company employee appointed to a fiduciary role wears two hats—one as an employee with an obligation to the company and one as a fiduciary with a loyalty to the plan and its participants. In most situations, these roles operate in harmony, or at least not in conflict. Nevertheless, situations may arise where the company's interests are not necessarily aligned with the participants. Many times these situations are solely settlor functions and therefore not subject to ERISA's fiduciary standards. Yet, the distinction is often a fine line. In these incidences competent outside ERISA counsel for the plan will prove invaluable. When considering an appointment as a fiduciary, the availability of an outside attorney for the plan should be considered a "deal breaker."

Review Existing Due Diligence File

Wise ongoing plan management should include proper documentation of fiduciary decisions and the process of making the determination. In reviewing the due diligence of current fiduciaries, prospective fiduciaries should focus on decisions related to vendor selections; investment selection and monitoring; review of fees and expenses; and previous committee minutes, notes and attachments. Throughout each decision, proper documentation should reveal a prudent process conducted with the exclusive benefit of the participant in mind. Additionally, an assessment of what education has been offered and how often is critical in understanding the tools that will be provided going forward.

ONGOING MANAGEMENT OF FIDUCIARY RESPONSIBILITY

Managing fiduciary responsibility is no easy task. Still, there are many resources available, including financial advisors, attorneys, and consultants. In attempts to better manage fiduciary responsibility, employers should engage the appropriate resources and follow the steps highlighted in this section. While the law defines fiduciary duty differently in different circumstances, the basic elements are the obligation to act in the best interests of the beneficiary of the fiduciary relationship (the duty of loyalty) and the obligation to act prudently in exercising power or discretion over the property or the interests that are the subject of the fiduciary relationship (the duty of prudence). These principles are most stringently applied to trustees and have been well developed in the various aspects of trust law.

Act in the Best Interest of the Plan and Its Participants

The most defining theme in fiduciary responsibility is placing the interests of participants and beneficiaries above all others. The fundamentals necessary to satisfy this requirement are maintaining personal loyalty, monitoring the loyalty of other fiduciaries, avoiding conflicts of interest, and avoiding entering into prohibited transactions. The fiduciary has to determine the beneficiaries to whom a duty of loyalty is owed under the legal regimes relating to the various roles the fiduciary has undertaken and the standard of loyalty to which they will be held. The fiduciary must clearly identify conflicts of interest and act scrupulously in investigating and considering independently what course of action will benefit each group of beneficiaries. He or she must not favor one group of beneficiaries over another (duty of impartiality) and must put the beneficiaries' interests before his or her own or those of third parties. If the conflicts of interest resulting from the fiduciary's various roles and the particular set of circumstances are such that the fiduciary cannot comply with the legal mandates, he or she should consider relinquishing one of the roles, at least as regards the decisions affected by the conflict, or delegating decision making to an independent fiduciary.[245]

Employ Prudent Processes

The courts have consistently given more weight to the process than the actual result. All actions of a fiduciary should be conducted by exercising prudence and due diligence. The law is concerned with the "conduct of the fiduciary, not the success of the investment."[246]

Moreover, fiduciaries should implement and launch appropriate internal controls to prevent inadvertent breaches of fiduciary duty. Prudent and responsible fiduciaries should fully familiarize themselves with the technical provisions of ERISA and adopt a compliance strategy designed to avert violations and expeditiously recognize and remedy any violation that occurs.

Document Decisions

Of equal importance to employing prudent processes, fiduciaries must be able to demonstrate through properly documenting and memorializing deliberations that, in fact, prudence was exerted. Written records should be maintained, including at a minimum fiduciary committee minutes, participant communications, internal memorandums regarding fiduciary decisions or activities, plan vendor contacts and due diligence files, invoices detailing expenses of the plan, and expert reports or opinions that the fiduciary relied on in making any decisions.

Fiduciaries can limit their liability in certain situations. Documenting the process used is one way fiduciaries can demonstrate that they have carried out their responsibilities properly. Documentation is one of the main ways to reduce legal liability, and it is becoming an essential component of pension plans. Exhibiting that such policies are in place to respond to different market scenarios can help demonstrate diligence and follow-through by the fiduciary.

Claims against fiduciaries are always brought with twenty-twenty hindsight. In that context, if the fiduciary has followed established procedures to satisfy the four basic responsibilities has documentation to show that, he or she should prevail. ERISA fiduciaries are not insurers. In summary, proper documentation will protect plan fiduciaries against most lawsuits brought by plan participants.

Scrutinize Fees and Expenses of the Plan

ERISA requires that pension plan fiduciaries appropriately manage plan expenses. A common obstacle to satisfying this duty is the bundled defined contribution plan where many expenses are hidden in the plan's structure and are not common knowledge. A more challenging issue is the rampant use of unreported soft-dollar expenses. In a typical pension plan, an investment's fees and expenses reduce any investment gains experienced. A fee increase of 1% can cause a 28% difference in an asset's value over a thirty-five year career.

Maintain and Follow the Provisions of an Updated Plan Document and Summary Plan Description

Following the terms of the plan document is also an important responsibility. This document serves as the foundation for plan operations. Employers will want to be familiar with their plan document, especially when a third-party service provider draws it up, and periodically review the document to make sure it remains current. For example, if a plan official named in the document changes, the plan document must be updated to reflect that change.

Appoint and Monitor Qualified Plan Fiduciaries

Named fiduciaries may delegate their responsibilities to other persons in accordance with plan provisions. Nonetheless, as this book previously notes under ERISA, fiduciaries are required to prudently select and monitor these individuals. It is a good idea to document which duties are being delegated and to whom. Fiduciaries should also make sure that each party understands his or her specific responsibilities. When delegating responsibilities a fiduciary should always (1) use reasonable and informed judgment when selecting a co-fiduciary or appointing other fiduciaries, (2) evaluate and monitor the ongoing performance of all fiduciaries and service providers, and (3) maintain a due diligence file documenting the information reviewed and the decisions made. In summary, delegating responsibilities does not relieve the fiduciary of ultimate responsibility, but it can assist in better managing fiduciary risks.

Conduct an Annual Retirement Plan Meeting to Review Plan Investments and Operations

At least annually, fiduciaries should conduct a fiduciary review meeting. This meeting helps fiduciaries to fulfill their fiduciary obligations and evaluate the company's pension plans. Topics proposed should include the following:

- Overview of fiduciary responsibility
  - Compliance with 404(c), if applicable
  - Investment policy statement processes
  - Appropriateness of the plan's funds
  - Documentation of minutes of each meeting and plan decisions
- Review of current funds
  - Performance
  - Diversification
- Discussion of investment fund alternatives
  - Due diligence process
  - Objectives the investment should satisfy
  - Frequency with which performance will be evaluated
  - Documentation of any investment change
- Evaluation of administrative issues
  - Plan design changes and implementation
- Review of employee communications
  - Enrollment workshops
  - Communication videos
  - Investment options and changes
  - Interactive Web site
  - Toll-free telephone services
- Analysis of operational issues
  - Governmental filings
  - Contributions
  - Discrimination testing
- Appraisal of legislative updates
- Discussion of future actions

Maintain an Investment Policy Statement

Although there is no formal ERISA requirement that a written investment policy statement be adopted for a pension plan, ERISA mentions the necessity of a written investment policy statement under several provisions. First section

402(b)(1) states, "Every employee benefit plan shall provide a procedure for establishing and carrying out a funding method consistent with the objectives of the plan and the requirements of this subchapter." Second, section 404(a)(1)(D) reads in part, "A fiduciary shall discharge his duties with respect to a plan ...in accordance with the documents and instruments governing the plan."

Furthermore, the DOL, in an interpretation of ERISA, has written "the maintenance by an employee benefit plan of a statement of investment policy designed to further the purpose of the plan ...is consistent with the fiduciary obligations set forth in ERISA."[247] Moreover, the DOL or IRS will routinely request a copy of the plan's investment policy statement during a plan audit.[248] Notwithstanding the language of ERISA and the DOL, an investment policy should be in writing for two reasons. First, having a written investment policy statement provides a fiduciary with a well-calculated framework from which to construct the investment portfolio. Investment decisions should be based on strategic objectives rather than market emotion or persuasive salespersons. Second, a written investment policy statement establishes rationale and diligence against which ensuing judgments can be made and evaluated.

In summary, an investment policy statement provides a fiduciary with a roadmap to use in evaluating and monitoring various investment issues. Adopting and following an investment policy statement can prevent problems before they develop. Assuming it is properly drafted, implemented, and followed, a written investment policy statement is the best insurance against liability. If fiduciaries follow a well-developed investment policy statement, it is more likely that they will be protected in the event of losses. In addition, not only does a well-drafted and carefully implemented investment policy statement protect the fiduciary from potential liability, it increases the likelihood of strong investment performance over time, which increases participants' satisfaction with the plan.

Complete Fiduciary Education

Fiduciary education controls exposure to fiduciary liability. New fiduciaries need to fully comprehend their responsibilities, their liability, ERISA, and investment principles, and they must be aware of the most common fiduciary violations. All fiduciaries should periodically reinforce their understanding of these areas. ERISA is a complex statute and fiduciaries must be prudent investors and business people. Remember, ERISA does not say a fiduciary has to try hard to do the right thing; it requires that the actions of a prudent person are demonstrated. Obviously, this places a heavy burden on plan fiduciaries. Knowledge can go a long way in preventing future problems.

File Annual Reports with Government Agencies

Fiduciaries are responsible for providing certain information to participants and government agencies. As discussed in detail in previous chapters, examples of required information include the following:

- To Participants:
  - o Summary of plan descriptions
  - o Summary of material modifications
  - o Summary annual reports
  - o Benefit statements to certain separated employees
  - o Notice regarding a blackout period
  - o Annual reports (Form 5500), if requested
  - o Plan documents, including trust agreements, if requested
  - o Statement of benefits (once during a twelve-month period), if requested
- To the Internal Revenue Service
  - o Determination letter requests
  - o Annual reports (Form 5500)
  - o Merger, consolidation, or transfer of assets or liabilities (Form 5310)
- To the Department of Labor
  - o Annual reports (Form 5500)
  - o Summary plan descriptions, if requested
  - o Summary of material modifications, if requested
  - o Plan documents, including trust agreements, if requested
- To the Pension Benefit Guaranty Corporation (for defined benefit plans)
  - o Annual reports (Form 5500)
  - o PBGC premiums
  - o Notice of reportable event
  - o Notice of intent to terminate

Items Specific to Defined Contribution Plans

- Offer participants a well-diversified menu of prudently selected investment options

- Comply with ERISA section 404(c) if the plan is a participant-directed plan
- Ensure that participant deferrals and loan payments are deposited in a timely manner
- Review investments for trading issues

Eliminate Company Stock in the Plan

There are clearly benefits to employees owning stock in the company and thereby aligning their interests with those of outside investors. Nevertheless, such a practice creates inherent and potentially large litigation risks as demonstrated by the recent waive of ERISA tagalong claims. As a result some companies are eliminating company stock as an authorized investment option and as the employer's matching contribution under plans. This is unquestionably the safest strategy from a risk management perspective.

Nevertheless, a fiduciary will inevitably encounter a situation where for various reasons—usually political or plan-sponsor motivated—it is not possible to remove company stock from the plan. In this situation, the conservative approach is to engage an independent fiduciary to manage the company stock within the plan. Additionally, consideration should be given to eliminating hard requirements in the plan document limiting or restricting the capacity of any fiduciary from taking free and unmonitored action related to the company stock.

While the courts have historically held that a fiduciary who divests an ESOP made up of employer stock exposes himself to liability,[249] a recent case challenges that breach in a scenario in which the fiduciary acts under an amendment by the settlor of the plan document to remove such option. At the time of publication of this book, there is a case pending in which the participants allege that the plan fiduciaries breached their fiduciary duties under ERISA when they failed to exercise their discretion to maintain the company stock fund as an investment option.[250] In this example, the fiduciaries liquidated and removed the company stock fund just before the stock experienced a significant increase in price.

The courts, however, have generally been favorable to the defense that the divestment was prudent.[251] In a recent case, the court concluded that prudence was demonstrated by the fiduciary when removing and divesting employer securities in a pension plan. The key factors considered in this ruling were that the fiduciaries had retained expert advice, the stock had been volatile and the business risky, and the aging participant base had a declining ability to weather a downturn.

In summary, a decision to remove a company stock fund or liquidate a portion of a company stock fund is a fiduciary decision. As such, as much prudence, diligence, and loyalty should be exerted before making this determination as in any other investment decision.

ADDRESSING MISTAKES

In spite of diligent efforts to follow the applicable sections of the Internal Revenue Code, ERISA, or applicable regulations, an employer and fiduciary still may make a mistake. To the extent that a plan has been operated in a manner that violates even the most technical provisions of the IRS regulations, a plan may have subjected itself to disqualification for the period of time that it violated any such provision. This can result in substantial tax liability on the part of both employer and employees.

Qualification Failures

The IRS has established programs for employers who wish to correct plan defects that raise qualification issues.[252] These programs are consolidated under the Employee Plans Compliance Resolution System (EPCRS). EPCRS consists of the following three programs:

- **Self-Correction Program (SCP).** A plan sponsor that has established compliance practices and procedures may correct insignificant operational failures at any time without paying any fee or sanction. In addition, a plan that is the subject of a favorable determination letter may correct significant operational failures within a two-year period without paying any fee or sanction.

- **Voluntary Correction Program (VCP).** A plan sponsor at any time before an audit may pay a limited fee and receive the IRS's approval for the correction of a qualification failure. VCP includes special procedures for group and anonymous submissions.

- **Audit Closing Agreement Program (Audit CAP).** If a qualification failure is identified during an audit, the plan sponsor may correct the failure and pay a sanction. The sanction imposed will bear reasonable relationship to the nature, extent, and severity of the failure, taking into account the extent to which correction occurred before the audit.

Categories of Qualification Failures

The availability of a particular correction program under EPCRS depends on the type of qualification failure involved. There are four categories of qualification failures, which are as follows: (1) plan document failure, (2) operational failure, (3) demographic failure, and (4) employer eligibility failure. Only operational failures can be corrected under SCP; however, all categories can be corrected under VCP (with certain group exceptions) and Audit CAP.[253] Figure 11-2 shows which category may be corrected under which method.

Plan Document Failure

A plan document failure is a plan provision or the absence of a plan provision that violates the IRC. If a plan has not been timely or properly amended during an applicable remedial period, a plan document failure results. In addition, this category is a catch all. In other words, any qualification error that is not an operational failure, demographic failure, or employer eligibility failure is a plan document error. SCP is not available to correct a plan document failure.

Operational Failure

An operational failure is a failure arising solely from not following plan provisions. A plan does not have an operational failure if the plan can be amended retroactively to reflect the plan's operation.

Demographic Failure

A demographic failure is a failure to satisfy the discrimination requirements of Internal Revenue Code section 401(a)(4) or the coverage requirements of Internal Revenue Code section 410(b) that is not an operational failure or an employer eligibility failure. The correction of a demographic failure usually requires a corrective amendment. SCP and group submissions under VCP are not eligible to correct a demographic failure.

Employer Eligibility Failure

An employer eligibility failure is an error caused by certain ineligible entities adopting certain plan types during certain periods. SCP and group submissions under VCP are not eligible to correct an employer eligibility failure.

Figure 11-2: Qualification Failures and Correction Programs Compared

Which Programs Can Correct Which Type of Failures				
Type of Failure	SCP	VCP	Audit CAP	Group Correction
Plan Document	No	Yes	Yes	Yes
Operational	Yes (limited)	Yes	Yes	Yes
Demographic	No	Yes	Yes	No
Employer Eligibility	No	Yes	Yes	No

Fiduciary Failures

The DOL has adopted a voluntary compliance program—the Voluntary Fiduciary Correction (VFC) program that is intended to encourage the voluntary correction of certain possible fiduciary breaches.[254] On March 15, 2000, the DOL Pension & Welfare Benefits Administration (PWBA) (which has subsequently changed its name to the Employee Benefit Security Administration (EBSA)) published a notice[255] informing the public of the newly adopted VFC program. This program enables plan officials[256] to identify specific transactions[257] that constitute violations of the fiduciary provisions of ERISA and to voluntarily correct those specific violations using the "blue print"[258] of approved correction methodologies as detailed in the VFC program.

If the correction of the specific transaction(s) is considered by EBSA to be full and accurate correction in accordance with the notice, EBSA will issue a "no-action letter"[259] to that specific applicant with respect to that specific transaction and no 502(l) civil penalty will be assessed with regard to such correction. The VFC program allows fiduciaries to voluntarily correct breaches and prohibited transactions, thereby avoiding civil action and penalties. The program is available to a plan not currently under investigation by the DOL.

Overview of VFC Program

In order to participate in this self-correction program, essentially anyone[260] who is in the position to correct a plan breach of the fiduciary responsibilities contained in Part 4, Title 1 of ERISA may correct the specific ERISA violation detailed in the notice and submit an application to the local EBSA regional office[261] requesting a no-action letter.

There are two limitations to the above-mentioned meaning of "anyone."[262] First, neither the plan in question nor the applicant can be currently "[u]nder [i]nvestigation" (which is defined in the notice as meaning an investigation "pursuant to ERISA §504(a) or any criminal statute affecting a transaction which involves an employee benefit plan").[263] Second, it is not permissible for a party to participate in the program if the application in question contains evidence of criminal violations.

With regard to the impermissible use of the program in situations where the applicant or plan are under investigation,[264] the penalty of perjury statement as detailed in the notice further provides that a plan fiduciary must "further certify under penalty of perjury that at the date of this certification neither the DOL nor any other Federal agency has informed [him or her] of an intention to investigate or examine the plan or otherwise made inquiry with respect to the transaction described in this application."[265] This "under investigation" definition appears to include any government agency, such as the IRS or the Securities and Exchange Commission, with respect to the transaction detailed in the application narrative.[266]

In order to successfully participate in the program, each VFC program application must contain the following: a detailed narrative that identifies the specific transaction that is in violation of ERISA, the facts and circumstances surrounding the specific transaction, and the individuals involved in the transaction; evidence that the specific transaction has been fully and adequately corrected using the specified EBSA correction guidance, including, but not limited to, the restoration of any identified losses with interest, disgorgement of profits by plan officials, and the payment of supplemental benefits to participants; a copy of the written sample notice[267] to be furnished to each participant[268] entitled to receive benefits under the plan[269] detailing the correction under the program; a signed and dated VFC program checklist;[270] a copy of the plan document and other pertinent plan documentation; and a signed and dated penalty of perjury statement from the plan fiduciary.[271]

The cost of correction of the violation specified in the application may not be paid with plan assets, unless such cost would have otherwise been paid from the plan (assuming the plan document permits such payment of reasonable and necessary expenses to be paid from the trust). In other words, the plan (the participants or beneficiaries, or both), should be placed in the same position as it (or they) would have been in but for the fiduciary breach.

Specific Violations Permissible for Correction under VFC Program

Fifteen specific transactions may be corrected under the VFC program as specified in the notice. The specific transactions that are eligible[272] for the VFC program have been grouped into five subcategorizes in the Federal Register, as follows:

Contributions

- o Late deposit of participant contributions to a pension plan
- o Late deposit of participant contributions to an insured welfare plan
- o Late deposit of participant contributions to a welfare benefit trust

Loans

- o Loan at fair-market interest rate to a party-in-interest with respect to the plan
- o Loan at below-market interest rate to a party-in-interest with respect to the plan
- o Loan at below-market interest rate to non-party-in-interest with respect to the plan
- o Loan at below-market interest rate due solely to delay in perfecting plan's security interest

Purchases, Sales, and Exchanges

- o Purchase of an asset (including real property) by a plan from a party-in-interest
- o Sale of an asset (including real property) by a plan to a party-in-interest
- o Sale and leaseback of real property to employer
- o Purchase of an asset (including real property) by a plan from a non-party-in-interest at a price other than fair market value
- o Sale of an asset (including real property) by a plan to a non-party-in-interest at a price less than fair market value

Benefits

- o Payment of benefits without properly valuing plan assets on which payment is based

Plan Expenses

- o Duplicative, excessive, or unnecessary compensation paid by a plan
- o Payment of dual compensation to a plan fiduciary[273]

Each of the above-mentioned specific violations is identified in the notice, along with the formalized correction guidance that must be specifically adhered to and documented to EBSA.[274] The notice also provides detailed examples of each violation specified above and the required correction for each violation.[275]

The DOL tried to identify common fiduciary breaches that are easily correctable. All of these are straightforward violations.[276] Additionally, the DOL asserts that it did not intend to use this program as a targeting mechanism.[277] This is important because if plan officials were to anticipate increased exposure to PWBA enforcement action because of participation in the program, it would most likely have a chilling effect on the utilization of the VFC program.

The approved correction methodology of the specific fiduciary breach in the notice is not necessarily consistent with the correction methodology as desired by code section 4975. Nevertheless, "the IRS has indicated that except in those instances where the fiduciary breach or its correction results in a tax abuse situation or a plan qualification failure, correction under the VFC program will generally be acceptable under the [Internal Revenue Code]."[278] This is significant because if plan officials fear that correction pursuant to the VFC program will not suffice as adequate correction with regard to the IRS and that such participation in the VFC program may expose the plan to additional IRS correction, the program's success would be compromised.

As detailed later in the section entitled Cons of the VFC program, a plan's participation in this program will result in a referral to the IRS and most likely the imposition of IRS excise taxes.

Pros of the VFC Program

- **Benefits to Plan Officials**
  - One benefit of the program is that the applicant obtains a no-action letter with regard to the specific transaction detailed in the application. This no-action letter states that EBSA will not initiate an investigation with respect to the specific transaction addressed in the application or refer the matter to the Solicitor of Labor.[279] Thus, the applicant can obtain closure[280] with regard to the violation.
  - Additionally, as noted previously, if the correction is complete and adequate, a significant benefit of the program is that the 20% 502(l) civil penalty will not be imposed on the specific transaction in the application.[281]

- Benefits to the Private Pension World
  - o With a formalized correction initiative, plan fiduciaries are provided with information about how to remedy thirteen specific violations. Even if a particular violation is not one of the specified thirteen in the program, the notice provides guidance as to the types of EBSA-approved correction methodologies. These methodologies might be extrapolated to other violations.
  - o The VFC program will most likely deter future violations by creating awareness of ERISA fiduciary breaches and educating the public about such violations.[282] Perhaps most important, the program will result in the increased correction of breaches and the increased restoration of plan assets, thereby protecting the financial security of millions of participants. EBSA estimates that the benefit of the VFC program to participants and beneficiaries will total approximately $80 million.[283]
  - o EBSA will be able to focus its time and energy on investigations where violations are more complicated and egregious. This would result in EBSA utilizing its limited resources more efficiently, thus resulting in additional security to private pension plan assets.

Cons of the VFC Program

One disadvantage of the program is that the 502(l) civil penalty will be applied to any additional recovery amount repaid to the plan or participants in the correction of the breach(es).[284] Thus, even a plan official's good-faith effort to fully remedy a breach (utilizing the correction methodology in the application) could potentially result in additional repayments subject to a civil penalty.

Additionally, EBSA reserves the right to reject a VFC program application and may pursue enforcement action with regard to the transaction delineated in the application if, for example, such transaction is not eligible for the program. In addition, EBSA reserves the right to investigate the truthfulness or veracity of any application.[285]

Additionally, the desired result of participation in the program is EBSA's issuance of a no-action letter. However, the no-action letter provides relief only from further action by EBSA with respect to the specific transaction subject to the application and solely for the applicant who submitted the VFC program application. The no-action letter does not protect the applicant from actions or claims brought by third parties or other government agencies.[286]

Arguably, however, if one has adhered to the correction methodology in the notice, there is no monetary remedy to be sought by a third party.[287] Nonetheless, an equitable remedy may be sought and is not protected by the no-action letter. Additionally, in the situation of a third party action against a plan official for the breach remedied through the VFC program application, the application itself might be construed as an evidentiary "admission against interest" against the plan official in a court proceeding.[288] One case in which the application, if construed as an "admission against interest," would be clearly problematic would be in a situation where the plan official is correcting a "potential" violation, because the VFC program is available to correct actual breaches or potential breaches, or both, of ERISA.[289] The possible use of an application as an admission of fiduciary wrongdoing or ERISA breach must be considered before entering into the VFC program in a situation where the plan official is correcting a "potential" breach.[290]

Nevertheless, if the applicant is in possession of an EBSA no-action letter, a court would most likely look favorably upon the correction methodology adhered to by the plan officials and give deference to the no-action letter in the third party court action.[291] The VFC application might be advantageous to the applicant in a third party action as it provides evidence that the correction methodology adhered to pursuant to the VFC program is "adequate correction." In certain circumstances, this no-action letter might be a basis for resolving legal action by third parties.[292] Additionally, a court might give deference to the no-action letter as issued by EBSA and view such letter, although not binding, as persuasive authority.[293]

The no-action letter is not binding with the DOL, unlike an IRS closing agreement under the EPCRS.[294] Experience, however, indicates that EBSA generally will not reopen a closed investigation once the agency has issued a closing letter with respect to a violation. Thus, it can be assumed that once EBSA issues a no-action letter stating no further enforcement action will be taken by PWBA with regard to the corrected violation described in the narrative, it will stand by its promise. Technically, in court this no-action letter is not a document that binds the applicant or EBSA.[295]

Conceivably the principal disadvantage for most plan fiduciaries is the requirement that participants be notified of the fiduciary breach and ensuing correction pursuant to the VFC program. Additionally, this written notice must detail that participants may obtain a copy of the VFC application with all supporting documentation that was submitted to PWBA from the plan administrator.[296] The VFC program requires that plan officials in effect broadcast their ERISA mistakes to plan participants—a step that they are not required to make when they go through the standard voluntary compliance procedure during a department investigation. Moreover, notice to participants is not mandated when a DOL lawsuit against a plan results in a consent judgment, although information is available to plan participants who seek it.

Plan officials often want to correct their ERISA violations but do not want to publicize such errors to the participants. This notice requirement creates a disincentive to plan officials to utilize the VFC program. Although there are no detailed specifications as to what type of written notice must be given to participants regarding the correction[297], such notification to plan participants would most likely prove to be a human relations nightmare for the plan sponsor or plan official, or both. Nonetheless, such a written notice is a requirement that must be adhered to in order to participate in the program.

Additionally, plans that correct fiduciary breaches under the program also will be required to disclose the fact in their annual Form 5500 report.[298] Consequently, correction under the VFC program is open to public scrutiny by plan participants who receive the written correction notice or request a copy of the plan's annual Form 5500 return, or both.

Pursuant to ERISA section 3003(c), the DOL is required to refer the plan to the IRS for possible excise tax on each prohibited transaction corrected through the VFC program. Excise tax is a requirement of law.[299]

Summary

There are many advantages and disadvantages to the VFC program that must be weighed by plan officials and practitioners before entering into the program. One recommendation that would most likely increase the use of the VFC program and its effectiveness in obtaining voluntary compliance and utilization would be to allow for "John/Jane Doe" submissions.[300] To date, plan officials cannot submit applications anonymously under the VFC program.

The VFC program might be perceived as too rigid[301] because it details the exact correction methodology that must be adhered to in order to participate in the program. EPCRS allows for negotiation between the IRS and the plan official and demonstrates correction principles, citing examples of possible correction methodologies, but does not stipulate the only acceptable methods of correction, which would result in an "all or nothing proposition"[302] as in the VFC program.

The written notice requirement to the participants and as the referral to the IRS under Section 3003(c) of ERISA should be reconsidered in the VFC program in light of plan officials' potential resulting hesitancy to utilize the program.

With those additional modifications, the VFC program would prove to be even more beneficial and successful for plans, plan officials, and the private pension community, as well as EBSA. More practitioners and plan officials would be willing to enter into the VFC program and correct ERISA breaches in accordance with EBSA correction methodologies. Currently, it appears that most practitioners and plan officials will adopt a "wait and see"[303] approach prior to using the VFC program until all issues have been resolved through the notice and comments period or through the initial use of the program.

Examples of situations where a fiduciary may breach ERISA duties include the following.

- **Failure to prudently select:** When a plan fiduciary or committee fails to properly select the investment managers for the plan, the participants might seek to recover the difference between what they actually earned and what they might have earned had an appropriate selection been made.

- **Failure to provide for "actual participant control":** When a plan fiduciary of a participant-directed plan fails to provide participants with the requisite "broad selection" of investments or fails to allow participants the ability to make changes frequently enough, the fiduciary could be held liable for participants' individual investment allocation decisions. If those decisions were overly aggressive or ultraconservative, the plan fiduciary could be required to make up the difference between what the participant could have earned had he or she been "properly invested" and what he or she actually earned.

- **Failure to provide sufficient investment information:** In a participant-directed plan, if plan fiduciaries fail to provide "sufficient" information so that participants can make intelligent and informed long-term investment allocation decisions, plan fiduciaries could be held liable and responsible for the allocation by any participant who failed to understand the nature of his or her decisions. Again, the fiduciaries could be held liable for the difference between what the participant might have earned had he or she been "properly invested" and what he or she actually earned.

- **Mislabeling of investments:** In a participant-directed plan, the plan fiduciary communicated that one of the investment vehicles was "guaranteed" and could not lose principal. In fact, the issuer of that instrument is unable to pay in full the principal value of the investment or the accrued interest. In this event, the plan fiduciary could be held liable and required to make up the difference to participants under the theory that he or she imprudently selected the investment and imprudently represented that investment to participants as "guaranteed."

- **Failure to monitor:** In a participant-directed plan, if the plan fiduciary fails to monitor the plan's performance on a periodic basis and that performance over time is found to be deficient in comparison to benchmark indexes, the fiduciary might be charged to make up the difference between actual performance and the benchmark index performance under the theory that the fiduciary failed to monitor the investments and to take corrective action.

- **Failure to monitor volatility:** In a participant-directed plan, if the plan fiduciaries fail to monitor the volatility of the investment alternatives and it is found later that the volatility of one or more of the investment alternatives necessitated greater transfer frequency, the plan could lose all protections under section 404(c) and the fiduciaries could be responsible for participants' investment decisions.

- **Failure to perform due diligence:** In a participant-directed plan, if the sponsor performed no due diligence review over the investment advisors managing the assets in the plan and one of those advisors experienced extensive turnover of portfolio managers that later resulted in a performance decline, the plan fiduciaries might be held liable to make up the difference to the plan under the theory that the fiduciaries failed to perform due diligence on an ongoing basis with respect to the plan's asset managers.

CONCLUSION

Not since the groundswell of the 1970s have employee benefits seen the amount of reform, scrutiny, litigation, and legislation concerning pension plans. Over recent years, focus on fiduciary responsibility, investments, and documentation have conflicted with participant needs and corporate motives. Employers' exposure is heightened further by a volatile stock market, increased litigation, and zealous government scrutiny. While the concepts of fiduciary law have been in existence since the early Roman civilization and U.S. pension plans have been available for more than one hundred years, only in recent years have complexities arisen that warrant attention from the highest level within an organization.

Regardless of these recent trends, the core fundamentals of fiduciary responsibility remain unchanged—loyalty and prudence. All actions by a fiduciary must be carried out with loyalty toward the participants and beneficiaries and demonstrated by prudent actions. With the current hot topics—communications, investment management, fees and expenses, and securities issues, fiduciaries must know the law, acquire expertise or use experts, document their actions to demonstrate prudence, and above all remain loyal.

Fiduciaries must insure communication with participants and beneficiaries where necessary and appropriate. Recent developments in the law have further emphasized the principle that participants and beneficiaries need to be informed on an ongoing basis of any material information that would affect their interests in the plan. In the wake of mutual fund and corporate scandals, fiduciaries will be faced with difficult decisions regarding their disclosure obligations to plan participants. Little attention has been given to communications materials. The evolving ERISA case law indicates that plaintiffs' attorneys do a good job of exploiting and uncovering all of the weaknesses of communications when making their case for a fiduciary breach.

Investment management of pension assets has become noticeably complicated in recent years, bringing new challenges for fiduciaries. Fiduciaries must ensure that the investments are prudent and permitted under the plan document. Likewise, a fiduciary must monitor plan investments with the level of knowledge reserved for an expert. Finally, all investments—including employer securities—must be scrutinized with the intention that the fiduciary satisfies that no prohibited transaction rule.

Fiduciaries are responsible for making important decisions about the management of pension plans including the obligation that they evaluate and understand plan fees and expenses. ERISA section 404(a) requires, in part, that plan fiduciaries administer the plan by defraying "reasonable expenses of administering the plan." To fulfill this duty, fiduciaries must regularly monitor fees to ensure they remain reasonable in view of the services provided and the results achieved. In recent years, the DOL has made expenses paid by plans an audit priority.

It is important that all aspects of the prudent processes described above be fully and carefully documented. Plan fiduciaries should keep communication logs that record relevant information that has been considered, and they should document the decisions made and the decision-making process through preparation of minutes of their plan fiduciary meetings.

Fiduciaries should meet as frequently as needed. In addition, while pension plan committees may normally meet on a quarterly basis, the current mutual fund scrutiny will likely require more frequent meetings, otherwise known as "special meetings," to be called and attended by plan fiduciaries. In the recent *Enron* decision, the judge mentioned the lack of frequent meetings by plan committee members as one indication that fiduciaries may not have met their fiduciary standards under ERISA.

The purpose of ERISA was to "promote the interests of employees and their beneficiaries in employment benefit plans." ERISA regulates employee benefit plans of private employers. The comprehensive statutory regulation prescribed by ERISA affects over 85% of non-elderly American workers who have private health insurance through employee benefit plans. In passing ERISA, Congress was motivated by a desire to protect individuals against private sector mismanagement of employee benefit plans that places participants' potential benefits at risk. For example, the closing of the Studebaker automotive plant in 1963 left over ten thousand employees unable to receive pension plan benefits because the pension plan had not been adequately funded.

In short, the statutory language of ERISA contains many unanswered questions for fiduciaries, and guidance must be sought from case law. As such, ERISA is in a state of flux and evolving. Burying one's head in the sand is not an option as fiduciaries of companies referenced throughout this book have found out the hard way.

APPENDICES

APPENDIX A

INVESTMENT AND FINANCIAL MEASURES

Standard Deviation

A statistical measurement of dispersion about an average, which for a portfolio depicts how widely the returns varied over a certain period. Investors use the standard deviation of historical performance to attempt to predict the range of returns that is most likely for a given portfolio. When a portfolio has a high standard deviation, the predicted range of performance is wide, implying a greater volatility.

If a portfolio's returns follow a normal distribution, then approximately 68% of the time they will fall within one standard deviation of the mean return for the portfolio and 95% of the time within two standard deviations. For example, for a portfolio with a mean annual return of 10% and a standard deviation of 2%, one would expect the return to be between 8% and 12% about 68% of the time and between 6% and 14% about 95% of the time.

Beta

A measure of a fund's sensitivity to market movements. By definition, the beta of the market is 1.00. The beta is calculated by comparing a fund's excess return over T-bills to the market's excess return of T-bills. Therefore, a beta of 1.10 reflects that the fund has performed 10% better than its benchmark index in up markets and 10% worse in down markets—assuming all other factors remain equal. Conversely, a beta of 0.85 indicates that the fund's excess return is expected to perform 15% worse than the market's excess return during up markets and 15% better during down markets.

Beta is a useful tool when the market as a whole can explain some of the fund's performance history. Beta is appropriate when used to measure risk of a combined portfolio of mutual funds.

It is important to note that a low beta for a fund does not necessarily imply that the fund has a low level of volatility. A low beta signifies that the fund's market-related risk is low.

Alpha

A measure of the difference between a fund's actual returns and its expected return, given its level of risk as measured by beta. A positive alpha indicates the fund has performed better that its beta would predict. In contrast, a negative alpha indicates the fund's underperformance in light of the expectations established by its beta.

Alpha is useful to directly measure the value added or lost by a fund's manager. Alpha depends on two factors. The first is the assumption that market risk—as measured by beta—is the only risk measure necessary. The second factor is the strength of the linear relationship between the fund and the index as measured by R-squared. Additionally, a negative alpha can often result from the expenses that are present in the fund's returns but not in the returns of the benchmark index.

R-Squared

A measure that reflects the percentage of a fund's movement that can be explained by movements in its benchmark index. An R-squared of 100 indicates that all movements of a fund can be explained by movements in the index. Therefore, index funds that invest only in S&P 500 stocks will have an R-squared close to 100. Conversely, a low R-squared indicates that few of the fund's movements can be explained by movements in the benchmark index. For example, an R-squared of 35 means that 35% of the fund's movements can be explained by movements in the benchmark index.

R-squared can be used to ascertain the significance of a particular beta. Generally, a higher R-squared will indicate a more reliable beta figure. If the R-squared is lower, then the beta is less relevant to the fund's performance.

Sharpe Ratio

A measure calculated by using the standard deviation and excess return to determine the reward unit of risk. The higher the Sharpe Ratio, the better the fund's historical risk-adjusted performance. The Sharpe Ratio is calculated from the past 36-month period by dividing a fund's annualized excess returns by its annualized standard deviation.

The Sharpe Ratio is most appropriately applied when analyzing a fund that is an investor's sole holding because this ratio uses standard deviation as its risk measure. The Sharpe Ratio can be used to compare two funds directly on how much risk a fund had to bear to earn excess returns over the risk-free rate.

Price-Earnings Ratio (P/E Ratio)

A valuation ratio of a company's current share price compared to its per-share earnings.

Calculated as:
Market Value per Share divided by Earnings per Share

Earnings per Share

The portion of a company's profit allocated to each outstanding share of common stock.

Calculated as:
(Net Income less Dividends on Preferred Stock) divided by Average Outstanding Shared

Companies usually use a weighted average number of shares outstanding over the reporting term.

APPENDIX B

PENSION AND INVESTMENT TERMINOLOGY

Actuary	A statistical expert employed by an insurance company to figure out how much people should pay for insurance.
Active Management	The pursuit of transactions with the objective of profiting (adding value) from competitive information.
Annualize	To express a rate of return for a period greater than one year or less than one year in terms of 12 months.
Annuity	A combination of insurance and investing. An annuity contract (usually issued by an insurance company) assures that it will make certain payments back to the investor at a stated time in the future. An annuity can be either variable or fixed (i.e., dependent on market fluctuations or not). Annuities allow tax-deferred growth and therefore are often used as long-term savings, investment, and retirement vehicles. They tend to have high penalties for early withdrawal.
Asset	Anything having commercial or exchange value that is owned by a business, institution, or individual. In other words, anything worth something.
Asset Allocation	Investing assets in such a way as to build an investment portfolio that minimizes risk while maximizing return. Diversification is a key ingredient in successful asset allocation.

Asset Allocation Decision	A process that determines the optimal distribution of funds among various types of assets that offer the highest probability of consistently achieving investment objectives within the confines of a predetermined level of risk. The process often includes the use of a computer model program to assist in the processing of a myriad of data.
Basis Point	The smallest measure used in quoting yields. One basis point is .01%. One hundred basis points are equal to 1%.
Bear Market	When the investment market is in a slump or decline. In a bear market, stock prices are usually low. It is usually good to buy stock in a bear market. Unfortunately, people are not rational creatures and instead usually end up buying stock in a bull market when prices are high.
Blue Chip	Common stock of huge growth companies. Blue chip stocks are those stocks issued by big companies like GE, Coca-Cola, IBM, and, of course, Microsoft. Bond An issuance of debt by the government or a corporation. It basically is an IOU, which states that if an investor lends money to the government or a corporation now, then they will pay the money back at a stated time in the future while making small interest payments along the way. There are many different types of bonds.
Bottom-Up Manager	A common stock manager who places selection emphasis on recognizing favorable characteristics of individual companies, as opposed to developing the portfolio with an emphasis on the economy and industries (a top-down approach).
Bull Market	When the overall investment market is in a state of appreciation. Stock princes are usually going up.

Cash Equivalents	Short-term investments held in lieu of cash and readily converted into cash within a short time span (i.e., CDs, commercial paper, Treasury bills, etc.).
Common Stock	Securities that represent an ownership interest in a corporation. If the company has also issued preferred stock, both common and preferred have ownership rights. The preferred stock normally is limited to a fixed dividend but has prior claim on dividends and, in the event of liquidation, assets. Claims of both common and preferred stockholders are junior to claims of bondholders and other creditors of the company. Common stockholders assume greater risk but generally exercise greater control and may gain greater reward in the form of dividends and capital appreciation. The terms common stock and capital stock are often used interchangeably when the company has no preferred stock.
Corporate Bond	An instrument written under seal whereby a corporation acknowledges a stated sum is owed, which it will repay at a specified date. It also obligates itself to pay a stipulated amount of interest to the bondholders for the privilege of using their money.
Custodian	A depository of securities for purposes of safekeeping. A custodian does not have a fiduciary responsibility unless the account is a directed trust.
Discount Rate	The interest rate charged by the twelve Federal Reserve Banks for short-term loans to member banks. The discount rate is typically low when the economy is in a recession and the Federal Reserve Board is attempting to increase the money supply thus making loans more accessible to potential borrowers with enticing low interest rates. Member banks borrow money and set their interest rate a notch above that to make a profit, which is the rate that borrowers see. When the Federal Reserve Board wants to slow the

economy down to stop a potential inflationary period, the discount rate is set high so that when member banks borrow money they are forced to set their rate a notch above this higher rate. Essentially this action tightens the money supply because potential borrowers typically do not want to borrow at these higher rates thus slowing overall market spending and cutting demand for goods and services.

Diversification

One of the most important concepts when putting together an investment portfolio. Diversification is achieved by mixing assets between various types of stocks, bonds, and other investment vehicles in order to minimize risk while maximizing return.

EAFE

The Europe, Australia, Far East (EAFE) Stock Market Index. This is an unmanaged value-weighted index of more than nine hundred securities issued by foreign companies.

Equities

Refers to ownership of property, usually in the form of common stocks, as distinguished from fixed income bearing securities such as bonds or mortgages.

Fiduciary

An individual or trust institution given the duty of acting for the benefit of another.

Growth

A percentile ranking where 100 represents those companies with the greatest earnings growth potential, and 1 consists of those companies with the lowest.

High-Yield Bond

Also known as junk bonds. These fixed income instruments have a rating of BB or lower and pay a higher yield to compensate for their greater credit risk.

Index Fund

A fund (or account) made up of securities, the characteristics of which will produce a return that will replicate (or substantially replicate) a designated securities index.

Investment Consultant An individual, or firm, who provides investment advice for a fixed fee, a fee based upon a percentage of assets, or a fee derived from brokerage commissions. Such advice generally includes portfolio constraint analysis, performance objectives setting, asset allocation counsel, and investment manager evaluation, selection and monitoring services. It may or may not include performance measurement services.

Lehman Brothers Aggregate Index An index composed of securities from Lehman Brothers Government/Corporate Bond Index, Mortgage-Backed Securities Index, and Yankee Bond Index. It is generally considered to be representative of all unmanaged domestic, dollar-denominated fixed-rate investment grade bonds with maturities greater than one year.

Market A public place where buyers and sellers make transactions, directly or via intermediaries. Also used to mean the stock market.

Market Value The current or prevailing price of a security or commodity as indicated by current market quotations, and, therefore, the price at which additional amounts can presumably be purchased or sold.

NASDAQ An automated information network that provides brokers and dealers with price quotations for securities traded over the counter. NASDAQ is an acronym for National Association of Securities Dealers Automated Quotations.

New York Stock Exchange An unincorporated, voluntary association founded in 1792 and existing under a written constitution and bylaws. Membership is obtained by purchasing a SEAT from a retiring, deceased, or expelled member and must be approved by a Committee on Admissions. Privileges include the right to buy and sell securities on the trading floor of the exchange for one's own account or for others.

Passive Management   A management procedure that does not generate superior information. A typical example of passive management is the maintenance of index funds. Here, the process is known to all; there is no superior information. The opposite of passive management is active management.

Portfolio Optimization   A process that involves selecting the portfolio that minimizes risk for a given level of return. This starts with a universe of securities or asset classes that has been valued in terms of expected return, variances of expected return, and covariance of return with every other security under consideration. In practice, the computerized optimization programs can impose manifold constraints on the characteristics of the resultant portfolio. A typical constraint would be that the resultant portfolio has no more than a given weight in a portfolio asset class.

Russell 2000   Small stock index that is generally considered representative of unmanaged small capitalization stocks in U.S. markets. It represents stocks that rank from 1001 to 3000 in market capitalization.

Security   An investment instrument other than an insurance policy or fixed annuity issued by a corporation, government, or other organization that offers evidence of debt or equity. The official definition from the Securities Exchange Act of 1934 is "Any note, stock, treasury stock, bond, debenture, certificate of interest or participation in any profit-sharing agreement or in any oil, gas, or other mineral royalty or lease, any collateral trust certificate, preorganization certificate or subscription, transferable share, investment contract, voting-trust certificate, certificate of deposit, for a security, any put, call, straddle, option, or privilege on any security, certificate of deposit, or group or index of securities (including any interest therein or based on the value thereof), or any put, call, straddle, option, or privilege entered into on a national securities exchange relating to foreign currency, or in general, any instrument commonly known as a 'security'; or any certificate of interest or participation in, temporary or interim certificate for, receipt for, or warrant or right to subscribe to or purchase, any of the foregoing; but shall not include currency or any note, draft, bill of exchange, or banker's acceptance which has a maturity at the time of issuance of not exceeding nine months, exclusive of days of grace, or any renewal thereof the maturity of which is likewise limited."

Standard & Poor's 500   Stock price index. The primary objective of the S&P 500 is to be the performance benchmark for the U.S. equity markets. It is important to note, however, that the S&P 500 does not contain the five hundred largest stocks. Although many of the stocks in the index are among the largest, there are also many relatively small companies in the index. This is because the S&P 500 is a "bottom-up" index constructed by industry groups. Important industry groups within the U.S. economy are identified, and then a representative sample of stocks within each important industry group is allocated to the index. The index can therefore be used as a proxy for the whole market and for individual industry groups. The index was founded in 1923, although there were only 233 companies in the index at the time.

Stock   An instrument that signifies an ownership position (called equity) in a corporation, and represents a claim on its proportional share of the corporation's assets and profits. Ownership in the company is determined by the number of shares a person owns divided by the total number of shares outstanding. For example, if a company has 1000 shares of stock outstanding and a person owns 50 of them, then he or she owns 5% of the company. Most stock also provides voting rights, which give shareholders a proportional vote in certain corporate decisions. Only a certain type of company, called a corporation, has stock; other types of companies such as sole proprietorships and limited partnerships do not issue stock. Also called equity or equity securities or corporate stock.

Tactical Asset Allocation Shifting percentages of portfolios among stocks, bonds, and cash, depending on the relative attractiveness of the respective markets.

Top-Down Manager Investment manager who selects stocks by first looking at trends in the general economy and then selecting industries and finally companies that will benefit from those trends. Trustee An individual or institution that holds the legal title to an asset and administers it for the benefit of another person.

Universe The list of all assets eligible for inclusion in a portfolio.

Venture Capital Fund Investment vehicle organized to raise capital for startup companies or firms in the early stages of developing products and services. Investors in these funds expect higher rates of return due to the greater risks involved in investing in companies at this stage of development.

SOURCE NOTES

[1] *Shaw v. Delta Air Lines, Inc.*, 463 U.S. 85, 90 (1983).

[2] 29 U.S.C. S 1104(a)(1).

[3] 29 U.S.C. S 1104(a)(1)((B).

[4] *Donovan v. Bierwirth*, 680 F.2d 263, 272 n.8 (2d Cir.), cert. denied, 459 U.S. 1069 (1982).

[5] Ann L. Combs (U.S. Department of Labor, assistant secretary), remarks at the kickoff of the Fiduciary Education Campaign, *Getting It Right*, May 18, 2004.

[6] *Id.*

[7] ALICIA H. MUNNELL & ANNIKA SUNDEN, PRIVATE PENSIONS: COVERAGE AND BENEFIT TRENDS (2001).

[8] ROBERT H. HAHLO, THE SOUTH AFRICAN LEGAL SYSTEM AND ITS BACKGROUND, 517–519 (1973).

[9] R. W. LEE, INTRODUCTION TO ROMAN-DUTCH LAW, 5TH ED., 374 (1953); DAVID JOHNSTON, THE ROMAN LAW OF TRUSTS, 84 (1989).

[10] JUSTINIAN, JUSTINIAN'S INSTITUTES, Peter Burk & Grant McLeod trans. (CORNELL UNIVERSITY PRESS, 1987).

[11] WILLIAM W. BUCKLAND, A TEXTBOOK OF ROMAN LAW, 3RD ED., 355 (CAMBRIDGE UNIVERSITY PRESS, 1963); J. A. C. THOMAS, TEXTBOOK OF ROMAN LAW, 512 (ELSEVIER SCIENCE & TECHNOLOGY BOOKS, 1976).

[12] Buckland *supra* note 11 at 356; Thomas *supra* note 11 at 513.

[13] T. NADARAJA, THE ROMAN-DUTCH LAW OF FIDEICOMMISSA (1949).

[14] EDWARD GIBBON, DECLINE AND FALL OF THE ROMAN EMPIRE, 492 (DELL PUBLISHING COMPANY, INCORPORATED, 1974).

[15] FREDERIC W. MAITLAND, EQUITY: A COURSE OF LECTURES, 2D ED., 28 (GAUNT, INCORPORATED, 2001).

[16] Lee *supra* note 9 at 381.

[17] DAVID L HAYTON, COMMENTARY AND CASES ON THE LAW OF TRUSTS AND EQUITABLE REMEDIES, 11TH ED., 8–13 (SWEET & MAXWELL, LTD., 2001).

[18] AUSTIN WAKEMAN SCOTT, ABRIDGEMENT OF THE LAW OF TRUSTS, §1 (LITTLE BROWN, 1960).

[19] *Id.*

[20] DAVID J. HAYTON, THE LAW OF TRUSTS, 2D ED. (1993).

[21] *Meinhard v. Salmon*, 294 N.Y. 458, 464, 164 N.E. 545, 546 (1928).

[22] *Harvard College v. Amory*, 26 Mass. (9 Pick.) 446, 461 (1830).

[23] STEVEN A. SASS, THE PROMISE OF PRIVATE PENSIONS: THE FIRST HUNDRED YEARS. (CAMBRIDGE: HARVARD UNIVERSITY PRESS, 1997).

[24] *See* STUART D. BRANDES, AMERICAN WELFARE CAPITALISM: 1880–1940 (CHICAGO: UNIVERSITY OF CHICAGO PRESS, 1970).

[25] WILLIAM M. O'BARR & JOHN M. CONLEY, FORTUNE AND FOLLY: THE WEALTH AND POWER OF INSTITUTIONAL INVESTING. (THE MCGRAW-HILL COMPANIES, 1992). (The first pension in the United States was granted to disabled veterans of the Revolutionary War. The first military pension law was passed in 1818. In 1836, widows of soldiers of the Revolutionary War were covered by pensions.)

[26] MURRAY W. LATIMER, INDUSTRIAL PENSION SYSTEMS IN THE UNITED STATES AND CANADA, VOL. 1, 21–22 (NEW YORK: INDUSTRIAL RELATIONS COUNSELORS, 1932).

[27] Sass *supra* note 23.

[28] WILLIAM C. GREENOUGH & FRANCIS P. KING, PENSION PLANS AND PUBLIC POLICY, 154 (NEW YORK: COLUMBIA UNIVERSITY PRESS, 1976).

[29] Mary Conygton, *Industrial Pension for Old Age and Disability*, Monthly Labor Review, January 1926 at 45.

[30] James A. Wooten, *Regulating the "Unseen Revolution": A Political History of the Employee Retirement Income Security Act of 1974* (2003) (unpublished Ph. D. thesis, Yale Univ.).

[31] Ramon A. Aggabao, *Evolution of U.S. Pension Plans*, Contingencies, July/August 2003.

[32] PETER DRUCKER, THE UNSEEN REVOLUTION: HOW PENSION FUND SOCIALISM CAME TO AMERICA (NEW YORK: HARPER & ROW, 1976); O'Barr & Conley *supra* note 25.

[33] O'Barr & Conley *supra* note 25.

[34] Michael S. Gordon, *Overview: Why Was ERISA Enacted?* In *The Employee Retirement Income Security Act of 1974: The First Decade*, 6–24 (U.S. Senate, Special Committee on Aging) (1984).

[35] MICHAEL ALLEN, THE STUDEBAKER INCIDENT AND ITS INFLUENCE ON THE PRIVATE PENSION PLAN REFORM MOVEMENT (1985).

[36] KAREN FERGUSON & KATE BLACKWELL, THE PENSION BOOK: WHAT YOU NEED TO KNOW TO PREPARE FOR RETIREMENT (ARCADE PUBLISHING, 1996).

[37] Gordon *supra* note 34.

[38] *Central States, Southeast & Southwest Areas Pension Fund v. Central Transp. Inc.*, 472 U.S. 559, 570 (1985), *citing* S. Rep. No. 93-127, p. 29 (1973), 1974 U.S.C.C.A.N. (88 Stat. 832) 4639, 4865 ("The fiduciary responsibility section, in essence, codifies and makes applicable to these fiduciaries certain principles developed in the evolution of the law of trusts."); H.R. Rep., No. 93-533, p. 11 (1973), 1974 U.S.C.C.A.N. (88 Stat. 832) 4649 (identical language).

[39] ERISA §4(a).

[40] ERISA §403(a).

[41] ERISA §402(a).

[42] ERISA §3(21)(A).

[43] Restatement (Second) of Trusts §170(1) (1959).

[44] ERISA §404(a)(1)(A).

[45] Uniform Prudent Investor Act §1, comment (1994).

[46] Restatement (Second) of Trusts §174 (1959). ERISA §404(a)(1)(B).

[47] *Central States, Southeast & Southwest Areas Pension Fund v. Central Transport Inc.*, 472 U.S. 559, 570 (1985).

[48] *Firestone Tire & Rubber Co. v. Bruch*, 489 U. S. 101, 110 (1989).

[49] Restatement (Second) of Trusts §175 (1959).

[50] *Id.* at §§232-41.

[51] John H. Langbein, *The Secret Life of the Trust: The Trust as an Instrument of Commerce*, 107 Yale L. J. 165 (1997).

[52] ERISA §§3(1), 3(2); 29 U.S.C. §§1002(1), 1002(2).

[53] ERISA §4, 29 U.S.C. §1103 (1994); see also ERISA §§3(4), 3(5), 3(6), 3(11), and 3(12); 29 U.S.C. §§1002(4), 1002(5), and 1002(6), 1002 (11), and 1002(12).

[54] As defined in ERISA §3(32).

[55] As defined in ERISA §3(33).

[56] ERISA §4(b); 29 U.S.C. §1003(b).

[57] 29 C.F.R. §§2510.3-1 to 2510.3-3.

[58] ERISA §3(16)(B); 29 U.S.C. §1002(16)(B).

[59] ERISA §§3(7), 3(8); 29 U.S.C. §§1002(7), 1002(8).

[60] ERISA §3(16)(A); 29 U.S.C. §1002(16)(A).

[61] ERISA §3(21); 29 U.S.C. §1002(21).

[62] *Hozier v. Midwest Fasteners, Inc.*, 908 F.2d 1155, 1161-62 (3d Cir. 1990).

[63] ERISA §411; 29 U.S.C. §1111.

[64] Ted Benna, creator of the 401(k) plan.

[65] Munnell & Sunden *supra* note 7.

[66] Richard Ippolito, *The Reversion Tax's Perverse Result*, Regulations, Spring 2002; Jack VanDerhei & Craig Copeland, *The Changing Face of Private Retirement Plans*, EBRI Issue Brief no. 232, Employee Benefit Research Institute, April 2001.

[67] Krzystof Ostaszewskil, *Macroeconomic Aspects of Private Retirement Programs*, North American Actuarial Journal, July 2001.

[68] VanDerhei & Copeland *supra* note 66; Ostaszewskil *supra* note 67.

[69] U.S. General Accounting Office, *Cash Balance Plans: Implications of Conversions to Cash Balance Plans*, GAO/HEHS-00-207 (2000).

[70] U.S. General Accounting Office, *Private Pensions: Implications of Conversions to Cash Balance Plans*, GAO/HEHS-00-185 (2000).

[71] Announcement 2003-1, 2003-2 I.R.B. 281, http://www.irs.gov/pub/irs-drop/a-03-1.pdf.

[72] *Id.*

[73] *Tootle v. ARINC, Inc.*, 222 F.R.D. 88 (D. Md. 2004).

[74] *Cooper v. IBM Personal Pension Plan*, 2003 U.S. Dist. LEXIS 13223 (S.D. Ill. July 31, 2003).

[75] *Berger v. Xerox Corporate Retirement Income Guaranty Plan*, 338 F.3d 755 (7th Cir. Ill. 2003).

[76] IRC §411 (d)(6)(B) (The code generally prohibits an employer from amending a plan's benefit formula to reduce benefits that have already accrued (the "anticutback rule"). For this purpose, an amendment is treated as reducing accrued benefits if it has the effect of eliminating or reducing an early retirement benefit or a retirement-type subsidy or of eliminating an optional form of benefit. The provisions do not, however, protect benefits that have not yet accrued but would have in the future if the plan's benefit formula had not changed.)

[77] In some cases, the plan may convert the protected benefit into a lump-sum equivalent for purposes of the opening account balance. Even if at the time of the initial calculation the opening balance equals the value of the protected benefit, the account balance may not continue to reflect the value of the protected benefit over time, depending on the actuarial assumptions used. Thus, a cash balance plan may not rely on the cash balance formula to protect accrued benefits because it may encounter problems under the anticutback rule (depending on the actuarial assumptions used).

[78] This is sometimes the reduction in benefits that is referred to regarding cash balance conversions, i.e., a reduction of expected benefits, not accrued benefits.

[79] ERISA §3(14).

[80] ERISA §3(21)(A).

[81] 29 C.F.R. §2509.75-5, FR-1.

[82] H.R. Conf. Rep. No. 1280, 93d Congress, 2d Sess. 297 (1974).

[83] 29 U.S.C. §1102(a).

[84] 29 C.F.R. §2509.75-8.

[85] *Id.*

[86] ERISA §3(21)(A).

[87] 29 C.F.R. §2509.75-8.

[88] ERISA §3(38).

[89] *Reich v. McManus*, 883 F.Supp. 1144 (ND Ill. 1995).

[90] *Chao v. Hall Holding Company, Inc. et al*, 285 F.3d 415 (6th Cir. 2002).

[91] Eileen Hess, It's a Dangerous Time to Be a Fiduciary (2003).

[92] *Tittle v. Enron Corp.*, 284 F.Supp.2d 511 (S.D. Tex. 2003); *In re WorldCom, Inc. ERISA Litigation*, 263 F.Supp.2d 745 (S.D.N.Y. 2003).

[93] Fundamentals of Employee Benefit Programs, 5th Ed. (Employee Benefit Research Institute, 1997).

[94] ERISA §404(a)(1).

[95] 29 U.S.C. §1104(a)(1).

[96] *Donovan v. Bierwith*, 680 F.2d 263, 271 (2d Cir.), *cert. denied*, 459 U.S. 1069 (1982).

[97] 29 U.S.C. §1104(a)(1).

[98] ERISA §404(a)(1)(A).

[99] *Donovan v. Bierwirth*, 680 F.2d 263 (2d Cir.), cert. denied, 459 U.S. 1069 (1982); ERISA §404(a)(1).

[100] *In re Unisys Sav. Plan Litig.*, 19 EBC 2392 (3d Cir. 1996); *See also, Devlin v. Empire Blue Cross & Blue Shield*, 274 F.3d 76, 88 (2d Cir. 2001) (a fiduciary has "'a duty to deal fairly and honestly with its beneficiaries'") (quoting *Ballone v. Eastman Kodak Co.*, 109 F.3d 117, 123-24 (2d Cir. 1997); *Mullins v. Pfizer*, 23 F.3d 663, 669 (2d Cir. 1994) ("'when a plan administrator speaks, it must speak truthfully'") (quoting *Fischer v. Phila. Elec. Co.*, 994 F.2d 130, 135 (3d Cir. 1993); *Berlin v. Mich. Bell Tel. Co.*, 858 F.2d 1154, 1163 (6th Cir. 1988).

[101] *Fischer v. Phila. Elec. Co.*, 994 F.2d 130 (3d Cir. 1993).

[102] *Mullins v. Pfizer Inc.*, 147 F.Supp.2d 95 (2001).

[103] *Fischer v. Phila. Elec. Co.*, 994 F.2d 130 (3d Cir. 1993).

[104] *Varity Corp. v. Howe*, 516 U.S. 489, 506 (1996).

[105] *See e.g., Devlin v. Empire Blue Cross & Blue Shield*, 274 F.3d 76, 88-89 (2d Cir. 2001)(trial court must be permitted to determine whether defendants either made affirmative misrepresentations or failed to provide completely accurate plan information) (citing *In re Unisys Corp. Retiree Med. Benefit ERISA Litig.*, 57 F.3d 1255, 1264 (3d Cir. 1995) ("[W]hen a plan administrator affirmatively misrepresents the terms of a plan or fails to provide information when it knows that its failure to do so might cause harm, the plan administrator has breached its fiduciary duty.")); *Becker v. Eastman Kodak Co.*, 120 F.3d 5, 9 (2d Cir. 1997) (because summary plan description and benefit counselor's advice together amounted to materially misleading information, fiduciary breached duty to provide participants with complete and accurate information); *Simeon v. Mt. Sinai Med. Ctr.*, 150 F. Supp. 2d 598, 604 (S.D.N.Y. 2001); *In re Bidermann Indus. U.S.A., Inc.*, 241 B.R. 76, 90 (Bankr. S.D.N.Y. 1999).

[106] *Horn v. Cendant Operations, Inc.*, 2003 U.S. App. LEXIS 13535 (10th Cir. 2003).

[107] *Bixler v. Cent. Pa. Teamsters Health and Welfare Fund*, 12 F.3d 1292 (3d Cir. 1994).

[108] *See, Franklin v. First Union Corp.*, 84 F. Supp. 2d 720, 735 (E.D. Va. 2000) (fiduciary had "a duty to notify the plaintiffs of the changes in the investment funds in such a manner as to prevent any misinformation to and misleading of the plaintiffs regarding their options"); *Hudson v. Gen. Dynamics Corp.*, 118 F. Supp. 2d 226, 256 (D. Conn. 2000) (recognizing a "'duty to correct,' in the face of a statement demonstrating a material misunderstanding of benefits information, on plan fiduciaries in certain situations"); *Mullins v. Pfizer, Inc.*, 899 F.

Supp. at 77 ("If such misrepresentations were made and defendant knew of them, defendant had an affirmative duty to correct material misrepresentations that it knew or should have known plaintiff would rely on.").

[109] *Griggs v. E.I. DuPont de Nemours & Co.*, 237 F.3d 371, 381 (4th Cir. 2001) (citation omitted); *See also, Davis v. Bowman Apple Prods. Co.*, No. CIV.A. 5:00CV00033, 2002 WL 535068, at 6-7 (WD. Va. Mar. 29, 2002) (citing Griggs for "duty to correct"), aff'd, 50 Fed. Appx. 138 (4th Cir 2002).

[110] Latin term meaning "friend of the court." The name for a brief filed with the court by someone who is not a party to the case.

[111] ERISA §404(a)(1)(B).

[112] *DeBruyne v. Equitable Life Assur. Socy. of U.S.*, 920 F.2d 457, 465 (7th Cir. 1990); *See also*, Norton Bankruptcy Law and Practice 2d, sec. 156:9 (1997-98).

[113] *See*, James F. Forden et al., *Handbook on ERISA Litigation* @ 3.03[A], at 3-53 (1994).

[114] 29 U.S.C. §1106(b).

[115] *Donovan v. Bierwirth*, 680 F.2d 263, 271 (2d Cir. 1982).

[116] *NLRB v. Amax Coal Co.*, 453 U.S. 322, 329-30 (1981).

[117] *Lowen v. Tower Asset Management, Inc.*, 829 F.2d 1209, 1213 (2d Cir. 1987).

[118] *Donovan v. Bierwirth*, 680 F.2d 263 (2d Cir. 1982).

[119] *Geils Band Employee Benefit Plan v. Smith Barney Shearson*, 76 F.3d 1245 (1st Cir. 1996)

[120] *Harley v. Minnesota Mining and Manufacturing Company*, 42 F. Supp. 2d 898, 907 (D. Minn. 1999).

[121] DOL Reg. §2509.95-1(c)(6).

[122] *Liss v. Smith*, 991 F. Supp. 278, 297 (S.D.N.Y. 1998).

[123] *Bisceglia v. Bisceglia*, 17 F3d 393 (9th Cir. 1994).

[124] *In re: Unisys Savings Plan Litigation*, 74 F.3d 420, 435-36 (3d Cir. 1996), *cert. denied*, 519 U.S. 810 (1996).

[125] DOL Interpretive Bulletin §2509.75-78.

[126] *See, Moench v. Robertson*, 62 F.3d 553, 568-572 (3d Cir. 1995); *Kuper v. Iovenko*, 66 F.3d 1447, 1457-60 (6th Cir. 1995).

[127] *Liss v. Smith*, 991 F.Supp. 278, 297 (S.D.N.Y. 1998).

[128] *Id.* at 300.

[129] *Gregg v. Transportation Workers of America International*, 343 F.3d 833, 841 (6th Cir. 2003).

[130] ERISA §§404(a)(1)(A)(ii), 406(a)(1)(C), and 408(b)(2).

[131] *A Look at 401(k) Plan Fees*, U.S. Department of Labor, Employee Benefits Security Administration.

[132] ERISA §§406(b), 408(b)(2).

[133] Fred Reish, *Consents to Advice: Should Plan Sponsors Offer Investment Advice?*, Plan Sponsor Magazine, December 2002.

[134] DOL Interpretive Bulletin 94-1.

[135] DOL Adv. Op. 2001-09A.

[136] H. R. 93-1280, 93d Cong., 2d Sess. at p. 304.

[137] *See, Cent. States Pension Fund v. Cent. Transps., Inc.*, 472 U.S. 559 (1985).

[138] *Tittle v. Enron Corp.*, 284 F.Supp.2d 511 (S.D. Tex. 2003).

[139] 29 U.S.C. §1104(a)(1) (In addition, fiduciaries must discharge their duties "(B) with the care, skill, prudence, and diligence under the circumstances then prevailing that a prudent man acting in a like capacity and familiar with such matters would use in the conduct of an enterprise of a like character and with like aims; "(C) by diversifying the investments of the plan so as to minimize the risk of large losses, unless under the circumstances it is clearly prudent not to do so; and "(D) in accordance with the documents and instruments governing the plan insofar as such documents and instruments are consistent with the provisions of this subchapter and subchapter III of this chapter.").

[140] 29 U.S.C. §1002(7).

[141] *Firestone Tire & Rubber Co. v. Bruch*, 489 U.S. 101 (1989).

[142] *See*, 29 U.S.C. §1002(6) (an employee is any individual employed by an employer). *Nationwide Mut. Ins. Co. v. Darden*, 112 S. Ct. 1344 (1992) (The application of the common law test for employee status uses a thirteen-factor test).

[143] ERISA §3(8).

[144] *Hughes Aircraft Co. v. Jacobson*, 525 U.S. 432 (1999).

[145] ERISA §3(21)(A).

[146] DOL Reg 2550.404c-1. *See also*, Perdue, *ERISA Liability of Fiduciaries and Plan Service Providers Is a Growing Concern*, 2JTEB 19, May/Jun 1994, and Jenkins, *Fiduciaries of Participant-Directed Accounts Must Plan to Protect Themselves*, 2JTEB 116, Sept/Oct 1994.

[147] DOL's regulations under ERISA section 404(c).

[148] *See*, 29 C.F.R. §2550.404c-1(b)(1).

[149] *Id.*

[150] *See*, Don Carlson & Timothy Goodman, *Are You Protected? Demonstrating Compliance with Section 404(c) of ERISA*, Employee Benefits Update, February 12, 2004.

[151] House Report to ERISA, H. Rep. No. 93-1280; 93rd Cong., 2nd Sess. *See, Donovan v. Guaranty National Bank*, 4 Emp. Benefits Cas. (BNA) 1686 (S.D. W. Va. 1983).

[152] Under ERISA section 404(c) plan must at a minimum provide a participant or beneficiary an opportunity to give investment instructions at least once within any three-month period (referred to elsewhere herein as the "three- month minimum"). Paragraph (b)(2)(ii)(C)(1) of the final regulation clarifies that the minimum of three core alternatives subject to the three-month minimum must itself constitute a broad range of investment alternatives.

[153] ERISA §404(c).

[154] Preamble to ERISA §404(c).

[155] DOL Reg. §2550.404c-1(b)(2)(B)(1).

[156] *Id.*

[157] *See*, DOL Reg. §2550.404c-1.

[158] *Id.*

[159] 29 C.F.R. §2509.75-8 at FR-17.

[160] Preamble to DOL 404(c) Regulations, 57 Fed. Reg. 46906,46922.

[161] Internal Revenue Code §401(a)(28)(B).

[162] *Chao v. Hall Holding Company, Inc. et al*, 285 F.3d 415 (6th Cir. 2002).

[163] DOL Interpretive Bulletin 75-8.

[164] *In re CMS Energy ERISA Litigation*, No. 02-72834, 2004 WL 737335 (E.D. Mich. 2004).

[165] *Id.*

[166] 29 C.F.R. §2509.75-8.

[167] DOL Adv. Op. 97-15A (1997); DOL Adv. Op. 92-23A (1992); DOL letter to Jerry D. Shook (April 10, 1998); DOL information letter to Mark Sokolsky (September 5, 1996).

[168] *See, Beachem v. Rockford Products Corp.*, 2003 WL 1562561 (N.D. Ill. Mar. 24, 2003); *LaLonde v. Textron, Inc.*, 270 F.Supp. 2d 272 (D.R.I. 2003); *Kling v. Fidelity Mgmt. Trust Co.*, 270 F.Supp. 2d 121 (D.Mass. 2003); *Maniace v. Commerce Bank of Kansas City, N.A.*, 40 F.3d 264 (8th Cir. 1994).

[169] *See, In re WorldCom, Inc.*, 263 F.Supp 745 (S.D.N.Y. 2003).

[170] *See In re: WorldCom, Inc. ERISA Litig.*, 263 F. Supp. 2d 745 (S.D.N.Y. 2003); *In re: Williams Co. ERISA Litig.*, 271 F. Supp. 2d 1328 (N.D. Ok. 2003); *Rankin v. Rots*, 278 F. Supp. 2d 853 (E.D. Mi. 2003)

[171] *See Hull v. Policy Mgmt. Sys. Corp.*, No. 3:00-778-17, 2001 U.S. Dist. LEXIS 22343, at *1 (D.S.C. 2001) and *In re: McKesson HBOC, Inc. ERISA Litig.*, No. C00-20030 RMW, 2002 U.S. Dist. LEXIS 19473, at *1 (N.D. Ca. 2002).

[172] ERISA §408.

[173] Prohibited Transaction Exemptions (PTE) 96-62

[174] ERISA §404(a)(1)(B).

[175] INVESTMENT COMPANY INSTITUTE, 2004 MUTUAL FUND FACT BOOK (2004).

[176] Investment Company Institute, *401(k) Plan: How Plan Sponsors See the Market Plan*, Winter 1995.

[177] ERISA §401(b)(1).

[178] ERISA §404(c).

[179] DOL Reg. §2550.404c-1(c)(2).

[180] Profit Sharing/401(k) Council of America (PSCA), 47th Annual Survey of Profit Sharing and 401(k) Plans (2003).

[181] SCARBOURGH GROUP, 401(K) PARTICIPANT STUDY.

[182] DOL, *Report on the Working Group on Guidance in Setting and Monitoring Service Providers*, November 13, 1996.

[183] Harry Markowitz, *Portfolio Selection*, Journal of Finance, March 1952, Vol 7, pp. 77–91. (This paper laid the groundwork for Modern Portfolio Theory, which earned Dr. Markowitz a Nobel Prize. The paper suggests that instead of asking the question "What is a good investment?" you ought to be asking "What is a good investment for my portfolio?" It turns out that the answer is heavily dependent on what else happens to be in your portfolio. All else being equal, it is more beneficial (from the standpoint of maximizing your risk-adjusted return) to take on an investment that is likely to have low correlations with other elements in your portfolio than to take on an investment that is likely to have high correlations with other elements in your portfolio. Thus,

investment selection should involve getting maximum diversification benefit (with respect to the rest of the portfolio) from each investment.)

[184] Modern Portfolio Theory refers to the idea that each investment ought to be selected in consideration of how it will interact with other assets in one's portfolio. Modern Portfolio Theory is the basis for Mean Variance Optimization.

[185] Federal Reserve Flow of Funds.

[186] MSCI Stock Index for Europe, Australia, and the Far East (EAFE) versus S&P 500 Index, 1971–2002.

[187] Venture Economics.

[188] *Hedge Funds Demystified*, Goldman Sachs & Co.

[189] BARRON'S, 21-Feb-2000, page 40

[190] DOL, *Understanding Retirement Fees and Expenses*, May 2004.

[191] Revere Coalition, Intermediary and Service Provider Annual Disclosure Statement (August 2004).

[192] DOL, *A Look at 401(k) Plan Fees for Employees*, 2004.

[193] *Id.*

[194] DOL, Adv. Op. 2001-01A (2001).

[195] DOL, Field Assistance Bulletin 2003-3 (2003).

[196] *Id.*

[197] *Id.*

[198] DOL *supra* note 194.

[199] DOL *supra* note 195.

[200] IRS Rev. Rul. 96-47.

[201] DOL *supra* note 195.

[202] ERISA §404(a)(1)(B).

[203] The Sarbanes-Oxley Act of 2002 was primarily intended to address fraud in financial reporting and lack of oversight by self-interested senior corporate management; however, it modifies the reporting requirements under Section 16 of the Exchange Act, and restricts the purchase and sales of executive officers and directors during any blackout period.

[204] The April 30, 1984, letter from the administrator of the Office of Pension and Welfare Benefit Programs (reorganized as the Pension and Welfare Benefits Administration) to John Welch, attorney for the trustee of the profit

sharing and retirement plan for employees of Carter Hawley Hale Stores, Inc. in connection with pending tender offer by The Limited, Inc. (Profit Sharing Retirement Income Plan for Employees of Carter Hawley Hale Stores, Inc. (*CCH Pension Plan Guide*, p. 653F, paragraph 23 and *BNA Pension Reporter*, 11, p. 663); and DOL Op. Ltr. (Feb. 23, 1989), Polaroid Stock Equity Plan (*BNA Pension Reporter*, 16, p. 390).).). The letter expresses DOL opinion that the extent to which a trustee may follow action approved by plan participants is limited. *See also Danaher Corp. v. Chicago Pneumatic Tool Co.*, 633 F. Supp. 1066 (S.D.N.Y. 1986) indicating that a fiduciary has an obligation beyond following the passed-through vote of plan participants. (EBC, 7, pp. 1616–1620)

[205] DOL letter to Ian Lanoff dated September 28, 1995; cited in *Herman v. NationsBank Trust Company*, 126 F.3d 1354 (11th Cir. 1997).

[206] *Id.*

[207] *Herman v. NationsBank Trust Company*, 126 F.3d 1354 (11th Cir. 1997).

[208] ERISA §404(c).

[209] Internal Revenue Code §410(b).

[210] *Id.* at §414(q).

[211] *Id.* at §410(b).

[212] *Id.* at §§415(b)(1)(A), 415(c)(1)(A).

[213] *Id.* at §415(b)(1)(A).

[214] *Id.* at §415(c)(1)(A).

[215] *Id.* at §§401(a)(17), 404(l).

[216] *Id.* at §402(g)(1).

[217] *Id.* at §414(v)(2)(B)(i).

[218] *Id.* at §408(p)(2)(E).

[219] *Id.* at §4979.

[220] *Id.* at §416(g)(1).

[221] *Id., See also,* Internal Revenue Code §416(i)(1) for the definition of a key employee.

[222] Internal Revenue Code §416(g)(4)(C).

[223] *Id.* at §416(c)(2)(A).

[224] Profit Sharing/401k Council of America, *46th Annual Survey of Profit Sharing and 401k Plans*, September 2003.

225 Profit Sharing/401k Council of America, *Investment Advice Survey 2001*, 2001.

226 DOL, Interpretive Bulletin 96-1, Participant Investment Education; Final Rule (06/11/1996).

227 ERISA §3(21)(A)(ii). The DOL has expressed the view that, for purposes of section 3(21)(A)(ii), such fees or other compensation need not come from the plan and should be deemed to include all fees or other compensation incident to the transaction in which the investment advise has been or will be rendered. *See*, A.O. 83-60A (Nov. 21, 1983); *Reich v. McManus*, 883 F. Supp. 1144 (N.D. Ill. 1995).

228 *See*, footnote 3 of Interpretive Bulletin 96-1 at 29 C.F.R. Section 2509.96-1.

229 DOL, Interpretive Bulletin 96-1, Participant Investment Education; Final Rule (06/11/1996).

230 *Id.*

231 *Id.*

232 Reish *supra* note 133.

233 Fred Reish & Bruce Ashton, *Fiduciary Responsibilities in Selecting Providers of Investment Advice*, 401k Advisor, March 2000.

234 Michael C. Giallourakis & G. Stephen Taylor, An Evaluation of Benefit Communication Strategy.

235 *Donovan v. Bierwirth*, 680 F.2d 263, 272 n.8 (2d Cir.), *cert. denied*, 459 U.S. 1069 (1982).

236 *See, Tittle v. Enron Corp.*, 284 F.Supp.2d 511 (S.D. Tex. 2003); *In re WorldCom, Inc.* ERISA Litigation.

237 *Tittle v. Enron Corp.*, 284 F.Supp.2d 511 (S.D. Tex. 2003).

238 ERISA §410(b).

239 *Baker v. American Mobile Power Corporation*, 64 F.3d 1397, 1404 (9th Cir.1995).

240 ERISA §410(b).

241 Retirement System Group, Inc., *Employee Benefit Advisory*, Spring 2002.

242 ERISA §3(21)(A).

243 *Maniace v. Commerce Bank*, 40 F.3d 264 (CA-8, 1995).

244 ERISA §412.

[245] *See e.g., Danaher Corp. v. Chicago Pneumatic Tool Co.,* 635 F. Supp. 246 (S.D.N.Y. 1986).

[246] *GIW Industries, Inc. v. Trevor, Stewart, Burton & Jacobson, Inc.,* 895 F.2d 729 (11th cir. 1990).

[247] DOL Interpretive Bulletin 94-2.

[248] Profit Sharing/401(k) Association, *Defined Contribution Plan Process–The Written Investment Policy Statement,* July 18, 2001.

[249] *E.g., Kuper v. Ovenko,* 66 F.3d 1447 (6th Cir. 1995); *Lalonde v. Textron, Inc.,* 270 F. Supp. 2d 272 (D.R.I. 2003); *Schoenholtz v. Doniger,* 657 F. Supp. 899 (S.D.N.Y. 1987).

[250] *Tatum v. R.J. Reynolds Tobacco Company,* 2004 WL 2857376 (4th Cir. (N.C.) 2004).

[251] *See Thompson v. Avondale,* 29 EB Cas. 2865, 2003 WL 359932 (February 14, 2003).

[252] Rev. Proc. 2003-44, 2003-25 I.R.B.

[253] *Id.*

[254] 67 Fed. Reg. 15061.

[255] *Id.* at 14164.

[256] 65 Fed. Reg. 14164, 14170 (This definition is broader than "plan fiduciary" and is defined in the notice as meaning a "plan fiduciary, plan sponsor, party-in-interest with respect to the plan, or other person who is in a position to correct a [b]reach.")

[257] There are thirteen specific transactions that are delineated in the notice, and detailed herein, that are eligible for correction under the VFC program.

[258] This phrase or term was used to describe the VFC program by Virginia Smith, *New Labor Department Compliance Program Will Help Plans Voluntarily Address Breaches,* 27 Pension & Benefits Reporter, No. 11, p. 705.

[259] *See,* 65 Fed. Reg. 14164, Appendix A.

[260] *Id.* at 14170. (The exact wording in the notice is "other person who is in a position to correct a [b]reach," which essentially means "anyone who is in a position to correct a breach.")

[261] 65 Fed. Reg. 14164, Appendix C (There are ten EBSA regional offices throughout the United States).

[262] PWBA Fact Sheet (March 14, 2000).

263 A PWBA investigation is defined as including oral or written notification of such an investigation to a plan official (or their authorized representative). However, notification of an investigation does not include mere contact or inquiry by PWBA officials, unless such contact relates to the underlying transaction described in the VFC program application. 65 Fed. Reg. 14164, 14170.

264 65 Fed. Reg. 14164, 14170.

265 *Id.* at 14173.

266 *Id.* at 14172.

267 *Id.* (There is no guidance as to the specific type or format of the required notice. The notice must be given no later than the due date of the furnishing of the plan's summary annual report (SAR) following the date of submission of the application. A special notice explaining the supplemental distribution is required in situations where supplemental distributions are made to participants. The notice may be furnished by regular mail, posting, or electronic mail so long as the method results in a manner, which is reasonably calculated, to inform plan participants. Presumably, the notice may be given within and as part of the SAR.)

268 *See, id.* (It is important to note that the notice requirement of Section 5(e) of the VFC program does not mention beneficiaries or alternate payees as entitled to receive a written notice of the correction under the VFC program.)

269 *Id.* (Note a written correction notice must be given to "all" plan participants, not merely "affected" participants. The VFC program as detailed in the Federal Register is contradictory in that section 5(e) specifies that notice must be given to "all" plan participants and section 6(e)(viii) states that the application must include "a copy of the sample notification to all affected participants." Nonetheless, PWBA's press release dated March 14, 2000, states that notice must be given to "participants," which implies all participants, whether or not affected by the transaction.)

270 65 Fed. Reg. 14164, Appendix B. (A current fidelity bond; the date the plan's most recent Form 5500 was filed; in the case of a correction regarding the under-valuation or over-valuation of plan assets, the correction includes the filing of amended Forms 5500.)

271 65 Fed. Reg. 14164, 14172.

272 *See,* 65 Fed. Reg. 14164, 14170. (There are no dollar limitations or percentages of plan asset limitations for eligibility in the VFC program, and there are no filing fees or user fees as required in the IRS voluntary compliance pro-

grams with the exception of the Administrative Policy Regarding Self-Correction.)

[273] 65 Fed. Reg. 15061.

[274] Smith *supra* note 258, at 755. (Unlike IRS guidance under the Employee Plans Compliance Resolution System (EPCRS), this provides proposed correction methodologies and allows for flexibility in the actual correction approaches. With the VFC program, there is no flexibility regarding correction methodology.)

[275] 65 Fed. Reg. 14164, 14175, n. 8.

[276] Smith *supra* note 258, at 705.

[277] White, *PWBA Voluntary Compliance Program Enables Plans to Right 13 Types of Wrongs*, 27 Pension & Benefits Reporter 12, at 754.

[278] *DOL Adopts Program Allowing Fiduciaries to Self-Correct Violations Without Penalty*, Pension & Benefits Week, March 20, 2000, at 4.

[279] 65 Fed. Reg. 14164, 14169.

[280] *Id.* (The no-action letter only provides relief to the applicant by PWBA with respect to the specific transaction. Thus, it can be assumed that if the application is submitted by the board of directors or trustees, ERISA counsel should be careful to name all members of the above-mentioned board.)

[281] *Id.; See also,* ERISA §502(l).

[282] 65 Fed. Reg. 14164, 14166.

[283] *Id.* at 14166.7.

[284] *Id.* at 14164.

[285] *Id.* at 14169.

[286] *Id.*

[287] White, *New Labor Department Compliance Program Will Help Plans Voluntarily Address Breaches*, 27 Pension & Benefits Reporter, No. 11, at 706.

[288] ABA-CLE Teleconference, *What You Should Know About DOL's New Fiduciary Correction Program*, April 20, 2000.

[289] *Id.*

[290] *Id.*

[291] *Id.*

[292] *Id.*

[293] *Id.*

[294] Internal Revenue Code §7121.

[295] ABA-CLE Teleconference *supra* note 288.

[296] 65 Fed. Reg. 14164, 14172.

[297] *Id.*

[298] White *supra* note 287.

[299] White *supra* note 277 at 753.

[300] White *supra* note 287 at 755.

[301] *Id.* at 755.

[302] White *supra* note 277 at 755.

[303] White *supra* note 287 at 754.

INDEX

A

accumulated benefit obligation (ABO), 122
active investment management, 107–108
administrator of plan, 19–20, 42
age discrimination, 27–28
American Express, 11–12
annuity provider, selecting, 149–151
appointment of fiduciary, 36
Arthur Andersen, 1
asset allocation
    for defined-benefit plans, 128–137
    for defined-contribution plans, 105–107
    versus diversification, 60
asset allocation managers, 109–110
Audit Closing Agreement Program (Audit CAP), 217

B

balanced managers, 109–110
Baltimore & Ohio (B&O) Railroad, 12
bank collective funds, 95
BARRA factors, 148
benchmarks, 137–142
benefit plan, defined in ERISA, 18
benefit statements, 178
Bisceglia v. Bisceglia, 53
blackout period, 160–164
broad range requirement, 69
bundled pension plan products, 158

C

care, 52–53
cash balance plans, 24–30

978-0-595-34429-1
0-595-34429-1

Printed in the United States
59474LVS00003B/160

9 780595 344291